# Reinventing the Family in Uncertain Times

Also Available from Bloomsbury

Locating Social Justice in Higher Education Research,
*edited by Jan McArthur and Paul Ashwin*
Rethinking Education for Sustainable Development,
*edited by Radhika Iyengar and Ozge Karadag Caman*
Judaism, Education and Social Justice, *Matt Plen*
Teaching for Peace and Social Justice in Myanmar,
*edited by Mary Shepard Wong*
Class, Race, Disability and Mental Health in Higher Education, *Mike Seal*
Gender in an Era of Post-truth Populism, *edited by Penny Jane Burke,
Julia Coffey, Rosalind Gill and Akane Kanai*
Issues and Challenges of Immigration in Early Childhood in the USA,
*Wilma Robles-Melendez and Wayne Driscoll*
Transnational Feminist Politics, Education, and Social Justice,
*edited by Silvia Edling and Sheila Macrine*
Immigration and Children's Literature,
*Wilma Robles-Melendez and Audrey Henry*

# Reinventing the Family in Uncertain Times

*Education, Policy and Social Justice*

Edited by
Marie-Pierre Moreau, Catherine Lee and
Cynthia Okpokiri

BLOOMSBURY ACADEMIC
LONDON · NEW YORK · OXFORD · NEW DELHI · SYDNEY

BLOOMSBURY ACADEMIC
Bloomsbury Publishing Plc
50 Bedford Square, London, WC1B 3DP, UK
1385 Broadway, New York, NY 10018, USA
29 Earlsfort Terrace, Dublin 2, Ireland

BLOOMSBURY, BLOOMSBURY ACADEMIC and the Diana logo are trademarks of
Bloomsbury Publishing Plc

First published in Great Britain 2023

Copyright © Marie-Pierre Moreau, Catherine Lee and Cynthia Okpokiri and
contributors, 2023

Marie-Pierre Moreau, Catherine Lee and Cynthia Okpokiri and contributors have
asserted their right under the Copyright, Designs and Patents Act, 1988, to be
identified as Authors of this work.

For legal purposes the Acknowledgements on p. vii constitute an extension
of this copyright page.

Cover design: Grace Ridge
Cover image © Sean Gladwell / Getty Images

All rights reserved. No part of this publication may be reproduced or transmitted in
any form or by any means, electronic or mechanical, including photocopying,
recording, or any information storage or retrieval system, without prior
permission in writing from the publishers.

Bloomsbury Publishing Plc does not have any control over, or responsibility for, any
third-party websites referred to or in this book. All internet addresses given in this
book were correct at the time of going to press. The author and publisher regret any
inconvenience caused if addresses have changed or sites have ceased to exist, but can
accept no responsibility for any such changes.

A catalogue record for this book is available from the British Library.

A catalog record for this book is available from the Library of Congress.

ISBN: HB: 978-1-3502-8710-5
ePDF: 978-1-3502-8711-2
eBook: 978-1-3502-8712-9

Typeset by Newgen KnowledgeWorks Pvt. Ltd., Chennai, India

To find out more about our authors and books visit www.bloomsbury.com
and sign up for our newsletters.

# Contents

| | | |
|---|---|---:|
| Acknowledgements | | vii |
| List of Contributors | | viii |

1 Introduction
*Marie-Pierre Moreau, Cynthia Okpokiri and Catherine Lee* — 1

2 Shifting Family Meanings: A Sociological Overview
*João Paulo Mendes Carvalho and Cláudia Casimiro* — 11

3 Children's Valuations of Kinship Care Family Life – Cost-effective
Substitute Care or Multiple Ambivalent Affiliations in Flux
*Paul Shuttleworth* — 27

4 Language of Instruction Choice and Family Disruptions in Ghana
*Vincent Adzahlie-Mensah* — 49

5 Black British Families: Liminality and the Liabilities of Language
*Parise Carmichael-Murphy* — 65

6 Older Lesbians and Families of Friends
*Catherine Lee* — 83

7 Queering Familialism? Lesbian and Gay Claims of Parenthood and
the Transformation of Intimate Citizenship in Italy
*Paolo Gusmeroli and Luca Trappolin* — 105

8 Kithship: Protective Aspects of a Family of Choice for Older
Transgender Persons
*Sara J. English* — 123

9 Family Practices and Strategies of Middle-class Teachers in
Argentina in the Context of Covid-19: Transformations and
Discomforts in the Face of Care Processes and Labour Relations
*Leila M. Passerino and Denise Zenklusen* — 149

vi       *Contents*

10  'In True Naval Fashion': Young People's Perspectives on Family
Communication       167
*Jo Bowser-Angermann, Leanne Gray, Abigail Wood,*
*Matt Fossey and Lauren Godier-McBard*

11  From Active to Activist Parenting: Educational Struggle and the
Injuries of Institutionalized Misrecognition       187
*Nathan Fretwell and John Barker*

12  Conclusion       209
*Cynthia Okpokiri, Marie-Pierre Moreau and Catherine Lee*

Index       215

# Acknowledgements

The editors would like to express their deepest gratitude to the chapter authors for their contributions to this volume. Thank you as well to the Bloomsbury team and to our colleagues Lucie Wheeler and Samson Tsegay.

# Contributors

**John Barker** is Senior Lecturer at Middlesex University, UK, in the Department of Education. His research interests focus on children and youth, mobility, space and place, and higher education. He has also published on research methods. His most recent publications were contributions to *The Palgrave Handbook of Auto\Biography* (2020), which explores the role of space and place within auto/biographies and maps student narratives.

**Jo Bowser-Angermann** is Associate Professor in Education and Director of Student Experience and Engagement for the Faculty of Health, Education, Medicine and Social Care, at Anglia Ruskin University, UK. Her research interests focus on lifelong learning and social justice.

**Parise Carmichael-Murphy** is a PhD Education student at The University of Manchester, UK. Her research interests are Black feminist thought, education policy and youth mental health.

**Cláudia Casimiro** is Assistant Professor of Sociology at the University of Lisbon, Portugal, Institute of Social and Political Sciences and full member researcher at CIEG – Interdisciplinary Centre for Gender Studies. Her research interests focus on family, family violence, gender, digital technologies and online dating. Her most recent co-edited book is *Connecting Families? Information & Communication Technologies in a Life Course Perspective* (2018).

**João Carvalho** is a doctoral student in Critical Social/Personality Psychology at the Graduate Center, City University of New York, USA. His research interests focus on LGBTQ immigrants, community and personal networks, structural inequalities and decolonial theory. He is currently working on a chapter titled 'Find Places to Belong: You Do You' for the edited volume *Living Well: Skills for LGBTQIA+ People* (2022).

**Sara J. English** is Coordinator of the Gerontology Program and Assistant Professor in the Department of Social Work at Winthrop University, USA. She studies the power of non-familial relationships among seniors and the power of social connections among older transgender persons. She is passionate about qualitative research and the depth of understanding it can offer to studies of persons who live on the margins of society.

**Matt Fossey** is Professor of Public Services Research and Director of the Veterans and Families Institute for Military Social Research at Anglia Ruskin University, UK. He is particularly interested in knowledge exchange and research impact. He is a member of several UK government and international academic advisory panels and research groups.

**Nathan Fretwell** is Senior Lecturer in Education and Early Childhood in the Department of Education at Middlesex University, UK. His research interests focus on home–school relations, education and family policy, and the philosophy of education, with a particular emphasis on alternative/radical education. Nathan's work has been published in leading education journals, including the *British Educational Research Journal* and *Educational Philosophy and Theory*.

**Lauren Godier-McBard** is Senior Research Fellow at the Veterans and Families Institute at Anglia Ruskin University, UK, and leads the institute's Women & Equalities research programme. Her current research focuses on understanding the needs and experiences of women in the military community with the aim of improving services.

**Leanne Gray** is Senior Lecturer in Education in the School of Education and Social Care at Anglia Ruskin University, UK. Her research interests focus on early childhood and mathematics education.

**Paolo Gusmeroli** is Research Fellow at the Department of Philosophy, Sociology, Education and Applied Psychology, University of Padova, Italy. His research interests focus on gender, sexuality, family practices and social reproduction. He has published on transformations and conflicts around intimate citizenship in Italy.

**Catherine Lee** is National Teaching Fellow and Professor of Inclusive Education and Leadership at Anglia Ruskin University, UK. She is also Deputy Dean for Education in the Faculty of Health, Education, Medicine and Social Care. Catherine has published extensively on the theme of LGBTQ+ inclusion, and her research has created national and international impact.

**Vincent Adzahlie-Mensah** is Associate Professor at the Department of Social Studies in the University of Education, Winneba, Ghana. His current research interests are in national security, social justice and development education.

**Marie-Pierre Moreau** is Professor in Sociology of Education, Work and Inequalities at Anglia Ruskin University, UK, where she is also Education Research Lead and Director of the Centre for Education Research on Identities and Inequalities (CERII). She is the editor of the 'Bloomsbury Gender and Education' book series and of the open-access journal *Access: Critical Explorations of Equity in Higher Education*.

**Cynthia Okpokiri** is Lecturer in Social Work at University of East Anglia, UK, and Fellow of Anglia Ruskin University, UK. Cynthia's research and pedagogy have mostly focused on Black and Black African parenting and family dynamics. She explores how Eurocentric childrearing norms, practices and theories influence professional and ordinary understandings of Black parenting in Western and African contexts.

**Leila M. Passerino** is a researcher at National Scientific and Technical Research Council (CONICET) and Associate Professor in Citizenship, Human Rights and Education Seminar at Universidad Nacional de Rafaela, Argentina. Her research interests focus on studies on gender, citizenship and rights, health and corporality.

**Paul Shuttleworth** is an independent social worker, Researcher, Lecturer and Associate Tutor at the University of Sussex, UK. His research focuses on child participation, social work, dialogical participation, critical realism, social policy, permanence and kinship care. His most recent publication 'Recognition of Family Life by Children Living in Kinship Care Arrangements in England' was derived from his ESRC-funded thesis 'What Matters to Children Living in Kinship Care'.

**Luca Trappolin** is Assistant Professor of Sociology in the Department of Philosophy, Sociology, Education and Applied Psychology, University of Padova, Italy. He is the author of several papers on the social construction of homosexuality and homophobia, as well as on lesbian and gay parenthood in Italy. He is the co-author of *Confronting Homophobia in Europe. Social and Legal Perspectives* (with Gasparini and Wintemute, 2012).

**Abigail Wood** is Research Assistant in the Veterans and Families Institute at Anglia Ruskin University, UK. Much of her work focuses on the impact of service life on military children and families. Other research interests include women in the military community and military sexual violence.

**Denise Zenklusen** is a Postdoctoral Scholar at National Scientific and Technical Research Council (CONICET); Associate Professor in Education, Local and

Territorial Development at Universidad Nacional de Rafaela and Associate Professor in Methodology and Techniques of Qualitative Analysis at Universidad Nacional de Entre Ríos, Argentina. Her research interests focus on studies on gender, migration and cities.

1

# Introduction

Marie-Pierre Moreau, Cynthia Okpokiri and Catherine Lee

## The ties that bind: Disrupting and reinventing 'the family' in uncertain times

During the second half of the twentieth century, families and intimate lives were reclaimed as a political issue. The 1960s liberation and civil rights movements, which emerged in a range of countries, led to a redefinition of minoritized groups' position in society and challenged the then prevailing essentialist and functionalist understandings of identities and families. These struggles have retained their topicality, as exemplified by contemporary social movements such as #metoo and Black Lives Matter. Simultaneously, the revival of far-right politics observed in various countries has been associated with calls for a return to more conservative identity politics and family norms.

In a context characterized by a climate of profound socio-economic, cultural and political uncertainties, 'family' has become a more fluid, expandable concept, yet one that remains to this day the subject of fierce debates. Roseneil and Budgeon (2004) state that 'the idea of "family" retains an almost unparalleled ability to move people, both emotionally and politically' (135). Indeed, throughout history, changes in family law or practices have led some to claim that such changes would result in the collapse of the (heterosexist, patriarchal, post-colonial) social order (Moreau 2018). Suffice here to recall how the enactment of same-sex marriage and of child adoption by same-sex couples have been associated with social and political upheavals. The recent decision of the US Supreme Court to overturn the 1973 legal ruling known as *Roe v. Wade* and endthe right to abortion also illustrates the gendered, classed, raced and ableist implications of family discourses.

Set against this context, this edited volume is concerned with the reproduction and transformation of family norms in contemporary times. It is underpinned by two main ambitions. First, we wish to document and question what 'counts' as a family. Which families are rendered in/visible and mis/recognized; and how are these processes of in/visibility and mis/recognition framed by the discourses of power which operate in various institutional and geopolitical contexts? Second, we consider how family forms are changing in the current climate of uncertainties and profound socio-economic, cultural and political shifts alluded to earlier. How are these uncertainties disrupting family norms and facilitating or hindering the emergence of new ways of 'doing' family?

This volume focuses on discourses of families in the contexts of education and social care, understood broadly, as we acknowledge the embedding of discourses in specific environments and the socio-historic influence of education and social care institutions in framing what counts as family. It gathers contributions which critically engage with four themes. First, this collection explores the socio-cultural diversity of family formations and what makes a family in contemporary times, including work concerned with non-traditional, non-heteronormative, non-Eurocentric definitions of the family, such as single-parent families, one-person families, childless families, lesbian, gay, bisexual, transgender, queer or questioning (LGBTQ+) families, extended families, racialized families, transnational families, families with children under state care, blended families and families of friends. Second, the volume considers how power relationships linked to gender, class, ethnicity, sexuality, faith, dis/ability and other in/equalities intersect and operate in defining what counts as a family. Third, the volume is concerned with family narratives and their negotiation. Some of the questions we ask include how individuals and groups negotiate discourses of the family and their implications with regard to power relationships. This concern includes how activists, minoritized and dominant groups reproduce or challenge family norms and work towards the promotion of alternative definitions. Fourth, the volume considers the contemporary (including, though not only, Covid-19-related) disruptions to prevailing family norms, including the shift in private–public boundaries and the use and impact of social media on family dynamics.

On a theoretical level, this volume brings together contributions exploring families through a theoretical lens broadly borrowing from critical, feminist, and post-structuralist frameworks. Beyond the diversity of their precise theoretical positioning, the contributions are brought together by two shared concerns. First, all seek critical engagement with family formations and shift away from the normative and functionalist studies of the family which continue to permeate policy and, sometimes, research debates. Second, this critical engagement gives central consideration to identity and equity issues, with these understood as fluid, negotiable and intersectional, as individuals are positioned at the nexus of multiple power relations. This concern for the diversity and intersectionality of identities and family norms is reflected in our consideration of a broad range of equity matters, including gender, class, ethnicity, sexuality and nationality, to quote a few. As a result, the book benefits, yet strays away, from a sociological tradition which has, more often than not, maintained a focus on one specific equity aspect or one specific group. This encompassing approach is of course facilitated by the edited nature of this volume.

In adopting an intersectional lens, this collection takes inspiration from earlier sociological studies of the family in education and other settings. Diane Reay's work, in particular, has interrogated inequalities at the nexus of social class and gender (Reay 2005). Reay argues that, in spite of persistent claims that education enables significant social mobility, social class divides are reproduced through schools and other institutions. She highlights how parenting work, mothering work in particular, impacts on the educational attainment of children, with middle-class parents drawing on their cultural and economic capital to ensure their children succeed. Whilst the workplace is, in contemporary Britain as in many other countries, the domain of both men and women, Reay argues that it is overwhelmingly women as mothers who on top of their paid work put in additional hours with children, securing and perpetuating the advantage of middle-class children. While Reay's work precedes the pandemic, recent research shows how the disruption of schooling norms, including, in some instances, the schooling of children within the home, has considerably aggravated the gendered imbalance of the division of school and care work within households, with some considerable impact on mothers' well-being, retention in the labour market and career development (Ronksley-Pavia et al. 2022).

Another inspiration to this volume lies in the work of Sandra Paton-Imani, who also critically interrogates family norms while focusing on other intersectionalities (i.e. intersections of race, gender, socio-economic status and sexual orientation) in contrast to Reay (who primarily focused on the intersections of class and gender). For example, in her book *Queering Family Trees: Race, Reproductive Justice, and Lesbian Motherhood* (2018), Patton-Imani reflects on the intersection of her identity as a lesbian, a mother, an adopted child and someone in an interracial marriage. She examines the way in which, for lesbian mothers of colour, becoming a parent can sit uncomfortably with other oppressions. Patton-Imani exposes considerable tensions that sat beneath the celebration of equality in the United States when equal marriage became legal. Citing complications with her own marriage status, Patton-Imani argues that for her as a woman of colour, same-sex marriage was in fact not a celebration of inclusion but a protest against it, observing that marriage led for her personally to a compulsory and unwanted performance of citizenship.

A recent edited collection by Nadia von Benzon and Catherine Wilkinson (2019), *Intersectionality and Difference in Childhood and Youth*, considers more specifically the experiences of young people whose lives sit outside the 'normalcy' of childhood, in national and transnational contexts. Bringing together a series of contributions to understandings of alterity, agency and precarity, the book covers a broad range of childhood experiences disruptive of the prevailing family norms. While the volume's teaching primarily relates to 'doing' childhood, its critical underpinnings, broad scope and, for the most part, intersectional take on identities and inequalities echo our own endeavour.

The edited nature of this volume also enables us to bring together contributions exploring a vast range of organizational and national contexts (including Argentina, Ghana, Italy, Portugal, Spain, the UK and the United States), equity matters and family norms, ultimately allowing us to capture some of the diversity of family formations. Unexpectedly, the Covid-19 pandemic has reminded us that some families are more 'at risk' in the face of uncertainties and that the resources available to them are considerably affected by matters of equity. This has been made worse as a result of the neoliberal ideologies which, for several decades now, have withdrawn their support to the education, health and social care sectors and, linked to this, have called for individuals and communities to 'take responsibility' (Fraser 2013).

This concern for the diversity and intersectionality of families also encourages us to consider new directions for 'doing' family and the affordances of social change. One of the significant questions this book asks is how one 'does' family when they are positioned by others as, precisely, outside the family. Unsurprisingly, the literature on family diversity is often informed by queer studies or considers the experiences of LGBTQ+ households. In a collective piece (Crimmins et al. 2023), Genine Hook argues that, following Halberstam (2011: 89), 'my queer critique of family is "one method for imagining, not some fantasy of an elsewhere, but existing alternatives to hegemonic systems". To include the stories of sole parents as a queer critique of "the family" is a useful way to introduce the structural framework of families and to contrast this with the individual experiences within the broader expectations and mechanisms of the normative family' (forthcoming).

Oswald, Blume and Marks (2005) observe that in heteronormative discourses, only heterosexual families are deemed 'real', with 'pseudo families' (144) their binary opposite. Morgan (2011) refers to family as a set of practices that create a social dynamic that challenges the more traditional and heteronormative notion of the family as a social construct. Drawing on Butler's theory of gender performativity, they reject essentialist notions of the family and, like Morgan, argue for family as a performance in which dynamic and diverse representations of family can prevail. According to Hudak and Giammattei (2010), the performative act of family or 'doing family' (53) entails 'intentionally committing to add elements of responsibility and caretaking to the bonds of love, which usually embody roles traditionally assigned to kinship networks' (52). 'Doing family' transforms it from a fixed entity to a verb, encouraging new representations of caretaking and responsibility within loving relationships. Linked to this, this volume is also a call for a more inclusive consideration of 'doing family' and, as such, an encouragement to explore avenues for social change.

## An overview of the volume's contributions

The first contribution, 'Shifting Family Meanings: A Sociological Overview' by João Paulo Mendes Carvalho and Cláudia Casimiro provides a sociological overview of the shifting meaning of family. Drawing on current social practices, Carvalho and Casimiro argue that there have been significant theoretical and social advancements on what constitutes family, meaning such a term has become insufficient to answer the wide entanglements of everyday life. They highlight new understandings of how people are reinventing the family as well as paving the way to the gain of social legitimacy and protection of diverse families through inclusive policies.

The second chapter, 'Children's Valuations of Kinship Care Family Life – Cost-effective Substitute Care or Multiple Ambivalent Affiliations in Flux' by Paul Shuttleworth, focuses on children who are placed in the full-time care of family members when they cannot remain with their birth parents. Around the world, kinship care is the fastest growing care option for children who cannot live with their birth parents, yet this is a family formation which is under-researched, under-theorized and subjugated. Analysis of the children's views shows how they trouble commonly held notions of family, leading the author to call for theories of doing family challenging the static traditional hierarchical, gendered, white, Eurocentric, institutionalized, heteronormative ideals of family.

In 'Language of Instruction Choice and Family Disruptions in Ghana', Vincent Adzahlie-Mensah draws attention to how family dynamics and power are shifting in relation to the legislating of English language as the medium of instruction in Ghana. Using critical anti-colonial theory as an epistemological stance to discuss evidence from school-based ethnographic research in a Ghanaian rural community, the author argues that legislating English as language of instruction has disruptive effects within this African family setting. The chapter highlights the need for critical discussion of the language of instruction policy in Ghana, and the problematic persistence of neocolonial sentiments in domestic as well as public spaces in former colonies.

In 'Black British Families: Liminality and the Liabilities of Language', Parise Carmichael-Murphy explores how language is employed and mobilized in ways which marginalize Black British families. Reflecting upon the historical politicization of Blackness in Britain and the changing demographic of the British-born population, Carmichael-Murphy observes that the discourse of the 'absentee father' has perpetuated harmful stereotypes about Black British families which are rooted in deficit-based terminology which upholds the positioning of the British family as 'led' by a patriarch.

In 'Older Lesbians and Families of Friends', Catherine Lee shares her findings from research undertaken with a group of twelve lesbians over the age of fifty, who have known each other over a period of approximately thirty years. Drawing on social capital theory, the research explores the social structures and social relationships that connect these women and form 'norms of reciprocity and trust' (Putnam 2000: 19). Lee's chapter shows that these lesbians rely less on their family of origin for help, support and care as they approach later life and instead turn to friends, partners and ex-partners. Through long-established bonds of kinship, these women provide mutual bonds of support more typically associated with the traditional family, leading them to conceive of their friendship group as a 'family of friends'.

In 'Queering Familialism? Lesbian and Gay Claims of Parenthood and the Transformation of Intimate Citizenship in Italy', Paolo Gusmeroli and Luca Trappolin pursue the discussion about same-sex families. While, in 2016, the Italian Parliament approved the law on same-sex civil unions, lesbian and gay couples were not given access to medically assisted fertilization or adoption. Drawing on interviews conducted with lesbian and gay parents as part of two qualitative research projects carried out between 2015 and 2020, Gusmeroli and Trappolin highlight how this group challenges the nuclear and heteronormative ideal of Italian familism at a political level and in everyday practices.

Transgender people are the focus of Sara J. English's contribution. In 'Kithship: Protective Aspects of a Family of Choice for Older Transgender Persons', English argues that all persons are provided with the opportunity of two families: kin – the family of chance to which one is born and kith – the family of choice, formed through intentional, reciprocal relationships. Focusing on older transgender people – a group who has been broadly ignored in research on families – she introduces a conceptual model examining social ties, explaining how *kith* provides protective aspects for older transgender persons, who are aging alone in uncertain times.

In 'Family Practices and Strategies of Middle-class Teachers in Argentina in the Context of COVID-19: Transformations and Discomforts in the Face of Care Processes and Labor Relations', Leila Martina Passerino and Denise Zenklusen examine the impact of Covid-19 on the education workforce in Argentina. Focusing on the narratives of middle-class heterosexual women teachers of different civil statuses (married, separated, living with their partner) and with children under age twelve, the chapters explore the tensions arising from the (over)demands of paid and unpaid work. Passerino and Zenklusen consider the gendered impact of the unequal division of domestic and care work for mothers, as well as the discomforts and emotions that mediate their experiences in a Covid-19 context and the strategies they deploy.

In their chapter 'In True Naval Fashion': Young People's Perspectives on Family Communication', Jo Bowser-Angermann, Leanne Gray, Abigail Wood, Matt Fossey and Lauren Godier-McBard consider the lived experiences of military children as they reflect on communication with their serving parent during various military deployments throughout their childhood. In her now classic work, Segal (1986) described the military and the family as greedy institutions and therefore open to increased conflict where they intersect. The changing digital landscape has made it possible too for military children to communicate with their serving parent using a range of social media and internet-based communication. The chapter offers an insight into the military family through its engagement with emotions and feelings and the role internet-based communication plays within these.

Finally, Nathan Fretwell and John Barker examine the experiences of parents fighting for educational justice. In 'From Active to Activist Parenting: Educational Struggle and the Injuries of Institutionalized Misrecognition', parental involvement is shown to be a key tenet of the British education system. Drawing on qualitative data collected from three parent-led campaign groups contesting either funding cuts to education or the academization of local schools, Fretwell and Barker detail how parents' activism disrupts dominant rationalities of parental involvement, subverts neoliberal self-interest and contributes to redefining what counts as 'good' parenting by centring the importance of activism and political engagement for children's civic development. The authors argue for a more expansive and socially just understanding of parental involvement that recognizes the importance of parents' political and civic engagement and call on educational authorities to value this engagement and work with, rather than against, parents.

In the concluding comments, we tease out some of the key themes drawn from the various chapters. We reflect on how this volume privileges notions of family that reside at the periphery of traditional Western family discourses and practice and how, in doing so, it seeks to render visible the norms that minoritize some family formations. In doing so, we renew with our original concern for social justice and strive to create spaces for the inclusion of other voices and other ways of 'doing family'.

# References

von Benzon, N., and C. Wilkinson (2019), *Intersectionality and Difference in Childhood and Youth*, London: Routledge.

Crimmins, G., S. Casey, J. McIntyre, G. Hook and T. Gates (2023), 'Collective Feminist Resistance and Agitation from within Australian Universities – Slaying the Dragon', in M. Ronksley-Pavia, M. M. Neumann, J. Manakil and K. Pickard-Smith (eds), *Academic Women: Voicing Narratives of Gendered Experiences*, 58–82, London: Bloomsbury.

Fraser, N. (2013), *Fortunes of Feminism: From State-Managed Capitalism to Neoliberal Crisis*, New York: Verso.

Halberstam, J. (2011), *The Queer Art of Failure*, Durham, NC: Duke University Press.

Hudak, J., and S. V. Giammattei (2010), 'Doing Family: Decentering Heteronormativity in "Marriage" and "Family" Therapy', *Expanding Our Social Justice Practices: Advances in Theory and Training*, Winter issue: 49–58.

Moreau, M. P. (2018), *Teachers, Gender and the Feminisation Debate*, London: Routledge.

Morgan, D. H. J. (2011), *Rethinking Family Practices*, Basingstoke: Palgrave.

Oswald, R. M., L. B. Blume and S. R. Marks (2005), 'Decentering Heteronormativity: A Model for Family Studies', in V. Bengston, A. Acock, K. Allen, P. Dilworth-Anderson and D. Klein (eds), *Sourcebook of Family Theory and Research*, 143–65, Thousand Oaks, CA: Sage.

Putnam, R. (2000), *Bowling Alone: The Collapse and Revival of American Community*, New York: Simon Schuster.

Reay, D. (2005), 'Doing the Dirty Work of Social Class? Mothers' Work in Support of Their Children's Schooling', *The Sociological Review*, 53: 104–16.

Ronksley-Pavia, M., M. M. Neumann, J. Manakil and K. Pickard-Smith (eds) (2022), *Academic Women: Voicing Narratives of Gendered Experiences*, London: Bloomsbury.

Roseneil, S., and S. Budgeon (2004), 'Cultures of Intimacy and Care Beyond "the Family": Personal Life and Social Change in the Early 21st Century', *Current Sociology*, 52 (2): 135–59.

Segal, M. (1986), 'The Military and the Family as Greedy Institutions', *Armed Forces and Society*, 13 (1): 9–38.

2

# Shifting Family Meanings: A Sociological Overview

João Paulo Mendes Carvalho and Cláudia Casimiro

## Introduction

Researchers in the social sciences have become increasingly interested in the family as a social institution, especially in the decades following the 1960s. In disciplines ranging from law to sociology, family studies has been established foremost as an interdisciplinary field that articulates knowledge from public policy, history, psychology and anthropology (Karraker and Grochowski 2012), and the various theoretical and methodological perspectives of these areas have resulted in a diverse body of knowledge regarding the understanding of the family (Smyth 2016). However, when taken as an element of social structure, it is important to keep in mind that the family will reflect the political and cultural dynamics of a given time and place. As a result, ongoing transformations occurring in various contexts will undoubtedly affect the meaning of what is understood as family.

Nevertheless, due to the social, political and personal changes that have occurred over the last few decades, the traditional family notion has been constantly challenged by new arrangements that reflect its own changes (Morgan 2011; Nguyen-Trung 2018). Theorists in the field of family sociology have already attempted to explain what lies behind some of these trends. The breakdown theory, for example, argues that the increasing divorce to marriage ratio and number of people living alone could be evidence of a growing individualization as opposed to adherence to notions of family responsibility and obligation. Conversely, the democratization theory highlights a progressive move towards a more flexible understanding of relationships that allows people to invest in mutual interactions rather than in contractual obligations based on biological ties. Finally, the continuity theory claims that practices of caring and trust, along with personal values, have remained unaltered (Gillies 2003), and therefore strategies capable of following such transformations must be developed within the various disciplinary fields even if this implies the reformulation of traditional understandings. This would certainly help provide a more rigorous analysis, sparkling important outcomes in different domains, such as policy and law, thus ensuring the legitimacy of new family configurations and practices that are no longer supported by the Western, heteronormative notion of marriage and reproduction.

## Sociological interest in the family

Sociology has long been devoted to the study of the family and its role in society as well as the effects of societal trends on the family, and this commitment continues today. From the classic tradition, including Émile Durkheim's contributions to the sociology of the family as a subject (Torres 2010), and Georg Simmel's work *On the Sociology of the Family*, first published in 1895 (Frisby 1998; Torres 2010), to contemporary authors such as Elizabeth Beck-Gernsheim (2002), Philip N. Cohen (2018) and Carol Smart (2007), investigations into the family have covered a wide range of themes, dealing with complex elements that play a crucial role in this social institution. However, the dominant theoretical and methodological framework in this scientific area has been shaped by a hegemonic Western knowledge, which has relied on stereotyped conceptualizations of the family as a biologically constituted relationship between father, mother and children that is legally recognized under the statute of marriage (Eldén 2016; Karpman, Ruppel and Torres 2018; Schadler 2016).

As stated by May and Dawson (2018), the development of sociological interest in the family has passed through distinct stages. At first, the meaning of family was strictly attached to the notion of family as a fixed entity. By the end of the 1980s, a move away from the traditional perspective allowed the inclusion of other themes in discussion of the family, such as unemployment, gendered dynamics and patriarchy (Ryan and Maxwell 2016). At this point, social class gained special attention in family matters, especially in comparative studies focused on highlighting the differences between families from distinct social classes. However, it was during the 1990s that a deeper shift gained momentum, and the traditional meaning of the family broadened towards a more plural, inclusive perspective on families and relationships (May and Dawson 2018).

While certain social phenomena – such as a growing individualization, decreasing birth rates, childhood sentimentality, the deinstitutionalization of marriage, increasing marriage to divorce ratios and an increasing number of couples 'living apart together' (Qiu 2022) – represent processes of deep transformation in family status and practices (Morgan 2011), this does not mean that society is experiencing the decline or a transition towards the end of the family. Rather, families are in transition (Karraker and Grochowski 2012), and there is a complexity in the ways in which individuals have expanded the definitions and constitutions of their families, representing a distancing from the traditional nuclear family perspective (Finch 2007; Morgan 2011; Nguyen-Trung 2018; Roseneil 2005; Schadler 2016; Stoilova et al. 2016).

In an attempt to shed light on some existing practices of decentring the Western, urban, nuclear notion of the family, Tam, Findlay and Kohen (2016, 2017) argue against the monocultural definition of family that excludes the complexities present in other cultures, such as those of indigenous people. Values such as cultural identity, language, kinship systems and household compositions appear to play a more fundamental role than blood ties in the definition of family within such groups. However, even among indigenous communities, family practices and definitions can be rather diverse and can take on a variety of different meanings and forms (Castellano 2002). Considering the unique characteristics of such communities, the institutions that share responsibility for the care of indigenous families face the complex task of delivering strategies for the protection of children, the promotion of education and the reinforcement of health practices while remaining sensitive to the particularities of their culture and identity.

Focusing on the Australian context, Morphy (2006) also emphasizes the importance of cultural and linguistic sensitivity, as well as the critical importance of the national census, which is a cornerstone in the development of public policies and the understanding of different family arrangements. In turn, Marchetti-Mercer (2006) emphasizes the need to question the notion of house, as opposed to the notion of home, when it comes to breaking the customary limitations of the prevailing narrative of family, since the house is typically seen as the fulcrum of the family. The author convincingly argues that, in many circumstances, rather than serving as a source of belonging, safety and love, house may represent a source of oppression, violence and conflict. As a result, home might be more of a feeling than a physical location, and it may or may not involve members of the family of origin.

Aside from the specific examples from non-Western contexts described earlier, the feminist and LGBTQ movements have also contributed to significant advancements in the expansion of the notion of family as a whole (Marques, Tavares and Magalhães 2002). The widespread use of contraceptive technologies, the increased participation of women in the labour force and the struggles for the legalization of same-sex marriage have all indicated significant shifts in the biographies of traditional life (Schadler 2016; Smyth 2016). Such events have brought about significant changes in social life, compelling the scientific community to advance new trends in sociological thought that are capable of drawing attention to important aspects of daily life, such as friendships, intimacy and personal and sexual relationships. Essentially, this has constituted a significant change towards a more flexible conceptual framework that mirrors the continual diversity of practices and meanings within the family (Jamieson 2020; Roseneil 2005; Wall and Gouveia 2014).

## 'Doing family': A relational frame of family dynamics

In recent decades, the strengthening of perspectives that criticize outdated assumptions of traditional approaches used in family sociology has been particularly helpful in advancing the concept of 'doing family'. Morgan (2011) developed the concept of 'family practices' to challenge the dominant perspective that referred to the family as a social structure. Based on a critical stance regarding 'the family', Morgan (1996) argued in favour of the family as a set of daily practices across different realms of interactions, that is, 'people doing family as they act pragmatically within their circumstances' (Duncan 2011: 138), in opposition to the structuralist idea of the family. In the wake of Morgan's argument that 'contemporary families are defined more by "doing" family things than by "being" a family', Finch (2007) emphasizes the creative capacity of individuals to establish their practices and, above all, to display them, demonstrating that the notion of family is subject to transformations and that displaying practices of care and support configure unique meanings of family.

The 'doing family' perspective has gained visibility and provided a productive ground in some sociological investigations, namely those considering the wide diversity of realities, such as the bonds and mechanisms of transnational families (Vivas-Romero 2017), the dynamics and negotiations of families living apart together (Stoilova et al. 2016), family and friendship bonds mediated by communication technologies (Nedelcu and Wyss 2016; Policarpo 2016; Takasaki 2017) and strategies of care and solidarity among immigrants (Bayramoğlu and Lünenborg 2018; Kaplan 2016; Reyes-Santos and Lara 2018).

In this sense, to respond to the uncertainties and complexities of recent decades regarding family issues, it is essential to decentralize traditional perspectives in sociology to allow the emergence of perspectives that broaden the understanding of family beyond the traditional biological order, while actively exploring new personal-life dynamics and practices constituting different meanings of family (Allen and Mendez 2018; Budgeon and Roseneil 2004; Eldén 2016; Finch 2007; Morgan 2011; Schadler 2016). Research dedicated to the formation of families of choice (Weston 1991) and the deconstruction of the myth of the nuclear family (Lehr 1999) has galvanized the search for such new perspectives.

Historically associated with the LGBTQ community, the formation of families of choice emerged as a support strategy among peers experiencing discrimination and rejection by their family of origin and by members of their social circles (Weston 1991). With a strong expression in the United States, ballroom culture represented the subversion of the consanguineous family logic: the bonds of friendship and solidarity became the centre of family logic (Hull and Ortyl 2019). Friendship bonds then take centre stage in personal networks, serving as the primary source of emotional, financial and social support (Takasaki 2017), particularly among queer Latino and African-American communities (Karpman, Ruppel and Torres 2018). Although the practice of setting up families of choice is still strongly associated with the LGBTQ community, Hull and Ortyl (2019) state that the definitions of family among LGBTQ individuals are quite confluent: they consist of expansive and innovative strategies without abandoning the importance of biological family ties. Such an understanding confirms what May and Norqvist (2019) identified as the core of the sociology of personal life, which undeniably brings valorous insights into the discussion, when they link the importance of non-familial relations established on a daily basis to a larger dimension that encompasses the complex understandings of what counts as family.

## Sociological overview of the topic

Based on a literature review of the SAGE Journals database, we sought to analyse how sociological production has contributed to new meanings of the family. The SAGE Journals were chosen given their international relevance and large amount of published work in the social sciences. The following keywords were used to identify the relevant literature: kinship, personal life, family, personal relations, intimacy and chosen family. Eligible articles had to be in the field of sociology and published between 2011 and 2021. Duplicated work was removed and book chapters were not included. We performed a qualitative analysis, since our main goal was to provide an overview of the sociological contribution to the topic of new family meanings while critically discussing the findings (Pautasso 2020). Most of the reviewed studies relied on qualitative research methodologies, and the most frequently used technique in these was the interview. Focus groups, non-participant observation, surveys and mixed methods techniques were also employed in some of the studies, but less often.

Despite the methodological homogeneity present across the reviewed studies, both the plurality of the topics covered and the variety of samples reveal the versatility underlying the approaches to the topic of interest. Both the notion of 'doing family', proposed by Morgan (1996, 2011), as well as the practice of 'displaying' (Finch 2007) are extensively explored by authors who challenge the traditional perspective dominant in family sociology. Dyson, Berghs and Atkin (2015), for example, show how the idea of 'displaying family' can be used in the context of sickle cell clinics to understand the experiences of fathers by considering race, age and class among other aspects of identity.

Other than a coherent use of the 'doing family' and 'displaying' frameworks the intersectional perspective was also employed to explore social trends that may impact cultural, political and personal dynamics. This reflects a greater theoretical capacity to understand the phenomenon of family practices (Allen and Mendez 2018; Karpman, Ruppel and Torres 2018), especially among groups whose identities have been historically marginalized and oppressed.

The diversity of groups included in the reviewed studies favours the understanding of trends pointed out by the authors regarding the diffusion of family practices. That is, the notion of family beyond that of nuclear or biological family, historically portrayed as a practice of the LGBTQ community, is already dominant even among groups of heterosexual people (Roseneil 2005; Smyth 2016). Hull and Ortyl (2019) show that a greater social acceptance of homosexuality has promoted changes in the personal networks of LGBTQ individuals to the extent that families of choice do not imply a replacement of biological families but rather their being complemented through meaningful connections established by choice.

Research focused on friendship ties has highlighted the growing importance of friends in everyday life (Policarpo 2016; Takasaki 2017) due to the central role they play in support networks at social, emotional, informational and financial levels. Cronin (2015) also investigated friendship ties with regard to how gender norms prevail among friends and heterosexual couples, calling attention to the relational qualities of the ties. Adopting a qualitative perspective, Cronin (2015) demonstrated that friendship and coupledom represent different elements of personal life in the social ordering of intimacy. Moreover, given its ideological strength, the couple culture is questioned mainly when a person experiences a serious relationship breakdown or is single for a long time, which allows space to reflect on the importance of friends in the past. Cronin (2015) also argues that similarly to the family, friendship is a set of practices and should be understood accordingly, given that it will often represent the largest part of an individual's personal networks.

Exploring the complex ties that bind people to communal housing, Törnqvist (2019) explored the experiences of people living in such settings, helping shed light on discussions about the institutionalization of friendship. The author presents poignant arguments that bring the social dimension into play in the matter of people's ability to make choices regarding their housing composition, especially when such choices arise due to financial difficulties or simply as a negotiation of intimacy.

Additionally, some scholars mention the increasing importance of information and communication technology (ICT) as relevant to maintaining long-distance relationships (Bayramoğlu and Lünenborg 2018; Policarpo 2016; Wood et al. 2022). ICT plays a crucial role in the case of immigrants whose friends and family members live in their country of origin or in a different one (Brown 2019; Vivas-Romero 2017). ICT can also play an important role in helping immigrants to find a sense of belonging in virtual spaces, based on individual preferences or personal identities (Bayramoglu and Lünenborg 2018). Furthermore, ICT may help to enhance the feeling of 'being together at a distance' and can create a sense of everyday life through certain rituals, despite the challenges imposed by at-distance relations, as pointed out by Nedelcu and Wyss (2016). Such literature corroborates what Schout and De Jong (2018) called 'centrality of personal communities', which refers to the increasing importance of chosen bonds, mainly of friendship, and of decentring family ties based on biological kinship, although the importance of the latter for individuals is undeniable. Not surprisingly, faced with the Covid-19 pandemic, virtual communication has gained dramatic importance not only in the daily lives of immigrant families but in society as a whole, given the need for confinement and reduction in physical contact (Casimiro and Neves 2021).

The unprecedented impact of the pandemic has resulted in shifts in different spheres and dynamics of social life, disrupting established norms of home, space and social relations. Nevertheless, caring and support practices outside the family context have gained increasing attention, with particular focus on the role that community resources and personal networks play under such circumstances. Impoverished countries have been disproportionally affected by the pandemic (Nayak et al. 2021) and face scenarios of greater hardships in terms of food insecurity, poverty and joblessness (Chan 2021), alongside a worsening of existing social inequalities (Martins-Filho et al. 2020). In the face of insufficient or non-existent governmental responses to such scenarios, the importance of local communities' responses in mitigating the negative effects of the pandemic becomes even greater (Fisher et al. 2020). Acts of solidarity have arisen across diverse communities, with a sharing of responsibilities for the most vulnerable and marginalized individuals and families (Martinez and De Gasperi 2021; Nayak et al. 2021). Mobilizing communities' resources has proven to be very efficient in fostering resilient, innovative and sustainable responses through collective engagement.

Eldén (2016) explored children's understandings of family and found that they considered those who provide care as part of their families, even if those people do not have any biological or kinship tie. This study goes some way to corroborate Finch's (2007) argument regarding 'display', that is, that the demonstration of care practices plays a fundamental role in the individuals' perceptions about what counts as family.

In a different context, Bian, Hao and Li (2018) explored the relationship between formal and informal support networks and well-being by means of a transnational analysis comparing Australia, England and China. They found that strong effectiveness of informal support networks such as those based on kinship, friendship and acquaintance were more highly correlated with subjective well-being than formal support networks, such as work ties and formal organizations. The authors argue that this may be related to the greater emotional functions performed by informal networks compared to formal networks, which are mostly related to instrumental or practical functions in daily life.

Several authors have indicated the need to provide a suitable theoretical framework regarding changes in the family (Jamieson 2020; Oláh 2015; Roseneil 2005; Roseneil and Ketokivi 2015; Schadler 2016), while others have strongly critiqued family sociology as being unable to capture the complexity of existing everyday life practices and have stressed the relevance of investigating personal relationships (Roseneil and Ketokivi 2015). Despite the existence of approaches opposed to the dichotomy of the family as an institution versus the family as a practice (Smyth, 2016), a more significant transformation regarding family types (from organized to disorganized) has been emphasized rather than the theory of family 'dismantlement'.

The feminization of care work has also been identified as a relevant phenomenon in the question of family meanings. Brown (2019) pointed to the different family typologies presented by immigrant caregivers, which subvert the biological notion of kinship, expanding them to the relationships built in the context of their role as care workers. The author emphasizes, however, that the gendered approach must be critically analysed since it sheds light on the need to redefine solidarity networks, redistribution and collectivization of care, and this should include a criticism of the very structures that lead women to disproportionately opt for 'care functions' (Brown 2019). According to this perspective, it would be possible to imagine a profound transformation in the social fabric from the practices of solidarity and collective care, especially regarding the engagement of men in such activities.

Holmes, Jamieson and Natalier (2021) explored interpersonal relations in the domestic sphere with the aim of better understanding the emotional reflexivity of women in non-normative relationships, which the authors defined as those that challenge normative notions of coupledom such as gender roles, childcare responsibilities and cohabitation. Their findings point to women's challenges and bravery in imagining queer futures and their agency to stand against the dominant gender paradigm, while negotiating their own intimacy more broadly.

Russel (2019) makes a compelling argument as to why the discussion should include the social implications that a rigid definition of family may have on the lives of those whose family meanings and compositions do not fit such a definition. In other words, the dominant discourse legitimizes some kinds of relations, placing them in the family realm, while considering anything else to not represent 'real family'. Not surprisingly, this has negative implications on the health and well-being of diverse families, reiterating the need to respect their right to be recognized as family regardless of their composition.

In summary, important conceptual discussions have taken place among certain scholars regarding the understanding of the family, allowing space for more inclusive meanings. Brynin and Ermish (2008) highlight the transition from a very structured view of family to a more complex and dynamic network of relationships, in which new arrangements can now be perceived as family. The evident move towards a broader conceptualization of family has been facilitated by contributions in the field of family studies regarding concepts such as intimacy, personal life and kinship. Along these lines, Edwards and Gillies (2012) cast doubt on the argument that the concept of family is outdated and thus should no longer be employed as a main unit of analysis. In accordance with the broadening of the definition of families, in the plural sense, the authors emphasize the enduring importance of this concept, especially regarding the related public and political discourses.

## Reflections on family trends and social implications in the Portuguese context

As discussed earlier, in recent decades, rapidly changing social dynamics have been of the utmost importance in promoting a more inclusive understanding of family, despite its remaining limitations. However, there is no doubt that the call to pay more attention to family practices has positively contributed to new debates in various areas, particularly in the law and social policies.

As an illustration, developments in European family life, such as shifting household composition, concerns about work–life balance, increasing divorce to marriage ratios and changes in gender roles have all been shown to have had distinct impacts on the dynamics of family life in recent decades (Silva and Jorge 2018). Furthermore, in recent decades, the sheer relevance of such tendencies has revealed the need for new, updated family policies. Regarding divorce rates, an increasing tendency can be observed across the European context. According to the database PORDATA – Statistics about Portugal and Europe (FFMS 2020), Portugal showed a relatively high divorce to marriage ratio. This increasing tendency may be related to trends in policies that work either as causes or as consequences of social and family changes (Jorge and Silva 2018). Conversely, Hungary showed a lower divorce to marriage ratio in the same year, the lowest in the European Union (FFMS 2020). Such trends can be partly attributed to the strong influence of traditional church values and the government's efforts to tackle the country's demographic decline, such as family-building policies focused on encouraging marriage, providing better conditions for childbearing and improving work–life balance (Fűrész and Molnár 2021).

Compared to other European countries, Portugal was late to enter the demographic transition towards the diversification of the traditional family due to its many years under dictatorship. As a result, while many European countries were already witnessing changes in the family context, such as higher divorce-marriage ratio and increasing numbers of non-traditional households and young people living alone, Portugal remained strongly attached to the family principles of the Catholic Church. However, following the fall of the Portuguese dictatorial regime, the growth in the number of diverse families surged rapidly and acutely, leading Portugal to join those countries experiencing the most intense family transformations, namely the decrease in catholic marriages, the increase in single-parent families and the already mentioned increase in marriage to divorce ratios. According to Silva and Smart (2004), the link between policies and current family configurations is marked by a lack of congruence in the kind of support provided as well as in the very understandings and definitions of what family is.

Concerning the social changes that have occurred in Portugal, it can be inferred that two main movements marked the transformations in family values and practices. The first movement, which took place around the 1940s and 1950s, was characterized by a strong coupledom norm of the family – the 'conjugalisation' of family life – (Gouveia and Widmer 2014) and by very strong and well-defined gender roles. The second, which advanced after the 1960s, pointed to greater equality in gender-role dynamics within family life, access to contraceptive methods and valourization of individual life (Gouveia and Widmer 2014).

The rapidly changing and increasingly complex social and family contexts pushed social institutions to the edge, demanding support for and legitimization of non-dominant family arrangements. The early 2000s represented a turning point for family policies in Portugal, paving the way for the protection of same-sex relationships despite a tenacious resistance to recognizing such relationships as belonging to the realm of family (Marques, Tavares and Magalhães 2002). Examples are the right to adoption by same-sex couples achieved in 2016 and the changes in parental employment leave for men that allowed fathers to be more engaged in caring activities instead of relying exclusively on mothers. These also point to a policy transformation that reflects family practices and needs. Noticing the shifts occurring in the past decades regarding the broader understanding of the family, it is possible to argue that new perspectives of families are not only more widespread within society, pointing to its importance in current social dynamics, but are also essentially more complex in terms of composition, fluidity and commitment. Lastly, since family is also constructed through discursive practices, the need to broaden its political, social and cultural definition will be imperative in achieving a more inclusive and diverse understanding of what can be understood as a family.

## Final remarks

The literature analysed herein has allowed a rich understanding of a very broad thematic range that is able to challenge traditional sociological thought regarding the family. The theoretical proposals have provided a robust understanding of family practices that subvert the traditional notion of coupledom, legitimized by the marriage statute. Contributions from the sociology of personal life have proven very promising for refining methodology, theory and epistemology in sociological studies into the ways in which people organize, define and display their understandings of family.

The sociological thought built on the concept of 'doing family' enabled and expanded the understanding of the promotion of care and solidarity practices among individuals whose definitions of family are not primarily based on the biological ties. The literature has also shown that such chosen bonds neither replace nor minimize the importance of biological ones; rather, they can assume a complementary feature that may compensate the needs of an individual at some specific level. Future studies should focus on comparative investigation between young and elderly cohorts, to understand how historical shifts may impact the way they negotiate and construct their definitions of family.

Finally, the urgent need for a paradigm shift, particularly in traditional family sociology, is re-emphasized in this chapter. Choosing the nuclear family as the yardstick for determining what constitutes a family ignores the wide diversity of family configurations, dynamics and practices that exist in reality. Notably, when non-traditional arrangements are assimilated into one's everyday life and into society as a whole, they develop new connotations that invariably compel the broadening of the fundamental concept of family. Furthermore, it is critical to remember the social role that families play in the process of bringing about structural changes. Once we have examined how social definitions have an impact on families, it is equally important to evaluate the dialects that are involved in this process, that is, the activities that occur in various families that reverberate socially and, as a result, help to build new meanings. The heuristic significance of the family, however, continues to have substantial value despite the obvious and compelling need to rethink the notion of the family. This is particularly true when it comes to how people nourish their sense of belonging and identity on both a personal and a community level.

# References

Allen, S. H., and S. N. Mendez (2018), 'Hegemonic Heteronormativity: Toward a New Era of Queer Family Theory', *Journal of Family Theory & Review*, 10: 70–86.

Bayramoğlu, Y., and M. Lünenborg (2018), 'Queer Migration and Digital Affects: Refugees Navigating from the Middle East via Turkey to Germany', *Sexuality and Culture*, 22: 1019–36.

Beck-Gernsheim, E. (2002), *Reinventing the Family. On Search of New Life Styles*, Cambridge: Policy Press.

Bian, Y., M. Hao and Y. Li (2018), 'Social Networks and Subjective Well-Being: A Comparison of Australia, Britain, and China', *Journal of Happiness Studies*, 19: 2489–508.

Brown, R. (2019), 'Reproducing the National Family: Kinship Claims, Development Discourse and Migrant Caregivers in Palestine/Israel', *Feminist Theory*, 20 (3): 1–22.

Brynin, M., and J. Ermish (eds) (2008), *Changing Relationships*, London: Routledge.

Budgeon, S., and S. Roseneil (2004), 'Editors' Introduction: Beyond the Conventional Family', *Current Sociology*, 52 (2): 127–34.

Casimiro, C., and B. Neves (2021), 'Vida familiar e tecnologias de informação e comunicação num mundo globalizado', *Análise Social*, 56 (2): 308–21.

Castellano, M. (2002), *Aboriginal Family Trends: Extended Families, Nuclear Families, Families of the Heart*, Ottawa: The Vanier Institute of the Family.

Chan, H. Y. (2021), 'Mental Wellbeing in a Pandemic: The Role of Solidarity and Care', *Public Health Ethics*, 14 (1): 47–58.

Cohen, P. N. (2018), *The Family: Diversity, Inequality, and Social Change*, second edition, New York: W.W. Norton.

Cronin, A. (2015), 'Gendering Friendship: Couple Culture, Heteronormativity and the Production of Gender', *Sociology*, 49 (6): 1167–82.

Duncan, S. (2011), 'Personal Life, Pragmatism, and Bricolage', *Sociological Research Online*, 16 (4): 129–40.

Dyson, S., M. Berghs and K. Atkin (2015), '"Talk to Me. There's Two of Us": Fathers and Sickle Cell Screening', *Sociology*, 50 (1): 178–94.

Edwards, R., and V. Gillies (2012), 'Farewell to the Family? Notes on an Argument for Retaining the Concept', *Families, Relationships and Societies*, 1 (1): 63–9.

Eldén, S. (2016), 'An Ordinary Complexity of Care: Moving beyond "The Family" in Research with Children', *Families, Relationships and Societies*, 5 (2): 175–92.

FFMS (2020), 'Statistics about Portugal and Europe', *PORDATA – Statistical Facts about the Municipalities, Portugal and Europe*, retrieved from: https://www.pord ata.pt/en/Europe/Number+of+divorces+per+100+marriages-1566. Accessed on 1 October 2022.

Finch, J. (2007), 'Displaying Families', *Sociology*, 4 (1): 65–81.

Fisher, J., J. C. Languilaire, R. Lawthom, R. Nieuwenhuis, R. J. Petts, K. Runswick-Cole and A. Y. Mara (2020), 'Community, Work, and Family in Times of COVID-19', *Community, Work & Family*, 23 (3): 247–52.

Frisby, D. (1998), 'Introduction to Georg Simmel's "On the Sociology of the Family"', in *Theory, Culture & Society*, Special Issue on Love and Eroticism, 15: 3–4.

Fűrész, T., and B. Molnár (2021), 'The First Decade of Building a Family-Friendly Hungary', *Quaderns de Polítiques Familiars*, 7: 6–17.

Gillies, V. (2003), 'Family and Intimate Relationships: A Review of the Sociological Research', Families & Social Capital ESRC Research Group, London: South Bank University.

Gouveia, R., and E. Widmer (2014), 'The Salience of Kinship in Personal Networks of Three Cohorts of Portuguese People', *Families, Relationships and Societies*, 3 (3): 355–72.

Holmes, M., L. Jamieson and K. Natalier (2021), 'Future Building and Emotional Reflexivity: Gendered or Queered Navigations of Agency in Non-Normative Relationships?' *Sociology*, 55 (4): 734–50.

Hull, K., and T. Ortyl (2019), 'Conventional and Cutting-Edge: Definitions of Family in LGBT Communities', *Sexuality Research and Social Policy*, 16: 31–43.

Jamieson, L. (2020), 'Sociologies of Personal Relationships and the Challenge of Climate Change', *Sociology*, 54 (2): 219–36.

Kaplan, D. (2016), 'Social Club Sociability as a Model for National Solidarity', *American Journal of Cultural Sociology*, 6 (1): 1–36.

Karpman, H. E., E. H. Ruppel and M. Torres (2018), '"It Wasn't Feasible for Us": Queer Women of Color Navigating Family Formation', *Family Relations*, 67 (1): 118–31.

Karraker, M. W., and J. R. Grochowski (2012), *Families with Futures: Family Studies into the 21st Century*, second edition, London: Routledge.

Lehr, V. (1999), *Queer Family Values: Debunking the Myth of the Nuclear Family*, Philadelphia: Temple University Press.

Marchetti-Mercer, M. (2006), 'New Meaning of "Home" in South Africa', *Acta Academica*, 38 (2): 191–218.

Marques, C., M. Tavares and M. Magalhães (2002), 'Políticas e família: orientações legislativas em Portugal nos últimos anos. Actas do Colóquio Internacional "*Família, Género e Sexualidade nas Sociedades Contemporâneas*"', Lisboa, Associação Portuguesa de Sociologia.

Martinez, A. W., and F. De Gasperi (2021), 'Who Cares for What? Care Networks and New Urban Activisms in Madrid: Restating Solidarity', *Culture, Practice & Europeanization*, 6 (1): 15–38.

Martins-Filho, P. R., A. A. de Souza Araújo, L. J. Quintans-Júnior and V. S. Santos (2020), 'COVID-19 Fatality Rates Related to Social Inequality in Northeast Brazil: A Neighbourhood-Level Analysis', *Journal of Travel Medicine*, 27 (7): 1–3.

May, V., and M. Dawson (2018), 'Families and Relationships', Introduction, *Sociology*, special e-issue 52 (4): 1–10.

May, V., and P. Norqvist (2019), *Sociology of Personal Life*, second edition, London: Red Globe Press.

Morgan, D. (1996), *Family Connections*, Cambridge: Polity Press.

Morgan, D. (2011), 'Locating "Family Practices"', *Sociological Research Online*, 16 (4): online. Accessed on 1 March 2023, https://doi.org/10.5153/sro.25.

Morphy, F. (2006), 'Lost in Translation? Remote Indigenous Households and Definitions of the Family', *Family Matters*, 73: 23–31.

Nayak, S. S., A. J. Scoglio, D. Mirand, A. Oates, M. Rabow and E. M. Molnar (2021), 'Movement and Solidarity: Community Mobilization to Mitigate the Adverse Impact of COVID-19 on Families with Young Children Receiving Care from Early Childhood Systems', *Child Care in Practice*, published online: https://doi/full/10.1080/13575279.2021.2002810.

Nedelcu, M., and M. Wyss (2016), ' "Doing Family" through ICT-Mediated Ordinary Co-presence: Transnational Communication Practices of Romanian Migrants in Switzerland', *Global Networks*, 16 (2): 202–18.

Nguyen-Trung, K. (2018), 'From Sociology of the Family to Sociology of Personal Life: A Review of the Literature', *Sociology*, 6 (2): 22–33.

Oláh, L. (2015), 'Changing Families in the European Union: Trends and Policy Implications', analytical paper, prepared for the United Nations Expert Group Meeting, 'Family Policy Development: Achievements and Challenges', New York, 14–15 May.

Pautasso, M. (2020), 'The Structure and Conduct of a Narrative Literature Review', in Mohammadali M. Shoja, A. Arynchyna, M. Loukas, A. V. D'Antoni, S. M. Buerger, M. Karl and R. S. Tubbs (eds), *A Guide to the Scientific Career: Virtues, Communication, Research, and Academic Writing*, New York: John Wiley.

Policarpo, V. (2016), ' "The Real Deal": Managing Intimacy within Friendship at a Distance', *Qualitative Sociology Review*, 12: 22–42.

Qiu, S. (2022), 'Negotiating Intimacy and Family at Distance: Living Apart Together Relationship in China', in S. Quaid, C. Hugman and A. Wilcock (eds), *Negotiating Families and Personal Lives in the 21st Century – Exploring Diversity, Social Change and Inequalities*, 77–92, London: Routledge.

Reyes-Santos, A., and A. Lara (2018), 'Mangú y mofongo: Intergenerational Dominican-Puerto Rican Kinship, Intra-Latinx Subjectivities, and Latinidad', *Centro Journal*, 30 (1): 48–81.

Roseneil, S. (2005), 'Living and Loving beyond the Boundaries of the Heteronorm: Personal Relationships in the 21st Century', in L. Mackie, S. Cunningham-Burley and J. McKendrick (eds), *Families in Society: Boundaries and Relationships*, 241–58, Bristol: Policy Press.

Roseneil, S., and K. Ketokivi (2015), 'Relational Persons and Relational Processes: Developing the Notion of Relationality for the Sociology of Personal Life, *Sociology*, 50 (1): 143–59.

Russel, S. (2019), 'Social Justice and the Future of Healthy Families: Sociocultural Changes and Challenges', *Family Relations*, 68 (3): 358–70.

Ryan, L., and C. Maxwell (2016), 'Social Class and Sociology: The State of the Debate between 1967 and 1979', *Sociology*, 50 (4): E1–E11.

Schadler, C. (2016), 'How to Define Situated and Ever-Transforming Family Configurations? A New Materialist Approach', *Journal of Family Theory Review*, 8: 503–14.

Schout, G., and G. De Jong (2018), 'The Weakening of Kin Ties: Exploring the Need for Life-World Led Interventions', *International Journal of Environmental Research and Public Health*, 15 (2): 203.

Silva, E., and C. Smart (2004), *The New Family?* London: SAGE.

Silva, M. C., and A. R. Jorge (2018), 'Conjugal Dissolution and Gender (In)Equalities: A Study of Divorce Processes in Portugal', *Sociology Study*, 8 (6): 267–86.

Smart, C. (2007), *Personal Life – New Directions in Sociological Thinking*, Cambridge: Polity Press.

Smyth, L. (2016), 'The Disorganized Family: Institutions, Practices and Normativity', *The British Journal of Sociology*, 67 (4): 678–96.

Stoilova, M., S. Roseneil, J. Carter, S. Duncan and M. Phillips (2016), 'Constructions, Reconstructions and Deconstructions of "Family" amongst People Who Live Apart Together (LATs)', *The British Journal of Sociology*, 68 (1): 78–96.

Takasaki, K. (2017), 'Friends and Family in Relationship Communities: The Importance of Friendship during the Transition to Adulthood', *Michigan Family Review*, 21 (1): 76–96.

Tam, B., L. Findlay and D. Kohen (2016), 'Indigenous Families: Who Do You Call Family?', *Journal of Family Studies*, 23 (3): 243–59.

Tam, B., L. Findlay and D. Kohen (2017), 'Conceptualization of Family: Complexities of Defining an Indigenous Family', *Indigenous Policy Journal*, 18 (1): 1–19.

Torres, A. (2010), *Sociologia da Família. Teorias e Debates*, Provas de Agregação. Lisboa: ISCTE-IUL.

Törnqvist, M. (2019), 'Living Alone Together: Individualized Collectivism in Swedish Communal Housing', *Sociology*, 53 (5): 900–15.

Vivas-Romero, M. (2017), 'More than Just "Friends"? Locating Migrant Domestic Workers' Transnational Voluntary Kin Relationships', *Journal of Family Studies*, 26 (3): 389–404.

Wall, K., and Gouveia, R. (2014), 'Changing Meanings of Family in Personal Relationships', *Current Sociology*, 62 (3): 352–73.

Weston, K. (1991), *Families We Choose: Lesbians, Gays, Kinship*, New York: Columbia University Press.

Wood, A., L. Gray, J. Bowser-Angermann, P. Gibson, M. Fossey and L. Godier-McBard (2022), 'Social Media and Internet-Based Communication in Military Families during Separation: An International Scoping Review', *New Media & Society*, available online https://doi.org/10.1177/14614448221117767.

3

# Children's Valuations of Kinship Care Family Life – Cost-effective Substitute Care or Multiple Ambivalent Affiliations in Flux

Paul Shuttleworth

## Introduction

Kinship care is a full-time caring arrangement within the family constellation for children unable to remain with their birth parents. Most countries recognize that the family members can be related by legal family ties, biologically, or through previous meaningful relationships (Winokur, Holtan and Batchelder 2018).

For children who are unable to remain living with their birth parents, kinship care is the fastest growing care option around the world (Leinaweaver 2014). It is seemingly natural, and it feels like the right thing to do, to want to care for our family's children if their parents are unable. Due to the increase in global poverty and death rates following the Covid-19 pandemic, the number of these arrangements is likely to increase. However, kinship care remains relatively under-theorized and subjugated in research, policy and practice (Brown et al. 2019). When acknowledged, it is typically seen in research, policy, legislation and practice as an alternative permanence option, substitute care and a cost-effective social work service. Often anthropological, sociological and historical explanations of family life are disregarded (Skoglund and Thørnblad 2019); the present chapter attempts to rectify this.

Using the findings from research, children's views provide insight into *how* family life is practised in kinship care arrangements (Shuttleworth 2021). The children in the study emphasized that family involves practices that are performed, developed and displayed. The children also use spaces, places, time and narratives in resourceful ways to explore and test the tensions of family life, which are situated in a world of seeming contradictions. After hearing from the children, in this chapter, I reflect on and further analyse their views. It demonstrates that the presumptive adult framing of family can often fall short in reflecting the reality of a child's life. Specifically, helpful theories that emerge from children's views challenge the traditional hierarchical, institutionalized, gendered, white, Global North, heteronormative family ideals. Most importantly, this chapter highlights that children can demonstrate a sophisticated and nuanced grasp of their family life experiences, intentions and needs. This gives weight to the value of children being experts in their own lives, so we must provide space for children to participate in discussions about the meaning of family life.

## What is our understanding of family life kinship care?

### Historical-socio-political understandings of kinship care

Kinship care is the quickest growing care route for children who are unable to live with their birth parents. However, the prevalence and concept of kinship care are not new. It is one of the oldest customs for bringing up children. Throughout history, kinship care as a concept and a practice can be found in international anthropological studies. For example, references to kinship care are found in accounts of ancient Greece and Rome, where it was seen as an efficient way to protect successors (Enke 2019). Kinship care, as a phrase, is thought to originate from documentation of those subject to slavery in the United States (Geen 2004).

A phrase, made famous by Hilary Clinton (2007), generally applied to kinship care, comes from communities in Africa – 'it takes a whole village to raise a child' (Swadener, Kabiru and Njenga 2000). This attitude is taken in many other societies. For example, In Poland and India, the more employable parents work away from the children, often abroad. At the same time, other family members, usually grandparents, take on the majority of care for the family's children. Therefore, family practices are collective ventures in many parts of the world. In such places, kinship care is seen as an everyday, efficient and effective way of doing family (Owusu-Bempah 2010).

As described throughout this book, the discourse surrounding family norms is subject to sociopolitical, historical and cultural contexts. In the past fifty years or so, there has been a rise in the acceptance of divorce, same-sex parents having children, chain migration and a shift away from the stereotyped work–family responsibilities. This has produced more fluidity and diversity in family life.

However, much thinking and many children and family governmental policies, especially for children's care away from their birth parents, favour the Global North, white, heteronormative middle-class ideal (Boddy 2019). They show a preference for idealized family, or 'family-like', upbringings. They routinely draw distinctions between 'normal' families and the 'troubled', or rather 'troublesome' or 'troubling' ones (Smith 2015). Therefore, in many high-income countries, it is assumed that the use of kinship care by families is only for troublesome families using an abnormal family arrangement (McCartan et al. 2018; Owusu-Bempah 2010; Pratchett and Rees 2017).

Gendered notions also impact such normative ideals that caregivers should be women. It is of little surprise, then, that kinship carers are more likely to be women (e.g. Wijedasa 2015). One of the reasons for this is that patriarchal capitalist doctrines assign women the labour of paid and unpaid care (Lara 2013). For kinship care, this means that despite ongoing concern around intergenerational cycles of abuse for kinship care, such as 'the apple does not fall far from the tree' (Peters 2005: 598), almost in contradiction, the responsibility of care falls to women who should undertake the task without payment, kudos or state intervention.

Such political, sociological and anthropological considerations are often disregarded in kinship care literature, research and policy. One of the main reasons for the move away from sociopolitical understandings is high-income countries' tendency to understand kinship care as a solution to child protection and child welfare concerns (Skoglund and Thørnblad 2019). This service-oriented understanding focuses on what are perceived to be more measurable outcomes. Typically, these are considerations to 'placement' stability for children and comparisons to other effects such as health and well-being, which are then pitted against other out-of-home care arrangements such as adoption and fostering. Kinship care in this context becomes viewed 'more as a technology and less as a family' (Skoglund and Thørnblad 2019: 4). The introduction of kinship care into the arena of state responsibility and as a technology for the care and protection of children also means that when it is considered, it is typically situated into discourses surrounding adoption and fostering. In particular, there has been an attempt to slot kinship care family life into notions of permanence.

## Social work, permanence discourses and cost-effective placements

Permanence is a construct that features heavily in social work theory. It centres on the philosophy of a child's position within their family. Permanence is typically aligned with discourses around belonging, affiliation, heritage, history, emotional continuity and for children (Boddy 2017). These concepts of what matters for family identity are embedded in attachment theories, socialization theories and child development studies (Simmonds 2014).

For some time, many academics and policymakers have maintained that emotional permanence and a sense of permanence are most fundamental (Thoburn 1994). Nevertheless, how a sense of permanence is achieved has been a source of ongoing debate within social work permanency literature. Two primary counterpoint arguments exist for a child acquiring a sense of permanence: substitute psychological parenting and the preservation of family or support post-separation (Shuttleworth 2021).

The concept of psychological parenting was initially conceived by Goldstein, Freud and Solnit (1979). Critical for kinship care, psychological parenting suggests that if the birth parents do not meet the child's psychological needs, their parenting should be entirely cut off. Instead, the children need a substitute family and parenting, forever completely severed from previous carers.

As a counterpoint, this notion of severance and substitute families has been interrogated by other literature. Some of the principal arguments against complete separation are:

1. It is now known that psychologically a child can manage several caregiving relationships (Cassidy, Jones and Shaver 2013).
2. Birth parents are often psychologically present, even if they are not physically present (Samuels 2009).
3. There are difficulties concerning the practicalities of complete post-separation severance in the backdrop of social media, which is constantly changing in modern times (Samuels 2018).
4. The complete severance stance takes particular concepts of heteronormativity (Hicks 2005), nuclear family norms and conventional gender roles that do not imitate current family set-ups (Goldberg 2019).

Kinship care adds another factor to the permanence debate. Because children in kinship care arrangements are separated from birth parents whilst remaining within their family constellation, complete severance will be difficult to sustain, even logistically. There will always be connections, either through continuing relationships elsewhere in the family or seemingly innocuous things such as family likeness. Therefore, whilst policy debates may often drag kinship care into such disputes, the continuity and discontinuity ones concerning fostering and adoption may not apply.

Whilst these debates on what arrangement is most effective to provide permanence continue, an even more pressing consideration for policymakers is that kinship care is a financially attractive child welfare solution for governments (McGhee et al. 2018). Economic pressures on governments have heightened following the 2008 financial crash, and the Covid-19 pandemic is likely to generate more stark years in an effort to reduce government debt (Emmerson and Stockton 2020). Governments have found that they can reduce spending by cutting the number of children looked after by the state. It is, therefore, cheaper for children to be in informal kinship care where practical and financial support is discretionary, and local authorities are often not notified. Even when the state finances and, to some extent, supports formal kinship arrangements, less training is given, there are no recruitment costs and start-up costs are lower (McCartan et al. 2018). This need to cut costs has impacted the demand to use kinship care, no matter how the family set-up is seen to conform, or not, to normative family or permanence ideals.

Overall, then, discourse around kinship care is typically constrained by the need for cost-effective and efficient solutions for child welfare issues and government debt. There has been a dominance of how kinship care can be used as a pseudo social work service to provide permanence for children in need. The permanence ideals for kinship care are usually drafted from adoption and fostering notions. Many of the discussions have ignored sociopolitical considerations of family life, changes in society and the diversity of different family forms.

The next part of the chapter engages a different starting point to such debates by introducing what matters to the children living in kinship care arrangements. The subsequent section uses quotes from children themselves from research (Shuttleworth 2021). The research used philosophies, theories and methodologies of critical realism and dialogical participation. Children's views of family life, and only children's views, became central to how we can start to analyse and understand kinship care. The main interest was how the children's views might match, contradict or supplement traditional understandings of safe flourishing kinship care family life.

## Children's views of family life in kinship care

### Family make-up

The children in the study described a wealth of genetically related family members, non-genetically connected family friends and personal friends

32 *Reinventing the Family in Uncertain Times*

involved with their lives and care. They were emphatic that all these various people should be considered family.

> **Sydney:** Well, I've got nan and grandad, aunts and uncles, mum and dad, and Anna [not genetically related] who now lives with us. So, I call her family, because she is my family really.

Feeling that various types of differently related people in children's lives can be family is usual for children living in kinship care arrangements (Farmer 2010). However, every child would have a particular way of differentiating family types. They would use terminologies such as 'close family' versus 'extended family' and 'proper family' versus 'relatives'.

For most children, family was reliant on the amount of time and effort others spent trying to relate to them:

> **Eliza:** We have friends that like, it's her granddaughter and her. They're not like our 'family family', [but] family like our extended family … they've made the effort to, like, be with us and stuff like that … I don't think for family you actually have to be about 'related to you', I just feel like they have to want to relate with you.

Relating to each other, then, matters to family formation. However, this does not just apply to human relationships. The children spoke about pets being part of the family (Cain 1985). The children signified pets as a shared possession that can be used to show how a family can unite (Sussman 2016). At the start of our discussions, many child participants asserted that pets allowed children to undertake responsibility. Yet, when asked explicitly whether they were the ones who would feed their pets, clean their hutches or litter trays, or give them walks, most conceded that often they did not.

> **Lucy:** Well I do try to look after them quite a lot, but grandpa looks after them more because it's a bit too early for me to take them out … I love training them and stuff, and going on walks of them when I can, and growing up with them, and watching them get told off by grandma.

The children often portrayed their pets as being like another child or a sibling. Pets were also frequently presented not only by name but also by the length of time they had been in the family. Also, the children often described how scared these animals were when they first came to live with the family.

> **Lucy:** They were quite scared, and they were really small, because it's a new habitat for them and because … grandma bought them toys and

everything and we played with them. And they're much better now. Well not [cat's name], but he lets you stroke him. But he's more of an outdoor cat.

It became apparent the children often established similarities to their pets' situations and their own experiences of joining a new arrangement with a family (Irvine and Cilia 2017). The pets were cared for mainly by the household's parental figures, and although they may have needed some time for readjustment, they were quickly recognized as a family member. Pets were a way to understand and compare their own evolving sense of permanence. The treatment of the family pets privileged them to anticipate their likely care experience and foresee how their connections might persist.

Such categorizations by the children may insinuate that family is just a fluid social construct based on feelings, beliefs and values. Nevertheless, most children conveyed that family also has a fixed genealogical quality.

> **Zack:** Everyone who I'm related to is important to me, even if you hate them. They're still important. Like have you heard the saying that you can't choose your family, but you can choose your friends. Like that.

Despite inferences of both the fluidity and the fixed nature of family, all the children presented a wish to consider themselves part of a broader family network. Other research suggests that this is normal for children in kinship care arrangements (Biehal et al. 2010). Eliza sums this up by speaking about gaining a feeling of wider family, of family growing, as one of kinship care's benefits.

> **Eliza:** Well for me, most people that I need, even if they're not like directly related to me, they're like, for me, they're still like family … So it's like, it's kind of not compensation, but it's like I've got so many other family members, so it kind of makes up for the fact that I don't have the like original house unit.

## Absence/presence

> **Sydney:** I don't know how you really lose family. It just keeps getting bigger. And it's just that if they're not there anymore, well they're still here, but they're like in heaven.

All of the children mentioned death in every interview at least once. The children spoke about the death of pets and members of their families and communities.

They demonstrated that they often reflect on how others will be more or less present in their lives. The children also contemplated how family members can change their responsibilities and roles throughout their lives. Such thoughts may be at the forefront of their thoughts because kinship carers are frequently older than non-kinship ones (Selwyn and Nandy 2014). Their past experiences of being placed from one part of their family to another also make such reflections prominent (Farmer, Selwyn and Meakings 2013). Therefore, for these children, broader conceptualizations of family also took on meaning about who may be next to take on their care.

> **Lucy:** And yeah Grandma said if she drops down dead the next day then we have to go and live with Uncle M and Auntie J, and her sister. We have to move all the way to where they are, and so then I'll have to, like, go to a different school when I'm, like, literally in my second term at secondary school.

This quote shows that Lucy is clearly thinking about and planning her permanence. As such, it is inferred that the children's sense of permanence is the desire to stay within their current family network. However, it is not just a dependence on one or two carers. It is not about desiring a permanent substitute care arrangement where there are specific caregivers throughout their childhoods. As such, permanence is not only about the guaranteed presence of specific carers, as suggested by most kinship care policies and social work practices. Instead, the variable absence and presence of people in the children's lives and how this manifests for the children needs to be acknowledged.

This was further demonstrated when the children explicitly spoke about the ways people and feeling connected to others could happen psychologically even when people are not physically present (Samuels 2009).

> **Rainbow:** Although my sister is not here, I can see her by phone by computer and by things that she's given to me, like love. And I talk about people that aren't here every day. And I have pictures of them. And this (shows a postcard). It says sisters will be forever friends. And my sister's fiancé taught me how to ride a bike.

## Ambivalence relationships – siblings and birth parents

The children often spoke about their full-siblings, step-siblings, half-siblings and siblings that lived in the same home but were genetically uncles and aunts. They also talked about siblings they could only see when supervised, as well as adopted siblings, siblings they had never seen but heard of, and siblings of half-siblings. This is despite little mention in kinship care research and literature concerning sibling relationships (Wellard et al. 2017).

Sibling relationships were often regarded by the children as valuable because siblings were thought to have had shared experiences. Many times, these experiences predated their current family care set-up. Often this could lessen the intensity and pain of separation. The children felt that they would have others who may be better able to empathize with them and that siblings also provided them with a sense of alliance and identity (White and Hughes 2017).

> **Lucy:** Because when grandma and grandad died, they said that we can have half of the house each and we'd still live in it and look after each other.

Here, Lucy also reiterates how the children in kinship care regularly think about their permanency and envisage the continuity/discontinuity entrenched in their lives.

However, the children spoke about how they and their siblings did not always get on. They felt that their sibling relationships were varied and depended on age, context and other personal and social factors. Therefore, the children revealed a range of emotions about their siblings. Siblings often had a sense of concern, responsibility and affection towards each other. However, there was also often rivalry, resentment and even aggression towards one another (Sanders 2004).

> **Jake:** Yeah, I only like talking to [my sister], because when I actually see her, she actually just says 'go away, you stupid bum head'. And so sometimes, I kicked her by accident like a Power Ranger.

Generally, the children indicated that sibling relationships, with all their ups and downs, could provide an effective way to learn to circumnavigate complex relationships and the intricacies of socialization.

Resonating with previous research, the children also often exhibited some ambivalence about their birth parents (Kallinen 2020). For example, Thomas expressed admiration for his father and his father's work. Yet, later on in the same session, he stated that his father was 'rubbish' and 'didn't do anything'.

There was a range of contact arrangements with previous carers and their birth parents for the children who participated in the study. Zack favoured his birth mum turning up on an impromptu, informal basis. Rainbow and Lucy had difficult relationships with their parents but understood they might see them when they were older. Megan wanted to only know about her mum through stories and recounting memories from other family members.

> **Megan:** And it's nice because they all, like remember, like, my mum and stuff, and they can talk about her … It's like when our mum was young, or when our nan was young, and she was bringing up my mum. Obviously, it was like very different. And memories would have been brought out in photos and everything like that. So, it's like she still there but not there.

Although the many ways to keep connected with birth parents were different, it was evident that any connection with them is emotive and complex, even when largely positive. The children demonstrated that keeping links can never be a benign experience (Neil and Howe 2004). Furthermore, the children suggested that maintaining connections must be done safely with everybody's agreement. They desired a shared consensus across the family, which included their own wishes.

> **Eliza:** If you're going to have contact with that person it needs to be regular, and you need to know what's going on all the time and it just makes things easier to keep healthy relationships. There needs to be a mutual … Everyone needs to know what's going on and what's going to happen. Like every time.

## Sharing time

Sharing time with others was central to the children's sense of family.

> **Zac:** You don't have to do things with people you can just, like, be with them … like watching a film could be one of the most specialest [*sic*] things in the life.

Throughout the interviews, the concept of time, or rather the context of time, was often raised. Pets, people, plants, books, toys and other objects were typically introduced by children timestamping how long they had been part of their family.

> **Lucy:** I don't know why, but I took a picture of the clock … It just makes me feel kind of safe.

Time, routine and timings can allow people to have a sense of safety (Forman 2015). For many of us, we must have some knowledge and control over what is likely to come. Furthermore, power relations are embedded in the use and the comprehension of time. Much critical time research suggests that controlling time can be used as a means of authority and hierarchical power. Time is relational and can allow inclusion and exclusion (Bastian 2014). One example is that time is often allocated for children. This may include 'free time', 'screen time' or 'family time' to see birth parents. Therefore, time is not allocated efficiently or compassionately; children may see this as unempathetic precariousness (Yuill and Mueller-Hirth 2019). In particular, children who have experienced abuse and neglect may worry that they are once again experiencing inadequate or chaotic care.

The children in the study expressed the need for families to have time-dependent events, routines and matching rhythms. However, this does not mean that children and carers necessarily have to be doing precisely the same activities. Instead, analysis of the children's views suggests the need for something called 'mush time' (Baraitser 2013). This is when the family members are together, not in the same area, such as a home, but not necessarily in the same room doing the same thing. In these moments, each person's rhythms ostensibly match, regardless of whether one person happens to be watching TV, another is on their games console, or another is working.

As such, the children demonstrated how time is often used as a commodity and something to be measured. Time with others is precious, even if it is used to appease someone else's passion.

> **Megan:** That it can be quite difficult being a child, and that they just need like time with people, but time alone as well … And it's just nice to be with just nan and like just grandad sometimes. Like there are some days when we go out fishing
> **Researcher:** OK, do you like fishing as well?
> **Megan:** It's alright (laughs).

Overall, connecting and devoting time is more important than the activities pursued. It is a vital way to attune to the feelings of each other (Baraitser 2013). It is a crucial way of building up affinities and a sense of belonging. Nevertheless, rhythms must match, and there must be an agreement from all concerned whether time together is used focusing on the past, the present or the future.

> **Erica:** We don't like it when we see her. She makes us upset. She says things about what we don't want her to say about the past and things we don't want to talk about.

## Sharing space

As well as the use of time, the use of space was important to the children. An example of this was when we spoke about siblings sharing a room. There continue to be debates for social work policy and practice about whether it is appropriate for children of certain ages and genders to share a room. Legislation for England asserts that children of the opposite sex over the age of ten years should have their own bedrooms (e.g. the 1985 Housing Act). However, the children in the study did not express concern either way.

> **Researcher:** What's it like sharing a room?
>
> **Purple:** Erm, it's sometimes nice. It gets a bit crowded because Danielle always takes up most of the space. Although sometimes if you share a room you get to, like, to speak to your sibling at night-time, and also, we get to like play games together.

Overall, the children stated that it mattered more that various spaces were available dependent on what they wished to do with their time. The children appreciated designated areas, such as living rooms, where the family could be together. However, they also valued specified places for them to be alone, such as a particular place at the table where they ate.

> **Eliza:** Yeah because I share a room and I don't ever feel like I don't have anywhere to go and just, like, build my own. So, I don't think it's necessarily about needing to have your own room. It's just like needing to know that there is somewhere that you can go if you need to be alone or whatever.

Another example of how the children used spaces to navigate connection and separation was beds. The children often pointed to their beds when we talked about what makes a home. For many children, beds helped them detach from the world and different worries that concerned them. However, beds simultaneously let the children feel they were being cared for and that they were not completely alone.

> **Jake:** And sometimes when I wake up in the middle of the night, I always go into that bed (Jake takes me into his grandparents' room to show me some blankets on the floor next to their bed).
>
> **Researcher:** Why do you come and sleep in here?
>
> **Jake:** Cos sometimes, I always wake up in the middle of the night … because my bed's not the comfy one.

Jake's bed was a cabin bed. It is unlikely that the floor was more 'comfy' than his own. It is more plausible that Jake would get anxious and need to feel comforted by sleeping next to his grandparents. Many of the children echoed this need for comfort during bedtime. They desired to feel connected even though sleeping is often thought of as a solitary activity.

Another example was the children's use of gardens. They expressed that gardens were where they felt connected to the family home, yet felt suitably disconnected and felt they had more independence.

> **Eliza:** I feel like if I go to the garden, I'm out of the house but I'm not like away from everyone … I'm not like detaching myself.

## Shared narratives

Throughout the sessions, many of the children would use the pronoun 'we' when we discussed their family lives. This use of the inclusive pronoun 'we' can be a way to establish and express feelings of affinity and belonging (Galdiolo et al. 2016). When placed in their perceptions of family, which they said was often huge but also constantly changing, it demonstrates an attachment which protects against further feelings of loss and rejection.

The children were also keen to share stories and narratives about their family members, including those who were deceased.

> **Erica:** And this is over there, that's our great grandma, our grandma's mum, and we never got to see her. She died when grandma was 7 years old. But erm we've seen pictures of her and Grandma looks like her, and she's very beautiful. And Grandma says we get, she gets her good looks from her, and we get erm … good looks from her as well.

Finally, the children appreciated having photos and recounting shared family narratives regarding their journey within the family.

> **Danielle:** (Points to photo on the fridge). That's the first morning we were here. My Grandad couldn't fit in. He went to the loo and when he came back there's no room in the bed (laughs).

# What the children's views mean for conceptualizing family life

## Recognition of family

As discussed in the first part of the chapter, many conceptualizations of kinship care family life are founded on kinship care being a service evaluated in terms of permanence and cost-effectiveness rather than being another way of family life.

However, a rich finding from the children's insights is that they portrayed their family life in ways that suggest more sociologically based theories.

David Morgan's (2011) notion of family practices is a compelling concept to help recognize how the children spoke about their family life. Like the children's accounts, Morgan challenged traditional understandings of family as a static grouping that consists solely of blood ties, legal bonds or living in the same space. Therefore, family is not exclusively about genealogical, legal or even cultural definitions of family and home. Instead, family encompasses those that do not have the same genetic relatedness, in the case of family friends, or even species relatedness, in the case of pets. As proposed by Morgan, the children agreed that family is in flux and continually growing. Evidently, the children felt this was one of the advantages of kinship care. Nevertheless, at the centre of family is how different members want to relate to one another.

As such, the capability of family to undergo change augments Morgan's proposal that family is something people do rather than what people are. This perception of family moves away from the traditional, idealized, gendered and Eurocentric recognitions of family that are often found central to policy and practice. Instead, there are multiple meanings of family, which are founded on members sharing time, space and narratives. Family includes how children navigate, think about and drive the ambiguities inherent in their sense of permanence, affiliation, connection, belonging and continuity. Children are, therefore, active participants in the continuous meaning and making of family. They are complicit in forming family and making it work.

The concept of family 'display' by Finch (2007) is also valuable for recognizing how the children spoke about their experiences of family life. The children explained about how they do family and, by doing so, were keen to show that it should be given credence in the eyes of others. For the children, they needed to be allowed to show to others that they were a genuine family.

## Permanence

In the UK, the current legislative definition of permanence is that it provides a child with the need for 'a sense of security, continuity, commitment and identity' with a family during childhood as well as into adulthood (Department for Education 2010: 12). Analysis of the children's views supports this onus on a sense of permanence that is enduring over the life course. However, it also suggests that, for the children, a sense of permanence includes notions of multiple family affiliations and even residences over the life course (Rustin 1994). Therefore, permanence is not just the shift from one or two carers to another through substitute care. Instead, the children envisage that a sense of permanence must be the responsibility of the family network as a whole. It is not an individual responsibility but rather a collective one. It is about having an ongoing and evolving sense of family where children are active in its meaning-making.

The children also acknowledged that different connections and separations with family members would change as they got older. They also understood that their level of need would change over time and that they would likely have newly emerging ones. This advocates for a life course approach which is not just dependent on the overly neoliberal, individualized, gendered, heteronormative precepts on which much of social work in Europe is often based (Webb 2016). A sense of permanence does not just conform to developmental stages and life trajectories which is embedded in much social work policy and practice, especially for permanence. Instead, broader meanings of family and kinship care, such as those from the Global South, should be considered (Davey 2016). These meanings must also rely on how children are active in mobilizing time. Child welfare academics, policymakers, practitioners and families should not forget that children have agency which they constantly think about, experiment with, test and revise.

## Working with ambivalence and change

The analysis drawn from the children's views reveals that maintaining their family lives and a sense of permanence is a challenging, complex, shifting process that is ongoing and involves many ambivalent thoughts and feelings. The children's insights show how they navigate such ambivalence and are constantly reflecting on and challenging the crude either/or perceptions of their family lives. They often are actively navigating the space in between simplistic binaries. These binaries are often referred to as dualisms by sociologists (Craib 2000).

Such dualisms are often present because kinship care, permanence, legislation, child welfare practice, families and research often try to indicate validity through discrete either/or thinking. For example, kinship care is typically framed as either a placement or a private family set-up. The lives of families are either troubling or trouble-free. Permanence is habitually perceived as either remaining with birth families or by substituting them. It is marked by either the absence or presence of others. Kinship care is either a safe, cost-effective way for children to remain in their families with a female caregiver, or else it is risky and, in the long run, will require more costs due to the likelihood of intergenerational cycles of abuse.

Moving away from dualisms was termed dialectical thinking by critical realist Roy Bhaskar (1993). The children indicated that they use dialectical thinking as they navigate feeling part of a new family whilst also remaining within their previous one. They, and their families, are vulnerable and dependent, yet also display agency. The children have ambivalent feelings about their birth parents and siblings as they want them to remain part of their lives, yet they also encounter difficulties maintaining relationships with them. For child protection practitioners, policymakers and researchers, being able to hear and work with such ambivalence is challenging. However, the first step is to move away from the binary thinking that traditionally dominates debates about family life. Importantly it is not always possible or even necessary for others to resolve such seeming dichotomies (Cree 2000).

## The sharing of time, place and space

A child's sense of permanence was also dependent on how they shared or sometimes did not wish to share time, place and space. By using time, place and space, the children would test out their feelings of affinity, belonging and their continuity of care. It was important that everybody used time and space efficiently and effectively. They were used as markers, commodities and predictors. For example, the children used time alone in the garden to manage the push and pull of the dialectical connections/separations in their lives. They explored their interdependence by using personal areas and places in the house and objects such as the toys they were given. Whilst the children engaged with these outwardly solitary activities, they still retained some safe connection to the environment and their worlds that surround them. Also, time spent in apparently separate spaces could be considered 'mush time' (Baraitser 2013), and it was on the knowledge that more engaged time would be spent later with those they believed would care for and protect them. Crucially, the children are constantly navigating time, place and space and how they do this should be a central deliberation to understanding how their family life works.

## Sharing narratives

Similarly, the children also used narratives, stories, photos, rituals and routines, such as collective times for meals and family celebrations, as a process of 'doing' and 'displaying' family. This provided the children with a mutual sense of narrative and embedded a sense of belonging, affinity and affiliation. It also supported them to see how they fit into the inter-generational life cycle of the whole family. Focusing on family practices in this way, rather than as one-off events, indicates the task of doing kinship can be upheld through such everyday exchanges (Cossar and Neil 2013).

Conversations and the sharing of family narratives should also include the prospect of death and different future caring arrangements. Often there is a wariness to engage in such conversations with children to preserve their innocence and protect them from upsetting information. However, the children who were part of the research demonstrated that those in kinship care arrangements show that such situations are being contemplated, whether or not they are openly talked about with others (see also Burgess et al. 2010; Farmer, Selwyn and Meakings 2013). Already, within their family, they have experienced major shifts in the responsibilities for their care, and they, therefore, recognize family and family narratives as an ongoing 'active process' which constantly shifts (Morgan 2011).

Pets (Carr and Rockett 2017) and siblings (Cossar and Neil 2013) were not only other ways that children and their families could share narratives, but they were also ways to explore and predict permanence. Again, they allowed the children to do and display family and kinship. Both pets and siblings frequently provided something to care about, comfort, play with and somebody to care for them. One advantage of pets was that they did not answer back and so would listen without prejudice. However, sibling relationships could often be more precarious, and so the children would typically work even harder to manage their interdependence with them. Again, this shows that children are negotiating relationships, and their thinking, through the dialectic.

## Conclusion

The children demonstrate that family life involves them and others, mobilizing time, space and family narratives. Central to this are how others, as Eliza states, 'have to want to relate with you'. Yet, if the children feel there are multiple meanings of family, this means that their perspectives are, to some extent, individual, subjective and often ambivalent. It is, therefore, crucial for family members, researchers, practitioners and policymakers to spend time with children by building relationships that are open, honest and safe. It is through these relationships that children feel OK about expressing their thoughts, feelings and ambivalences about how they negotiate their family lives. We need to find out how particular children and their families navigate time, space, family narratives and ambivalences for us to support their flourishing.

This brings me to my final and probably the most crucial point from the study and this chapter. It has been demonstrated that children, even younger children, can provide nuanced, sophisticated and considered understandings of their often seemingly fractured complex family lives. Therefore, a child's current methods of managing and of making do and getting by should be the starting point to what their family life means. Presumptive adult-centric beliefs of family and support can only go so far in recognizing the realities of children's lived experiences. Truly ensuring that children are included in the debates about their lives can ensure that support is matched to real-life experiences, especially in a changing society. The dilemma should not be whether we listen to children and make them central to our considerations. Instead, it is about finding ways to ensure that we do, so that we can learn from their insights to ensure that they have flourishing and safe family lives.

# References

Baraitser, L. (2013), 'Mush Time: Communality and the Temporal Rhythms of Family Life', *Families, Relationships and Societies*, 2 (1): 147–53.

Bastian, M. (2014), 'Time and Community: A Scoping Study', *Time & Society*, 23 (2): 137–66.

Bhaskar, R. (1993), *Dialectic: The Pulse of Freedom*, London: Verso.

Biehal, N., S. Ellison, C. Baker and I. Sinclair (2010), *Belonging and Permanence: Outcomes in Long-Term Foster Care and Adoption*, London: British Association for Adoption and Fostering.

Boddy, J. (2017), *Understanding Permanence for Looked After Children: Care Inquiry*, London: The Care Inquiry.

Boddy, J. (2019), 'Troubling Meanings of "Family" for Young People Who Have Been in Care: From Policy to Lived Experience', *Journal of Family Issues*, 40 (16): 2239–63.

Brown, R., K. Broadhurst, J. Harwin and J. Simmonds (2019), 'Special Guardianship: International Research on Kinship Care', Evidence Review, London: Nuffield Family Justice Observatory.

Burgess, C., F. Rossvoll, B. Wallace and B. Daniel (2010), ' "It's Just like Another Home, Just Another Family, so It's Nae Different" Children's Voices in Kinship Care: A Research Study about the Experience of Children in Kinship Care in Scotland: Children's Voices in Kinship Care', *Child & Family Social Work*, 15 (3): 297–306.

Cain, A. O. (1985), 'Pets as Family Members', *Marriage & Family Review*, 8 (3–4): 5–10.

Carr, S., and B. Rockett (2017), 'Fostering Secure Attachment: Experiences of Animal Companions in the Foster Home', *Attachment & Human Development*, 19 (3): 259–77.

Cassidy, J., J. D. Jones and P. R. Shaver (2013), 'Contributions of Attachment Theory and Research: A Framework for Future Research, Translation, and Policy', *Development and Psychopathology*, 25 (402): 1415–34.

Clinton, H. R. (2007), *It Takes a Village: And Other Lessons Children Teach Us*, UK edition, London: Simon & Schuster.

Cossar, J., and E. Neil (2013), 'Making Sense of Siblings: Connections and Severances in Post-Adoption Contact', *Child & Family Social Work*, 18 (1): 67–76.

Craib, I. (2000), *Classical Social Theory: An Introduction to the Thought of Marx, Weber, Durkheim and Simmel*, reprint edition, Oxford: Oxford University Press.

Cree, V. E. (2000), *Sociology for Social Workers and Probation Officers*, London: Psychology Press.

Davey, J. (2016), 'The Care of Kin: A Case Study Approach to Kinship Care in the South of England and Zululand, South Africa', PhD Thesis, Bournemouth University, Bournemouth.

Department for Education (2010), 'The Children Act 1989 Guidance and Regulations Volume 2: Care Planning, Placement and Case Review', London: HMSO.

Emmerson, C., and I. Stockton (2020), 'The Economic Response to Coronavirus Will Substantially Increase Government Borrowing', The IFS, available online: https://www.ifs.org.uk/publications/14771 (accessed 27 March 2020).

Enke, B. (2019), 'Kinship, Cooperation, and the Evolution of Moral Systems', *The Quarterly Journal of Economics*, 134 (2): 953–1019.

Farmer, E. (2010), 'What Factors Relate to Good Placement Outcomes in Kinship Care?', *British Journal of Social Work*, 40 (2): 426–44.

Farmer, E., J. Selwyn and S. Meakings (2013), '"Other Children Say You're Not Normal Because You Don't Live with Your Parents". Children's Views of Living with Informal Kinship Carers: Social Networks, Stigma and Attachment to Carers', *Child & Family Social Work*, 18 (1): 25–34.

Finch, J. (2007), 'Displaying Families', *Sociology*, 41 (1): 65–81.

Forman, H. (2015), 'Events and Children's Sense of Time: A Perspective on the Origins of Everyday Time-Keeping', *Frontiers in Psychology*, 6 (259): 1–5.

Galdiolo, S., I. Roskam, L. L. Verhofstadt, J. De Mol, L. Dewinne and S. Vandaudenard (2016), 'Associations between Relational Pronoun Usage and the Quality of Early Family Interactions', *Frontiers in Psychology*, 7 (16). doi: 10.3389/fpsyg.2016.01719.

Geen, R. (2004), 'The Evolution of Kinship Care Policy and Practice', *The Future of Children*, 14 (1): 130–49.

Goldberg, A. E. (2019), *Open Adoption and Diverse Families: Complex Relationships in the Digital Age*, Oxford: Oxford University Press.

Goldstein, J., A. Freud and A. J. Solnit (1979), *Beyond the Best Interests of the Child*, New York: Free Press.

Hicks, S. (2005), 'Lesbian and Gay Foster Care and Adoption: A Brief UK History', *Adoption & Fostering*, 29 (3): 42–56.

Irvine, L., and L. Cilia (2017), 'More-than-Human Families: Pets, People, and Practices in Multispecies Households', *Sociology Compass*, 11 (2): 1–13.

Kallinen, K. P. (2020), 'Family Relationships of Children in Kinship Foster Care', *Nordic Social Work Research*, 11 (4): 319–32.

Lara, M. S. (2013), *Kinship Care Policy: Women's Oppression & Neoliberal Familialization: Exacerbating Women's Multiple Oppressions through Developing Neoliberal Policy in Child Welfare*, Saarbrücken: LAP LAMBERT Academic Publishing.

Leinaweaver, J. (2014), 'Informal Kinship-Based Fostering Around the World: Anthropological Findings', *Child Development Perspectives*, 8 (3): 131–6.

McGhee, J., Bunting, L., McCartan, C., Elliott, M., Bywaters, P. and Featherstone and B. (2018), 'Looking After Children in the UK – Convergence or Divergence?', *The British Journal of Social Work*, 48(5): 1176–98.

McCartan, C., L. Bunting, P. Bywaters, G. Davidson, M. Elliott and J. Hooper (2018), 'A Four-Nation Comparison of Kinship Care in the UK: The Relationship between Formal Kinship Care and Deprivation', *Social Policy and Society*, 17 (4): 619–35.

Morgan, D. H. G. (2011), 'Locating "Family Practices"', *Sociological Research Online*, 16 (4): 174–82.

Neil, E., and D. Howe (eds) (2004), *Contact in Adoption and Permanent Foster Care: Research, Theory and Practice*, London: British Association for Adoption and Fostering.

Owusu-Bempah, K. (2010), *The Wellbeing of Children in Care: A New Approach for Improving Developmental Outcomes*, London: Routledge.

Peters, J. (2005), 'True Ambivalence: Child Welfare Workers' Thoughts, Feelings, and Beliefs about Kinship Foster Care', *Children and Youth Services Review*, 27 (6): 595–614.

Pratchett, R., and P. Rees (2017), 'Theories Underpinning Kinship Care', in J. Horton and M. Pyer (eds), *Children, Young People and Care*, 44–57, New York: Routledge.

Rustin, M. (1994), 'Multiple Families in Mind', *Clinical Child Psychology and Psychiatry*, 4 (1): 51–62.

Samuels, G. M. (2009), 'Ambiguous Loss of Home: The Experience of Familial (Im)permanence among Young Adults with Foster Care Backgrounds', *Children and Youth Services Review*, 31 (12): 1229–39.

Samuels, J. (2018), 'Adoption in the Digital Age', in J. Samuels (ed.), *Adoption in the Digital Age: Opportunities and Challenges for the 21st Century*, 29–50, Cham: Springer International Publishing.

Sanders, R. (2004), *Sibling Relationships: Theory and Issues for Practice*, London: Palgrave.

Selwyn, J., and S. Nandy (2014), 'Kinship Care in the UK: Using Census Data to Estimate the Extent of Formal and Informal Care by Relatives: Kinship Care in the UK', *Child & Family Social Work*, 19 (1): 44–54.

Shuttleworth, P. D. (2021), 'What Matters to Children Living in Kinship Care: "Another Way of Being a Normal Family"', PhD Thesis, University of Sussex.

Simmonds, J. (2014), 'Permanence Planning for Children in Family and Friends Care', in D. Pitcher (ed.), *Inside Kinship Care: Understanding Family Dynamics and Providing Effective Support*, 135–51, London: Jessica Kingsley.

Skoglund, J., and R. Thørnblad (2019), 'Kinship Care or Upbringing by Relatives? The Need for "New" Understandings in Research', *European Journal of Social Work*, 22 (3): 435–45.

Smith, R. (2015), 'Troubled, Troubling or Troublesome? Troubled Families and the Changing Shape of Youth Justice', in M. Wasik and S. Santatzoglou (eds), *The Management of Change in Criminal Justice: Who Knows Best?*, 49–63, London: Palgrave Macmillan UK.

Sussman, M. B. (2016), *Pets and the Family*, New York: Routledge.

Swadener, B. B., M. Kabiru and A. Njenga (2000), *Does the Village Still Raise the Child?: A Collaborative Study of Changing Child-Rearing and Early Education in Kenya*, SUNY Press.

Thoburn, J. (1994), *Child Placement: Principles and Practice*, second edition, Aldershot: Ashgate Publishing Limited.

Webb, S. A. (2016), 'European Individualism and Social Work', in F. Kessl, W. Lorenz, H.-U. Otto and S. White (eds), *European Social Work – A Compendium*, 114–38, Leverkusen: Barbara Budrich.

Wellard, S., S. Meakings, E. Farmer and J. Hunt (2017), 'Growing Up in Kinship Care', Grandparents Plus, Bristol: University of Bristol.

White, N., and C. Hughes (2017), *Why Siblings Matter: The Role of Brother and Sister Relationships in Development and Well-Being*, London: Routledge.

Wijedasa, D. (2015), *The Prevalence and Characteristics of Children Growing up with Relatives in the UK: Part I*, Hadley Centre for Adoption & Foster Care Studies, University of Bristol.

Winokur, M. A., A. Holtan and K. E. Batchelder (2018), 'Systematic Review of Kinship Care Effects on Safety, Permanency, and Well-Being Outcomes', *Research on Social Work Practice*, 28 (1): 19–32.

Yuill, C., and N. Mueller-Hirth (2019), 'Paperwork, Compassion and Temporal Conflicts in British Social Work', *Time & Society*, 28 (4): 1532–51.

# 4

# Language of Instruction Choice and Family Disruptions in Ghana

Vincent Adzahlie-Mensah

## Conceptualizing the African family

The family is at the centre of the dynamics which affect all societies. In all societies, it is recognized that the family is the basic unit of society around which major concerns for sustainable development are expressed. The family is the setting for demographic reproduction and the seat of the first integration of individuals to social life (Fomby and Sennott 2013; Ryan, Claessens and Markowitz 2013).

In Africa, the family is conceptualized within the African Union Plan of Action on the Family (2004) as consisting of three dimensions: (1) a psycho-biological unit where members are linked together by blood ties – kinship relationship, personal feelings and emotional bonds of its members; (2) a social unit where members live together in the same household and share tasks and social functions and (3) the basic economic production unit (African Union 2004). The family in Africa is extended to kinship systems and constitutes strength for guidance and support, thus providing members with a wide circle of relatives on whom they can fall back. The extended family is the prime mechanism for coping with social, economic and political adversities. For example, Samuel and Hertrich (2019: 1272) explained that 'the child's well-being depends in part on kin support, and certain people, such as grandparents or, more broadly, elders, can play a particular role'. The relationship is symbiotic as children can play a role in the well-being of the elderly. The extended family network is the principal focus for socialization and education of children. The extended family system ensures that the poor families are generally supported by rich ones (African Union 2004). In times of crisis, unemployment, sickness, poverty, old age and bereavement, most people rely on the family as the main source of material, social and emotional support and social security. The unity within the family ensures its survival in cases of internal conflicts, crises and adversity.

The African Union Plan of Action on the Family recognizes that the family is the basic and most fundamental unit of society, a dynamic unit engaged in an intertwined process of individual and group development. As the basic unit of society, shifts in family culture, systems and practices lead to corresponding changes in society. The reverse is true that macro level changes in society occasion significant shifts in family life. Therefore, the plan eulogized the need to place the African family at the core of society, and to advocate for the promotion, formulation, implementation and monitoring of policies and programmes to ensure the protection of and support to the African family so as to enable it to play a vital role more effectively in the development of Africa. In general, it is recognized that the formulation of policies and a review of legal frameworks for the family by governments would be the determinant factors in strengthening the structure of the family and a critical step forward for development. It is within this context that I seek to make a contribution to map out the disruptive events, processes and issues that threaten the formative and sustaining roles of the African family.

## Family disruptions

In Africa, the family is considered an important institution of society which is undergoing tremendous changes and facing many formidable challenges thus increasing pressures on the family (African Union 2004). There is plenty of research and literature discussing family disruptions, which show that the effects of disruptive events are usually negative (Fletcher 2013; Prevoo and Weel 2014; Thomas 2018). Parental life disruptions, such as divorce and job loss, could harm children by affecting their daily lives (Crosnoe et al. 2014; Thomas 2018). Children who experience family disruption suffer functional difficulties, including threats to security, health of familial bonds, depression, anxiety and academic failure, among other issues (Fomby and Sennott 2013; Ryan, Claessens & Markowitz 2013). Thomas's (2018) additive and cumulative hypothesis of family disruptions argues that the experience of multiple disruptive events within close time proximity fosters instability.

African family dynamics have been shifting in relation to several social changes (Samuel and Hertrich 2019) including the shift to cash economy, information technology, globalization, internal conflicts and wars. Such disruptions are evident in the increasing cases of female-headed households, consensual unions, rising rates of divorce, the impact of HIV/AIDS and other pandemics, domestic violence, sexual abuse and the rising phenomenon of street children and beggars.

School has been described as serving both horizontal and vertical functions. School builds stronger ties and capital within the family and communities while offering possibilities to leave behind those ties and binds (MacBeath 2010). Arguments for the positive side – how schools build ties and capital within families and communities – are well established (Lewin 2009). However, there is limited literature associated with schooling and family disruptions. Although the limited literature points to some ways in which school language choices are connected to identity issues (Adzahlie-Mensah 2014; Dunne and Adzahlie-Mensah 2016), there is little literature on family disruptions and school language practices, especially the role played by the use of foreign language as medium of instruction in ex-colonies. As such, this chapter explores family disruptions associated with language of instruction. The chapter presents the relationships and experiences of family members as being impacted, realigned or complicated by language of instruction.

## Language of instruction and family disruptions

There is little direct literature linking the language of instruction in schools to family disruptions although debates exist that proffer the native or home language as the best medium for working with children (Ball 2014; Peyton 2015; Zafeirakou 2015). Only scant literature argues that using English as the language in which everything is done within school affects family life and identity development in society (see Al-Nakhalah 2017; Painter 2010). However, critical understandings of language position it as a great force of socialization, an integrated component of culture, a symbol of social and cultural identity and a mode of communication and representation. Bhat (2008), for example, conceptualized language as a marker of identity that is drawn upon to reshape realities, beliefs and world views as well as acting as a tool for complete social control.

Critical studies elucidate language as a symbol of identity (Adzahlie-Mensah 2014; Bhat 2008; Painter 2010). For such scholars, the choice of language of instruction is associated with a sense of identity. By extension, they question the legislation of the colonizer's language as the medium of instruction in school on the grounds that 'language can only be interpreted and learned with reference to a specific cultural context' (Al-Nakhalah 2017: 56). In particular, critical pedagogy theorists argue that legislating that reading or writing must be taught in school instantiates power asymmetries in which to be illiterate is to feel powerless and dependent (Collins and Blot 2003; Freire 1993). Irvine and Gal (2000: 38) argue that legislating one language constitutes *erasure*: the process, in which ideology simplifies the sociolinguistic field, renders some persons and their sociolinguistic existence invisible or less important. 'Postcolonial psychology' similarly describes the replacement of Indigenous languages by a foreign language as *linguistic imperialism* (Macleod and Bhatia 2008: 581) which contributes to the silencing of a people; the erasure of an identity and the cutting of a tongue (Painter 2010). Bhat (2008: 4) explains that promoting a specific language is to promote particular systems of thought or 'system[s] of belief'.

Critical studies have questioned the rationale for using English as medium of instruction in post-colonial contexts (Adzahlie-Mensah and Dunne 2019; Dunne and Adzahlie-Mensah 2016; Painter 2010). As Painter (2010: 252) maintains, language is always 'tied up with politics of identity' such that using a foreign language for instruction in a post-colonial context meant that the post-colonial subject was caught up in an existential contradiction. For them, linguistic capital in the chosen language determines relationships beyond the school classroom to the extent of 'the amputation of ... being' as the post-colonial subject is not seen as 'having a language' (Painter 2010: 17). Bhat (2008: 2) presents the point clearer by arguing that in India, the legislation of English as medium of instruction represents a 'logical and structural dominance of one language over the other, the standard over the non-standard'.

In Ghana, one of the main arguments put forward to challenge colonial education, when Indigenous languages were condemned for being inadequate medium for teaching (GES, 2001), was that it was 'cut-rate education' below the British metropolitan standards, which 'largely functioned to maintain the colonial order of dependency' (Busia 1964: 7). Subsequently, the teaching and learning of Indigenous languages were abolished, as proficiency in English language became the indicator of good education (Quartey 2007). The effect was that many graduates became 'docile, dependent, low on initiative, and immoral' because the curriculum was 'predominantly academic and elitist' (Dzobo 1987: 2). The writers insist that the system of schooling promotes British racial superiority, as local languages were neglected from the curriculum (Dunne and Adzahlie-Mensah 2016; Woolman 2001). Other writers make the point that in using English as medium of instruction, the colonial school system in Ghana produced three nations – educated, the half educated and the uneducated – in one country (see Busia 1964; Woolman 2001). These three groups, they suggest, are always in conflict because each group is unable to communicate effectively with the others. In direct relation to the family, the creation of the three groups undermines the African family sense of collective responsibility (Woolman 2001) as the 'schooled' becomes a 'misfit in his own village' (Mazrui 1978: 16). As the Europeans had a civilizing mission, literacy in the English language is 'a key point for understanding the salvational overtones' (Adzahlie-Mensah, 2014: 59). In Malinowski's (1936) anthropological thinking, literacy in English language was the process 'to give the Native unstintingly … [English] knowledge' and to enable Africans to claim 'full citizenship and … personal dignity' (484). As language is the carrier of culture and identity, Malinowski's idea was that 'the Native' might be schooled in 'inverted anthropology' by which Africans would learn the habits and norms of Europeans, including Europeans' propensity to preach one thing but then do otherwise (503–4). Malinowski (1936: 497–8) described the effects of reorientation of the Natives as follows:

> At a dance there would be a group of people standing aside, looking on with keen interest and yet contemptuous, with envy and yet with a show of superiority … On the social side … a modernized African child develops a contempt for his African peers.

Thus, the use of English language as medium of instruction has a social disintegration effect of influencing systems of thinking, social organization and relationships. Johnson (2000: 177) argues that, to impose a language is to radically remove a significant and powerful dimension of personal and social identity. It is within this context that I discuss the effects of using English language as medium of instruction in Ghana. Although Ghana was the first country south of the Sahara to gain independence from imperial Britain, it has since retained the colonial language (English) as language of instruction at all levels of formal education (see Akyeampong and Adzahlie-Mensah 2018; GES 2001; Quartey 2007). The rationale for choosing to use English language for instruction is well established in the literature. Since 1852, the colonial authority declared Ghanaian languages as inadequate teaching media. The sustaining rationale is the status assigned to English language as an international language and a lingua franca in an ethnically diverse and linguistically polarized nation (Adzahlie-Mensah 2014). In discussing the epistemic effects, Esteva, Stuchal and Prakash (2005) contend that teaching in foreign language – as is the case of English language in Ghana – is capable of radically uprooting students from their ancestry because language also embodies the cultural and historical heritage of a people. However, students' direct experiences with English as the medium of instruction in Ghana is less visible in the literature on schooling in Ghana today. Herein lies our contribution to knowledge as I explore the connections between family disruptions and the use of English language as the medium of instruction.

## My approach

This work employs an anti-colonial discursive framework (Dei 2004) to explore the connections between the use of foreign language, the language of the former colonizer, as language of instruction and family disruptions in Ghana. The *colonial* in this sense is considered not simply as 'foreign' but also something 'imposed' and 'dominating' (Dei 2004:15). The aim is to interrogate the discursive dynamics associated with legislating the use of English language (the language of the colonizer) as medium of instruction in Ghanaian schools and the implications in family life within a Ghanaian community.

Purposive sampling is applied to select a typical case sample of fifteen participants, comprising five students, five community members and five teachers from a rural Ghanaian primary school. The study was conducted as a school-based qualitative ethnographic case study in a Ghanaian rural community. Data were collected through interviews and observation over a period of three months. I spoke to students in school and followed them to their homes to interview significant others (parents, guardians and out-of-school siblings). The purpose was to examine how school practices influenced by the choice of language of instruction impact family life.

## English as language of instruction and family disruption in Ghana

In Ghana, British colonizers legislated English language as the official language of instruction in 1852. This has persisted despite several reforms and research evidence that critique the practice (Alhassan and Adzahlie-Mensah 2010; Adzahlie-Mensah and Dunne 2019; GES 2001). In this research, I specifically explored views on the use of English language as the medium of instruction in Ghanaian basic schools and the epistemic implications for family life. I started by exploring student views on how English is deployed as medium of instruction

*Family Disruptions in Ghana*  55

in school. The interview responses from the students illustrate concerns about the use of English as medium of instruction.

> English is compulsory in this school. ... even class one children are forced to speak English. ... Everything is in English. From class one to class six. The teachers don't care if you understand or not. You can't speak any other language. They will say you don't know anything (Student 1)
>
> ... The teachers use English to teach everything ... . We do everything in English. They will beat you if you speak vernacular ... All of us, teachers and students, we use English (Student 2)
>
> Vernacular is not allowed on this compound, ... . they will beat you. Everything – class test, anything like quiz, exam, teaching – is done in English. (Student 3)

Three fundamental arguments can be made from the comments. First, everything in school was done in English language such that possession of English linguistic capital was a primary requirement. Teaching, class exercises, assignments and end-of-term examinations were conducted in English. All teacher–student and student–student interactions occurred in English no matter the grade level. Second, the Indigenous languages were subordinated pejoratively as formal prohibitions were placed on using them. Third, punishing students for speaking their Indigenous language gives expression to a regime of linguistic imperialism in which students were not treated as people having a language (Adzahlie-Mensah 2014; Painter 2010). The implication is that English is legislated as the only language in which teaching and learning as well as social interactions in school can occur. I explored the effects of this English-only regime on family life. From the perspectives of students, community members and teachers, the implications of legislating English as language of instruction for the family were clearly two directional. One understanding associated doing everything in English language with progress in an interconnected system of international benefits that needs to be acknowledged (Dunne and Adzahlie-Mensah 2019) while the other highlights its epistemic effects. Interviews with students reveal the following concerns:

> Everyone knows the value of speaking English. You can speak an international language, you understand the common language in Ghana. But it makes you a stranger among your people ... because of how they make English compulsory in school, ... you are always speaking English, English, English... . My father is a doctor [holds PhD degree] but he doesn't like us these days. He says we must speak in Ewe [the main Indigenous language in the Volta Region of Ghana]. He gets angry anytime we spoke English at home. ... He gets angry with mom that

she is helping us to speak English at home. Sometimes they can fight and not talk for three or more days because of this issue. I am afraid they may break up one day because we have become addicted to speaking English than the Ewe. We can't stop. ... And these days he doesn't stay at home much, more like an absentee father. (Student 1)

Me, my parents don't understand English. I am always confused ... . In school, the teachers like English. At home, my parents don't like it. Sometimes, I am confused about what to do. (Student 2)

When you speak English in the village, some people think you are bragging. Some people get angry with you. Some say you don't respect. ... Those people who went to school are happy when you speak English. But those people who didn't go to school don't like it at all. (Student 3)

Sometimes, I don't know if I am Effutu or English person ... . Using English for everything is not good at all ... . Sometimes it brings problems at home. Now my brother cannot speak Effutu well. My father is angry with him all the time. (Student 4)

I am Effutu from here. ... My mother tells me that I should marry a man who can speak English. She says that my father left her because the family said he cannot speak English. ... She also said some men have divorced or abandoned their wives because the women could not speak English. Sometimes she punishes us, especially my brother, for not speaking good English. But, sir, I am worried that I cannot speak Effutu well ... The other day one teacher said something like some of us don't have identity because we cannot speak our local language well. (Student 5)

These comments highlight several arguments that can be put forward. The use of English as medium of instruction affects family life in different ways. The main areas affected include child–parent attachment representations, interparental interactions and family stability (Hosny et al. 2020). It affects the capacity to transmit cultural knowledge through the use of the Indigenous language. Where English linguistic capital does not exist at home, it sets up tensions among family members, affecting children's capacity to communicate with their parents and grandparents. This has consequences for behavioural tendencies where some children are negatively perceived as 'disrespectful'. In acute cases, some children lose their Indigenous linguistic capital. Their inability to speak their Indigenous languages represents a loss of linguistic, cultural and social capital within their families. Interviews with people within the community affirm that the 'formal prohibitions' on speaking Indigenous languages produced an 'incitement to discourse' (Nayak and Kehily 2008: 79) far beyond the school site. The following quotes from community members reveal multiple discourses:

> I am not sure how to draw the relationship between English language use in school and our family crises of today and of yesterday. It is good to let children develop English language proficiency. But there are issues. … In summary, it has affected social organisation and cultural formations with severe consequences. In the early days the use of English in school helped us to understand the British colonizers, their mindset and cultural constructions. At the same time, it produced people who looked down upon their families as the use of the English language made them develop an adhesion to colonisers and their cultural ethos. … This fundamentally disrupted family structure and systems. Today, the same English language has created illiterates and literates, the educated and the uneducated, the drop outs and the completers. (Community member 1)

> There is much to say, but let me summarise by saying, it is good to learn English and become bilingual or even tri-lingual. But the bane of our society is how English is legislated in schools … This rule of using English in school has forced some to abandon their local languages … It is an affront to our culture and national identity. It is disrespectful to our values. How do you expect a child to start speaking English from the first day at school? … It means you want to change the child from one personality to another. Today, there are adults and children who cannot speak their local languages. (Community member 2)

> This issue of using English as medium of instruction has divided families and collapsed our value systems. It does not only affect family cohesion. There are people who can't communicate with their parents in their mother tongue. Grand children cannot communicate with their grandparents. … It's a crisis that goes beyond the family to the entire community and the Ghanaian society in general. It is an attack on our cultural heritage, a national security risk … Our language is an important part of family cultural heritage. These days there are Ghanaians who cannot speak any Ghanaian language. You can imagine what their children become. (Community member 3)

> It is pathetic how the use of English as medium of instruction has affected our family system. You have families divided such that some members cannot speak English while some cannot speak the local language. This is complete disorganisation! Today, we have terms like 'illiterate parents', 'illiterate wife', 'uneducated husband' etc. Emphasis on English has 'killed' our languages. … It is one of the major causes of disintegration in our families. It has destroyed our values. At the very foundation of the family, I am referring to the choice of marriage partner, people want to marry so called literates who can speak good English instead of women with values. These marriages collapse within few

years, creating broken homes for children and setting in motion a dangerous chain of broken homes. (Community member 4)

I want my children to learn English because it is an international language. It can help the children. I am happy they are bilingual. … But forcing them to speak English is causing more harm than good to our family heritage, language, identity and our culture. … I am afraid they are not able to speak Fante well. My children usually code-switch whenever we are in a conversation. I fear they may not be able to speak Fante one day. It means our heritage disappears. (Community member 5)

The comments acknowledge the positive rationale – the social and economic benefits that families derived from the use of English as medium of instruction. From a human capitalist view and functionalist view, the comments allow that the use of English as medium of instruction makes children bilingual. It offers them opportunities to improve proficiency in the official language and to acquire jobs that improve the lot and status of their families within global systems. However, it appears that the institutionalization of English as the medium of instruction, and the privilege assigned to it as good for socio-economic progress, endorses the hegemony of English as integral to family life. As in some earlier works (see Adzahlie-Mensah and Dunne 2019; Painter 2010), doing everything in English propels social disorganization and cultural dislocations by reducing the Indigenous languages to literary 'vernacular'. The use of English language for instruction meant that English cultural and epistemological codes subjugated local family values. It disparaged linguistic capital of families, denigrated family members who could take pride in English language while individual family members were compelled to abandon their language. In some cases, English language 'became foundations upon which the ideological edifice' of families was being built (Painter 2010: 120); the basis for family decision-making about marriage, family sustenance and child upbringing led to epistemic cultural violence. Perhaps the most violent finding was how the deployment of English as medium of instruction was separating family members from their 'other' language(s) – a central constituent of their personality, being and sociocultural identities. The interview comments from teachers emphasize the dual effects that the use of English as medium of instruction has on the family.

I don't know how this issue affects other people. What I know is that in my family we speak English at home … . This helps the children to improve their proficiency. We try to use the local language more when we visit my parents and grandparents. They don't like it when we speak English. … The other day, my grandmother was very angry with my mother for not teaching us Fante. My grandfather always says that it is good to speak and read English well for schooling purposes but we must speak Fante at home. We are struggling with this. I don't take my wife home at all because she cannot speak any Ghanaian language. The only way to protect my marriage is to keep her away from my grandparents. (Teacher 1)

See ... English is indirectly the main problem Ghanaian society faces at all levels. ... In our school, we say you are not intelligent because you cannot speak English well. ... There is a contradiction where children are supposed to develop competency in their local language. Many children cannot express themselves in their local tongues. This is terrible for the survival of our society beyond the family (Teacher 2)

When I was young, I heard from one of my friends that one man divorced the wife because ... the family members say she didn't go to school and cannot speak English. ... Now, I understand that this matter of English as a language of instruction is dangerous to our families, communities and national values systems ... Literacy is directly connected to using English language It denies us of our beings, our culture. It ... dictates ... how you should train your children. (Teacher 3)

There is evidence to suggest that the effects of using English as language of instruction goes far beyond the school. It has created problems in many families. As I speak to you, I have problems in my home because my wife thinks I speak too much English ... . The fact is I cannot speak the local language fluently. Some of my family members, especially my mother has stopped visiting because she said our children are always speaking English to her. That's how bad the situation is. I am sure people may have divorced, broken marriages may have occurred and some children may have been neglected because of this language issue. (Teacher 4)

English is a language. Why impose it on people ... . Using English to teach is like preparing the children against their families, culture, their community and themselves. I don't understand. Some of us cannot speak our languages fluently ... . Dreams have been shattered; families broken ... cultures forgotten because of this English problem. (Teacher 5)

The comments show that the use of English language as medium of instruction was considered an opening process that also has several epistemic effects for the family. As an opening process, it helps individuals to develop linguistic capital required for participation in national life, to gain jobs in the formal sector and to improve economic opportunities for their families. At the same time, the use of English language in school had some direct and indirect implications for family disorganization. First, some individuals can no longer speak their Indigenous languages. Second, the loss of linguistic capital affected their interactions with spouses, their children and extended family members. Third, the loss of linguistic capital, a salient aspect of cultural capital, affected cultural and epistemological codes that families sustain and vice versa. The teachers' comments held the cultural capital thesis in suggesting that possession of English language capital was a standard of measuring 'good' education in families. This works into arguments that educational language choice is neither neutral nor separable from issues of social and economic advantages (Adzahlie-Mensah 2014; Adzahlie-Mensah and Dunne 2019).

## Conclusion

The regime of using English as the medium of instruction is producing epistemic effects in terms of how family dynamics and power are shifting – how relationships and experiences of family members are being impacted, realigned or complicated as children encounter the use of English as a new language in school. It disparages Indigenous languages, concomitantly acceding false status to indigeneity – Indigenous culture, value systems, knowledges and identities. The regime disparages the status of Indigenous language as a force of socialization, a meaning-constituting system, a creator and carrier of cultural epistemological codes, symbol of social and cultural identity, a mode of communication and representation that has a deep connection to the development of identities that are structured by the slipperiness and instability of language. As Ghanaian children spend more time in school, to impose a language is to radically remove a significant and powerful dimension of their personal and social existence (Johnson 2000). I reflect that employing English as a medium of instruction limits spaces for students to think through concepts in their Indigenous languages, to develop Indigenous linguistic vocabulary and knowledge of their family's cultural and sociolinguistic identities. Legislating English as language of instruction represents an ideological de-legitimation of Indigenous languages, cultures and the identities of students thereby causing disruptions within the family structure. It shifts adult–child relations while reducing the socializing force of Indigenous languages of families. Therefore, there is the need for critical examination of the use of English language as medium of instruction in Ghana by examining the epistemic effects.

# References

Adzahlie-Mensah, V. (2014), 'Being "Nobodies": School Regimes and Student Identities in Ghana', Unpublished doctoral thesis, University of Sussex, http://sro.sussex.ac.uk/id/eprint/48419/. Accessed 1 March 2023.

Adzahlie-Mensah, V., and M. Dunne (2019), 'Continuing in the Shadows of Colonialism: The Educational Experiences of the African Child in Ghana', *Perspectives in Education*, 36 (2): 44–60.

African Union (2004), *Plan of Action on the Family in Africa*, Addis Ababa: African Union.

Akyeampong, K., and V. Adzahlie-Mensah (2018), 'Recent Trends in School Social Control in Sub-Saharan Africa', in J. Deakin, E. Taylor and A. Kupchik (eds), *The Palgrave Handbook of School Discipline, Surveillance, and Social Control*, 191–211, London: Palgrave Macmillan.

Alhassan, S., and V. Adzahlie-Mensah (2010), 'Teachers and Access to Schooling', *CREATE Pathways to Access Research Monograph No. 43*, Brighton: Centre for International Education, University of Sussex.

Al-Nakhalah, A. M. A. (2017), 'The Effect of Using English Language Only and Not Using the Mother Tongue in Teaching English Language for the Students of Primary Schools', *International Journal of Humanities and Social Science Invention*, 6 (6): 51–61.

Ball, J. (2014), 'Children Learn Better in Their Mother Tongue: Advancing Research on Mother Tongue-Based Multilingual Education', *Global Partnership for Education*, http://www.globalpartnership.org/blog/children-learn-better-their-mothertongue. Accessed 1 March 2023.

Bhat, M. A. (2008), 'Language: The Ultimate Tool of Social Control', *Interdisciplinary Journal of Linguistics*, 1: 111–18.

Busia, K. A. (1964), *Purposeful Education for Africa*, The Hague, The Netherlands: Mouton.

Collins, J., and R. Blot (2003), *Literacy and Literacies: Texts, Power, and Identity*, Cambridge: Cambridge University Press.

Crosnoe, R., K. Chambers Prickett, C. Smith and S. Cavanagh (2014), 'Changes in Young Children's Family Structures and Child Care Arrangements', *Demography*, 51: 459–83, https://doi.org/10.1007/s13524- 013-0258-5.

Dei, G. J. S. (2004), *Schooling and Education in Africa: The Case of Ghana*, Trenton: Africa World Press, Inc.

Dunne, M., and V. Adzahlie-Mensah (2016), 'Subordinate Subjects: The Work of the Hidden Curriculum in Post-Colonial Ghana', in D. Wyse, L. Haywood and J. Pandya (eds), *The SAGE Handbook of Curriculum, Pedagogy and Assessment*, 216–30, London: Sage.

Dzobo, N. K. (1987), 'Address at the National Workshop on the 1987 Educational Reforms', Accra: MOE.

62 *Reinventing the Family in Uncertain Times*

Esteva, G., Stuchal, D. L. and M. S. Prakash (2005), 'From a Pedagogy for Liberation to Liberation from Pedagogy', in B. A. Bowers and F. Apffel-Marglin (eds), *Re-Thinking Freire: Globalisation and the Environmental Crisis*, 39–50, New Jersey: Lawrence Erlbaum Associates.

Fletcher, K. A. (2013), 'Perceptions of Contemporary Effects of Colonialism among Educational Professionals in Ghana', University of Massachusetts, Amherst. Dissertation (Educational Doctorate).

Fomby, P., and C. A. Sennott (2013), 'Family Structure Instability and Mobility: The Consequences for Adolescents' Problem Behavior', *Social Science Research*, 42: 181–206.

Freire, P. (1993), *Pedagogy of the Oppressed*, London: Penguin.

GES (2001), 'Report of the Study on the Constitutional and Legal Framework for the Right to Pre-tertiary Education in Ghana', Accra: MOESS/GES.

Hosny, N. M., A. Danquah, K. Berr and M. W. Wan (2020), 'Children's Narratives of Family Life in Ghana: A Cultural Lens via Story Stems', *Journal of Child and Family Studies*. https://doi.org/10.1007/s10826-020-01839-6.

Irvine, J. T., and S. Gal (2000), 'Language ideology and Linguistic Differentiation', in P. V. Kroskrity (ed.), *Regimes of Language: Ideologies, Polities, and Identities*, 35–84, Santa Fe: School of American Research Press.

Johnson, F. L. (2000), *Speaking Culturally: Language Diversity in the United States*, London: Sage.

Lewin, K. M. (2009), 'Access to Education in Sub-Saharan Africa: Patterns, Problems and Possibilities', *Comparative Education*, 45 (2): 151–74.

MacBeath, J. (2010), *Living with the Legacy of Colonialism: The Ghana Story*, Cambridge: Cambridge University Press.

Macleod, C., and S. Bhatia (2008), 'Postcolonialism and Psychology', in C. Willig and W. S. Rogers (eds), *The SAGE Handbook of Qualitative Research in Psychology*, 576–89, London: SAGE.

Malinowski, B. (1936), 'Native Education and Culture Contact', *International Review of Missions*, 25: 480–515.

Mazrui, A. A. (1978), *Political Values and the Educated Class in Africa*, Berkeley: University of California Press.

Nayak, A. and M. J. Kehily (2008), *Gender, Youth and Culture: Young Masculinities and Femininities*, London: Palgrave Macmillan.

Painter, D. W. (2010), 'Tongue-Tied: The Politics of Language, Subjectivity and Social Psychology', Doctoral Thesis, University of South Africa.

Peyton, J. K. (2015), 'Language of Instruction: Research Findings and Program and Instructional Implications', *Reconsidering Development*, 4 (1): 16–34.

Prevoo, T., and B. Weel (2014), 'The Effect of Family Disruption on Children's Personality Development: Evidence from British Longitudinal Data', IZA Discussion Paper No. 8712.

Quartey, S. (2007), *Missionary Practices on the Gold Coast, 1832–1895: Discourse, Gaze, Gender in the Basel Mission in Pre-colonial West Africa*, New York: Cambria Press.

Ryan, R., A. Claessens and A. J. Markowitz (2013), 'Family Structure and Children's Behavior', *Focus*, 30 (2): 11–14.

Samuel, O., and V. Hertrich (2019), 'Introduction to the Special Collection on Children and Family Dynamics in Sub-Saharan Africa', *Demographic Research*, 41 (44): 1269–76.

Thomas, S. J. (2018), 'Dimensions of Family Disruption: Coincidence, Interactions, and Impacts on Children's Educational Attainment', *Longitudinal and Life Course Studies*, 9 (2): 157–87.

Woolman, D. C. (2001), 'Educational Reconstruction and Post-Colonial Curriculum Development: A Comparative Study of Four African Countries', *International Education Journal*, 2 (5), 27–46, WCCES Commission 6 Special 2001 Congress Issue.

Zafeirakou, A. (2015), 'The Power of Mother Tongue and Multilingual Education: Students Who Learn to Read in Their Mother Tongue Transfer These Skills to a Second Language', *Global Partnership for Education*. http://www.globalpartnership. org/blog/power-mother-tongue-and-multilingual-education.

5

# Black British Families: Liminality and the Liabilities of Language

Parise Carmichael-Murphy

## Introduction

This chapter seeks to contextualize contemporary constructions of Black British families within their socio-economic and historical contexts to draw attention to *how*, and *why*, social policy contributes to their marginalization in Britain. It aims to illuminate how liabilities of language and liminality in law sustain social inequities that affect Black British families, particularly concerning childhood and citizenship in Britain as conditional states. Social inequalities are a unique set of circumstances that can be re-enacted and re-enforced by single-issue policies which sustain liminalities and push Black British families into grey spaces where their discrimination is normalized. Interlocking discrimination at the intersection of age, race and class are enforced by British law and policy in ways that misrecognize Black British families' experiences of social inequality.

Education and social policies in Britain enforce universalism, normalize discriminatory language and mobilize harmful discourses in ways that position Black British families as 'out of place'. The politicization and policing of *Blackness* in Britain must be considered in historical context to comprehend how and why contemporary British policy may acknowledge difference, but fail to celebrate it. Consequentially, Black British families experience a fraught and unjust relationship with the education, justice, health and social care systems. This chapter will unpack: (1) existing social inequalities that affect Black British families, (2) the historical exclusion of Black British families in the UK, (3) how education and social policies sustain the discrimination of Black British families today and (4) why we need to move towards more critical practice in education, health and social care.

## Black British families

In Britain, 'Black' is typically used as an umbrella term for those who identify, or are identified, as Black African, Black Caribbean or Black other; Black British is typically used to describe a person who is Black and born in or lives in Britain (Office for National Statistics 2021). In Britain, Black ethnic groups make up 3.3 per cent (1.9 million) of the total population, including almost one million Black African and 0.6 million Black Caribbean individuals (GOV.UK 2018). 'Family' is used here broadly to describe members of a domestic social group who share common features (Kane 2019). Activists, practitioners, researchers and policymakers are illuminating how racial disparities across Britain disproportionately impact Black British families including, but not limited to, education, employment, health, social care and criminal justice domains. Passive policies that fail to identify, name and resist how social inequalities are sustained perpetuate the marginalization and misrecognition of Black British families.

'British life' is a socially constructed space where whiteness is naturalized and anything which deviates from the norm sensationalized as a threat to British morality (Gale and Thomas 2018). 'Nuclear family' is used in reference to a normative model of family as two biological parents and children built upon Westernized ideals (Bengtson 2001). During the mid-twentieth century, the 'nuclear family' came to be positioned as something ideal, thus supporting political narratives that placed value on family structure, particularly as part of the drive for economic independence at the household level (Sear 2021). A total of 14.9 per cent of British families are categorized as 'lone parent', with the majority of lone parents (86 per cent) considered to be mothers (ONS 2019). Black children in Britain are over twice as likely to live in a lone parent household (GOV.UK 2019). In Britain, deviation from the nuclear family structure is sensationalized as a determinant of social issues; tropes of 'absent father' and 'single mother' as diverse family structures are presented as in deficit. Parents who claim social assistance in the UK are often stigmatized (Jun 2019). This contributes to the sensationalizing of the Black family as incompatible with, and a direct threat to, the 'British way of living'.

Reynolds critiques assumptions that 'non-resident Black fathers' are inactive and absent, pushing for greater consideration of *why* fathers may reside in separate places from their children (Reynolds 2009). Using father's presence to describe disparities in Black children's outcomes perpetuates the stereotypical portrayal of Black fathers who reside in different homes away from their children as 'absentee' (Reynolds 2010). This disregards and devalues how Black fathers' parenting styles are influenced by community circumstances such as primary caregivers, familial relationships, resources and networks that impacted their access to care for their children (Reynolds 2009).

Reynolds (2009, 2020) further critiques universal and individualized notions of 'mothering' that typically misrecognizes Black women as mothers. Reynolds celebrates 'Black mothering' as a resistance beyond the family and the home that 'exists outside of biological function and instead encompasses collective acts of community activism' (2020: 3). Reynold's reconceptualization of Black mothering as community activism is pertinent, given the systematic dismissal of racialized disparities that impact Black British women. One example of such is how Black women in Britain are more than four times as likely to die during childbirth than their white counterparts (Knight et al. 2021). In response to this inequity, grassroots organization Five X More are pushing to reduce maternal mortality rates and improve health care outcomes for Black women. This sits within the wider response of Black-led collectives who, in response to the systematic denial of care to Black British parents, are mobilizing to care for their communities. Not-for-profit organization Southall Black Sisters is resisting domestic and gender-related violence against Black women, and community initiative Sistah Space is campaigning to improve access and quality of domestic abuse services for African heritage women and girls. Together, Southall Black Sisters and Sistah Space are drawing attention to exactly how the British social, economic, political and historical climates deter Black women from reporting domestic abuse. Black British women are less likely to report domestic abuse for fear of deportation and loss of public services for themselves and other parties involved (Women's Aid 2021). This *must* be considered and addressed within the context of the ongoing Windrush scandal, mass deportations, privatization of health care and 'hostile environment' measures.

## Britain, Brexit and 'Britishness'

As Britain post Brexit continues to negotiate its positioning internationally, a decade of austerity measures and vast cuts to public spending have contributed to a fraught sociopolitical climate within the UK. UK's exit from the European Union followed the 'anti-immigration Leave campaign' that was the culmination of decades of hostility towards immigrants (Gough 2017: 366). Intensified by the Nationality and Borders Bill as well as the No Recourse to Public Funds condition, British policy is contributing to 'hostile environments' that discriminate against migrant families by deprivation of British citizenship and access to public funds (Nationality and Borders Act 2022; Immigration and Asylum Act 1999). Clause 9 of the Nationality and Borders Bill means it is no longer a requirement for the government to give notice of any decision to deprive an individual of their British citizenship, should it be in the interests of national security, diplomatic relations or public interest. Section 115 of the Immigration and Asylum Act 1999 stops migrants from gaining access to welfare benefits. Expectations for households to be more autonomous are prevalent in requirements for joint Universal Credit applications; for any cohabiting couple who are assumed to be living as if married, the payment is made to only one household claimant (GOV. UK 2021c).

As Conservative governments continue to shift responsibility from the British state onto individuals and their families, the individualization and privatization of education, health and social care pushes social issues into the home (Millar 2019). This is evident in cuts to youth services across England and Wales, who have access to 70 per cent less funding; simultaneously, rates of knife crime, mental health difficulties and social isolation experienced by young people are increasing (YMCA 2020). British education is becoming characterized by a target-driven approach to schooling, with schools now experiencing greater accountability with less external help; during 2019, 65 per cent of secondary schools in England became academies, many of which served disadvantaged student populations (Eyles and Machin 2019). Under austerity, cuts across the education sector have contributed to: less spending per pupil, fewer teachers and teaching assistants, greater pupil numbers per class, reduced curricula and limited opening hours across English schools (Stop School Cuts 2020).

All of the issues cited earlier are compounding a culture of racial neoliberalism that draws responsibility away from the state by placing blame for experiencing social inequity with the communities that are racialized. Racial neoliberalism is a political tool that works to remove the state's responsibility to protect communities from discrimination and social injustice by criminalizing people for their social conditions (Kirton 2018). As the National Health Service (NHS) becomes privatized and the ability to sustain the self is individualized, collective approaches to caring are economically devalued; for many, this disregards community as a means of care (Reynolds 2003). Instead, racial neoliberalism attributes blame for an inability to meet needs with a person for *belonging* to the community. For Black British families, this hostile social, political, economic and historical climate criminalizes agency and autonomy within the Black British community.

## Policy is fundamental: British values

Under the 2010 Conservative and Liberal Democrat coalition government, the Department for Children, Schools and Families (DCSF) became the Department for Education (DfE). Subsequently, a 'back-to-basics' national curriculum introduced the fundamental 'British values', initiating a shift away from multiculturalism. The British values are a collection of ambiguous aspirations for all members of British society to demonstrate; these were introduced by the government in the 2011 *Prevent* strategy. 'Prevent' is a conduit for policing and securitization in schools. It reinforces harmful discourse about religious groups in Britain and has contributed to greater stigma, hypervisibility and Islamophobia towards British Muslims in education (Jerome et al. 2019). The 'British values' are intended to ensure that young people are prepared for 'life in modern Britain' (GOV.UK 2014). These values are defined as: (1) democracy, (2) the rule of law, (3) individual liberty and (4) mutual respect and tolerance of those with different faiths and beliefs, and of those without faith. Since 2019, the Office for Standards in Education, Children's Services and Skills (Ofsted) has instructed schools to equip students with 'cultural capital' as part of their inspection criteria.

The British values must be considered in the historical context of the British Empire and the imperial connotations of national identity and the superiority of 'Britishness' (Yıldız 2021). By asserting 'Britishness' as something that can be achieved through educational values, policy and subsequent practice, it contributes to the securitization of Black British families via schools, social services and health care. The British values indicate a politically ambiguous shift away from multiculturalism in Britain, albeit a passive one (Winter and Mills 2020; Yıldız 2021). To tolerate something suggests that it must be disliked or in disagreement; pushing for 'tolerance' alone disregards how or why difference is perceived as deficit in the first instance. The tolerance of difference passively sustains the existing power imbalances. By failing to adopt an *anti*-discriminatory stance, the British values reaffirm the naturalization of there being a *British way of life* that can be learned.

Black British families deserve *more* than tolerance; they need proactive movement towards anti-discriminatory approaches that acknowledge anti-Black rhetoric and practice and visible efforts to dismantle them. This would require acknowledgement of how the British values uphold essentialist and ethnocentric ideals (Winter and Mills 2020), to position Blackness as deficit of Britishness. In practice, this essentialism privileges whiteness and middle-class social capital

70       *Reinventing the Family in Uncertain Times*

in schools (Kirton 2018) and historically and systematically devalues culture and capital within Black British families. The British values are in stark contrast to the 2009 DCSF additional inclusion guidance 'Building Futures: Believing in Children. A Focus on Provision for Black Children in the Early Years Foundation Stage'. The 'Building Futures' guidance sought to challenge attitudes and ask difficult questions to improve the quality of Black children's experiences across the Early Years Foundation Stage (Department for Children, Schools and Families 2009).

## The policing of Blackness in British education

'Blackness' can typically be used to define one of two things: (1) a process of racialization and (2) a political reclamation of experience and identity. One might identify with Blackness as a reclamation of difference to subvert power by showing self-awareness and agentic self-definition (Lorde 1984). For some, self-definition with Black identities can provide individuals with a sense of group membership and community (Hunter et al. 2019). During the 1940s, Commonwealth migration to Britain was met with anti-Black and anti-immigration sentiment that filtered into social rhetoric, politics and policy. During the 1960s, the presence of Black labour migrants was sensationalized as a direct threat to the British 'way of living', and from the 1970s, the government began to 'scapegoat' young Black people for a failing economy as well as a rise in police violence (Christian 2005).

During the 1970s Bernard Coard documented how education practice in schools discriminated against Black child migrants from the West Indies, who represented 75 per cent of the pupil population in 'Educationally Subnormal Schools' (ESN). Coard's booklet *How the West Indian Child Is Made Educationally Subnormal in the British School System* (1971) drew attention to the discriminatory practices which saw the children of Caribbean immigrants more likely to be placed in ESN schools than their peers, particularly for a parental audience. The systematic exclusion of Black British students from education in Britain cannot be removed from discrimination of the Windrush generation. Currently, Black British students across schools are at greater risk of being permanently excluded (GOV.UK 2021b). Black British students are often categorized as 'Black Caribbean' or 'Black African' to separate the issue from idealized notions of 'Britishness'; this should be acknowledged as 'off-rolling' or 'off-shoring' a perceived problem (Akala 2018). The historical exclusion of

Black Caribbean people in Britain continues and is further evident in recent high-profile cases, where individuals who grew up in Britain are being deported to the Caribbean.

Education in Britain in relation to Black people reflects anti-Black politics and deficit-model thinking that disregards and devalues alternative ways of knowing (Yıldız 2021). British education has historically been positioned as a tool through which social problems in society can be fixed; the Schools Minister describes education as an 'engine of the economy', 'foundation of our culture' and 'preparation for adult life' (Gibb 2015). This conceptualization of education should not be viewed as distinct from the positioning of Black British communities as a threat to 'British life' and the presence of the Black child in British education as a long-standing 'problem' for Britain (Crozier 2005). As such, education based upon a cultural deficit model places 'responsibility' for experiencing inequity with the culture of the individual or community by *blaming* them for resisting assimilation (Solórzano and Yosso 2002).

The growing presence of police in schools is accelerating the early criminalization of Black students (Joseph-Salisbury 2020). Students who are excluded from school are placed at greater risk of experiencing unemployment, crime and imprisonment (Lammy 2017); arguably, education professionals should acknowledge their possible contribution to the early criminalizing of Black students *as well as* police. It is not surprising that young Black people report the least confidence in police than any other age or ethnicity group (GOV.UK 2020). Young Black people are progressively penalized throughout the criminal justice system; they are often perceived as less vulnerable and more excessively sanctioned by services that fail to meet their needs and legal rights (Goff et al. 2014).

The rapid privatization and growing academization of schools in Britain are contributing to: (1) a more target-driven approach to education (see Hamilton 2018), and (2) the securitization of individuals via policy (see Winter and Mills 2020). In turn, British education continues to attempt to deny economic and social capital to Black students; racism is concealed and repackaged as 'competition' amongst the educational market (Hamilton 2018; Winter and Mills 2020). This is evident in the numbers of Black students who are disproportionately excluded from schools and awarded General Certificate of Secondary Educations. For some context, only 1 per cent of pupils who are excluded achieve the five 'good' GCSEs needed to enter employment, and 42 per cent of the prisoners in the UK have been permanently excluded whilst 63 per cent have been temporarily excluded from school (Gill, Quilter-Pinner and Swift 2017). Out of the excluded pupils,

78 per cent are also identified as having special educational needs, eligibility for free school meals or were a child 'in need'; 11 per cent of all excluded pupils are identified as all three (Timpson 2019). Black students are the most likely to be excluded from school, and Black boys are least likely than any other gender or ethnicity grouping to achieve a strong pass in English and maths GCSEs (GOV. UK, 2021a,b).

As a significant means of socialization in Britain, education has historically and systematically discriminated against Black British families. This has sustained attempts to deny access to citizenship and care via disproportionate school exclusions, unemployment, incarceration as well as restricted access to social capital and social funds. In this sense, education policy plays a significant role in the material and ideological structuring of racial inequity that denies Black British children access to childhood, citizenship and care.

## Meritocracy is a myth

Meritocratic discourse in Britain sustains hostile environments that discriminate against Black British families and their communities; it disguises how capitalism and capitalized education benefit from institutional racism (Kapoor 2013). Deindustrialization, technological development, precarious employment and post-Brexit international negotiations are likely to continue to change the privatized and competitive climate of British education and social care moving forward. Moreover, this is likely to be further compounded by the ongoing global Covid-19 pandemic.

The growing privatization of schooling in a climate of neoliberal governance has enabled the securitization of individuals via policy, with racism being concealed and repackaged as competition amongst the educational market (Hamilton 2018; Winter and Mills 2020). Historically, British education has played a pivotal role in the systematic denial of social and economic capital to Black British families. Uncritical education disregards the role of the teacher, school or education system in sustaining competition, or failure to meet the needs of Black British families. Black British families are likely to benefit from greater accountability from gatekeepers of education, social care and healthcare to critically consider how their practices contribute to the discrimination of racialized individuals and communities across Britain (Solórzano and Yosso 2002).

The attribution of the cause of inequality to the individuals and groups who experience it is compounded by the strategic omission of 'race' from policy that makes it difficult to formally name racism. A linguistic 'burial of race' sustains the ambiguity that has culminated in the assignment of 'problematic' status of minoritized communities and their cultures (Kapoor 2013). As such, racialized disparities in education, employment and health outcomes are problematized as *because* of Black culture, rather than problematizing how Black culture is positioned as a threat to British society (Graham 2016). Black British families are more likely to experience social and economic circumstances that restrict their access to opportunities for social success (Glynn 2016). When the structure of Black British families (e.g. absent father, single mother) is emphasized as the cause of social inequality, this draws attention away from how British society positions Black families. For Black British families, policy that fails to name their discrimination pushes them into liminal spaces, where their experiences of inequality are disguised and sustained.

## Liminality and the liabilities of language

Tolerance will not foster a culture of equity, but given the strategic removal of 'race' from documentation and discussion, it becomes more difficult to name implicit and institutional racism. This disguises the marginalization and minoritization of communities under 'Equality, Diversity and Inclusion' (EDI) rhetoric that pushes inequality as a single issue. Single-issue policies do not acknowledge how language can reinforce discrimination; this is a strategic attempt to disempower and silence (Crenshaw 1991). Single-issue policy politicizes the problem amongst dominant groups; it fails to reflect the experience of intragroup difference or how 'singular' forms of discrimination influence others (Crenshaw 1991). Attempts to separate discrimination homogenize experiences by asserting that they are distinct from one another (Olson 1998). Inequality is not 'single-issue', yet essentialist distinctions of discrimination separate and redefine it in terms that serve dominant groups (Lorde 1984; Rankin-Wright, Hylton and Norman 2020).

Policy that pushes for equality of singular 'issues' pushes Black families in Britain into liminal spaces by disguising the social, economic, cultural and historical discourses that contribute to the subordination of Black British families. As such, policy that separates Black British families' experiences into single issues of 'Black', 'British' *or* 'family' obscures the social construction of their inequality that is upheld by dominant groups. To counter how policy subordinates racially minoritized groups, it must comprehend how social categorization recreates power imbalances (Crenshaw 1991). There is need to contextualize and unpack policy, with critical consideration on *why* they are created and who they are intended *for* to understand the active role of policy in the material and ideological structuring of racial inequity (Gillborn 2005).

Implicit nostalgia for the British Empire sustains the 'othering' of difference in British society (Yıldız 2021). Given the naturalization of middle-class capital as quintessentially British, any policy that pushes for social equity must grapple with the strategic separation of 'race' from 'class' as social categories. The naturalization of middle-class and meritocratic discourses in Britain positions Black children's restricted access to economic resource as low achievement or aspiration; this normalizes the perceived 'failure' of Black students in education (Hamilton 2018). In Britain, 'working class' is a politically loaded label that separates class discrimination from racism (Olusoga 2019). This cannot be separated from the socially constructed division of both Blackness and Britishness as distinct and incompatible identities (Boakye 2019). Undoubtedly, this feeds into divisive rhetoric about the 'white working-class crisis' and 'Black Caribbean underachievement' across research, policy and practice in education domains. Such rhetoric is not isolated to education alone, but feeds into social care and health services, which misrecognize Black British families and their experiences.

A major shift in perspective is needed, one that moves away from single-issue policy and law to a view that challenges the assumptions and ideologies that privilege ethnocentrism. This requires a move away from the polarizing 'British values' that perpetuate deficit discourse and contribute to assessments of 'Britishness' that perpetuate the marginalization of Black British families. Since 'invisibility only means misrecognition, not inexistence' (Ibrahim 2008: 57), it is vital that we spend time working to recognize theoretical misrecognition *within* Black British families – for example, those who identify, or are identified, as middle class, disabled, queer, adoptive, interracial, migrant, neurodiverse or religious. We need to consider how discourse sustains colourism, ableism, anti-Semitism, classism and xenophobia in ways that similarly position Black British families. Only then can we begin to address discrimination beyond words.

## Moving beyond misrecognition: Who cares?

Policy continues to position Black British families' divergence from the norm as deviance from Western ideals of the family. Systematically, policy and practice misrecognize Black British families' circumstances and experiences of discrimination in social, economic, historical and political contexts. They do not appreciate Black British families' distinct networks, resources, relations or household circumstances (Reynolds 2003, 2009) either. Such misrecognition positions Black British families as somewhat incompatible with idealized tropes of the 'British way of life'. In response, education, health and social care policy in Britain re-create and re-enforce hostile environments that police 'difference' for many Black British families. This policing is sustained by liminalities of language and policy that upholds childhood, citizenship and care in Britain as conditional.

Adultification is typically used to describe when a young person is 'forced into adult-like roles within the family' (Schmitz and Tyler 2016). There is a strong emphasis on adultification in the context of the family with little acknowledgement of the role of social settings, such as the school, and their role in pushing families into situations that require young people to 'grow up'. In Britain, adolescence reflects a transitionary point in the life course which sees a child 'become' an adult; during this time, the young person accrues legal accountability for their actions and is simultaneously expected to become economically successful and independent (Sundhall 2017). Legal protections afforded to 'childhood' in the Western context contribute to the romanticized ideals of safety. Yet, Black children and their families in Britain experience restricted access to societal capital and the protections associated with 'childhood', citizenship and children's rights (Goff et al. 2014; Hamilton 2018).

The paucity of research on Black early childhood and play reflects and sustains the normalization and universalization of 'childhood' as a white phenomenon (Bryan 2020). Further, it positions Black British families outside the constructions of safety whilst simultaneously restricting their access to economic capital. Arguably, social care fails to protect Black children from harm *outside* of the home, including criminal abuse or exploitation. Despite being more vulnerable to criminal exploitation, young Black people are less likely to report and less likely to access victim support about their experiences (The Child Safeguarding Review Panel 2020; Yarrow 2005). Further still, at the point of intervention, young Black people are more likely to encounter a youth offending service than a social one at the point (Davis and Marsh 2020).

The British child protection system was conceived of to respond to harm *within* the family; as such, its historical emphasis on the family or home in isolation misrecognizes risks in the wider environment. For example, uncritical social work intervention frames divergence from normative Western parenting ideals as deficit and pushes Black families to assimilate to Western ideals of parenting (Okpokiri 2020). Instead, we might work towards a contextual approach to safeguarding which takes account of the environments in which young people encounter harm or safeguarding risks, particularly beyond the family and in contexts where the families have little agency within (e.g. the school, neighbourhood or online) (Firmin 2020). Ideally, we should push for place-based critical practice that ensures Black communities are 'treated with care rather than suspicion' (Davis and Marsh 2020: 4).

Britain must acknowledge and unpack complicities that lie *within* British policies to sustain the systematic and historical discrimination of Blackness in Britain. If neither policy nor practice can make explicit authentic efforts to empower Black families, then we need to accept that what it does at present is contribute to their disempowerment. Without actively working to centralize the lived experiences of those who are pushed to occupy liminal spaces, services perpetuate the social, economic, political and historical conditions that discriminate against Black British families. This approach would require greater recognition of how migration, imprisonment and employment influence social circumstance. To counter how 'single-issue' approaches to equity disguise such experience, we need to embrace diversity and appreciate difference in British societies and *within* Black British families; and most importantly, we must do that with *care*.

## Conclusion

Liminalities in language and policy should be acknowledged as enforced misrecognition that sustains childhood, citizenship and care as conditional states. As such, misrecognition of the historical and systematic discrimination, exclusion, marginalization and oppression experienced by Black British communities disregard the socially constructed nature of Black British families' circumstances. Policy that positions inequity as a *consequence* of social characteristics conflates circumstance with choice; this positioning disguises how Black British communities are systematically restricted from access to social capital and economic goods such as exam grades or employment. The historical politicization of Blackness in Britain and the repackaging of neoliberalism as 'competition' systematically attempts to deny social economic capital from Black British families. This is disguised as meritocratic discourse that mythicizes 'Blackness' and 'Britishness' as distinct, and attempts to omit Black British families from the naturalized middle-class social policy rhetoric as enactment of the 'British way of life'. As such, British education, health and social care mobilize deficit discourse that polices Black British families' perceived differences and discriminates against them in education, health and social care spaces. Instead, we need critical approaches to research, policy and practice that work to understand, appreciate and counter *how* and *why* national services continue to misrecognize Black British families' experiences and push them into liminal spaces.

# References

Akala (2018), *Natives: Race and Class in the Ruins of Empire*, London: Hodder and Stoughton.

Bengtson, V. L. (2001), 'Beyond the Nuclear Family: The Increasing Importance of Multigenerational Bonds. The Burgess Award Lecture', *Journal of Marriage and Family*, 63 (1): 1–16, https://doi.org/10.1111/j.1741-3737.2001.00001.x.

Boakye, J. (2019), 'What It Means to Be Black and British Today', https://i-d.vice.com/en_uk/article/kzmey9/what-it-means-to-be-black-and-british-today.

Bryan, N. (2020), 'Shaking the Bad Boys: Troubling the Criminalization of Black Boys' Childhood Play, Hegemonic White Masculinity and Femininity, and the School Playground-to-Prison Pipeline', *Race Ethnicity and Education*, 23 (5): 673–92, https://doi.org/10.1080/13613324.2018.1512483.

Christian, M. (2005), 'The Politics of Black Presence in Britain and Black Male Exclusion in the British Education System', *Journal of Black Studies*, 35 (3): 327–46, https://doi.org/10.1177/0021934704268397.

Coard, B. (1971), *How the West Indian Child Is Made Educationally Subnormal in the British School System: The Scandal of the Black Child in Schools in Britain*, ERIC.

Crenshaw, K. (1991), 'Mapping the Margins: Intersectionality, Identity Politics, and Violence against Women of Color', *Stanford Law Review*, 43 (6): 1241–99. https://doi.org/10.2307/1229039.

Crozier, G. (2005), 'There's a War against Our Children': Black Educational Underachievement Revisited', *British Journal of Sociology of Education*, 26 (5): 585–98, https://doi.org/10.1080/01425690500293520.

Davis, J., and N. Marsh (2020), 'Boys to Men: The Cost of "Adultification" in Safeguarding Responses to Black Boys', *Critical and Radical Social Work*, 8 (2): 255–9, https://doi.org/10.1332/204986020X15945756023543.

Department for Children, Schools and Families (2009), *Building Futures: Believing in Children*, Department for Children, Schools and Families, https://www.foundationyears.org.uk/wp-content/uploads/2011/10/Believing_in_Children.pdf. Accessed 9 July 2022.

Eyles, A., and S. Machin (2019), 'The Introduction of Academy Schools to England's Education', *Journal of the European Economic Association*, 17 (4): 1107–46, https://doi.org/10.1093/jeea/jvy021.

# Reinventing the Family in Uncertain Times

Firmin, C. E. (2020), *Contextual Safeguarding: An Overview of the Operational, Strategic and Conceptual Framework*, England: University of Bedfordshire, https://uobrep.ope nrepository.com/bitstream/handle/10547/624844/Contextual-Safeguarding-Briefing. pdf?sequence=2&isAllowed=y.

Gale, R., and H. Thomas (2018), 'Race at the Margins: A Critical Race Theory Perspective on Race Equality in UK Planning', *Environment and Planning C: Politics and Space*, 36 (3): 460–78, https://doi.org/10.1177/2399654417723168.

Gibb, N. (2015), *The Purpose of Education*, GOV.UK. https://www.gov.uk/government/ speeches/the-purpose-of-education. Accessed 6 August 2022.

Gill, K., H. Quilter-Pinner and D. Swift (2017), *Making the Difference: Breaking the Link between School Exclusion and Social Exclusion*, Institute for Public Policy Research, https://www.ippr.org/publications/making-the-difference. Accessed 6 August 2022.

Gillborn, D. (2005), 'Education Policy as an Act of White Supremacy: Whiteness, Critical Race Theory and Education Reform', *Journal of Education Policy*, 20 (4): 485–505, https://doi.org/10.1080/02680930500132346.

Glynn, M. (2016), 'Towards an Intersectional Model of Desistance for Black Offenders', *Safer Communities*, 15 (1): 24–32, https://doi.org/10.1108/SC-05-2015-0016.

Goff, P. A., M. C. Jackson, B. A. L. Di Leone, C. M. Culotta and N. A. DiTomasso (2014), 'The Essence of Innocence: Consequences of Dehumanizing Black Children', *Journal of Personality and Social Psychology*, 106 (4): 526, https://doi.org/10.1037/ a0035663.

Gough, J. (2017), 'Brexit, Xenophobia and Left Strategy Now', *Capital & Class*, 41 (2): 366–72, https://doi.org/10.1177/0309816817711558e.

GOV.UK (2014), *Guidance on Promoting British Values in Schools Published*, Department for Education, https://www.gov.uk/government/news/guidance-on-promoting-british-values-in-schools-published.

GOV.UK (2018), *Population of England and Wales*. Ethnicity Facts and Figures, https:// www.ethnicity-facts-figures.service.gov.uk/uk-population-by-ethnicity/natio nal-and-regional-populations/population-of-england-and-wales/latest#by-ethnicity.

GOV.UK (2019), *Families and Households*. Ethnicity Facts and Figures, https://www. ethnicity-facts-figures.service.gov.uk/uk-population-by-ethnicity/demographics/ families-and-households/latest.

GOV.UK (2020), *Stop and Search*. Ethnicity Facts and Figures, https://www.ethnic ity-facts-figures.service.gov.uk/crime-justice-and-the-law/policing/stop-and-search/ latest#by-ethnicity.

GOV.UK (2021a), *GCSE Results (Attainment 8)*. Ethnicity Facts and Figures, https://www.ethnicity-facts-figures.service.gov.uk/education-skills-and-training/11-to-16-years-old/gcse-results-attainment-8-for-children-aged-14-to-16-key-stage-4/latest.

GOV.UK (2021b), *Permanent Exclusions*. Ethnicity Facts and Figures, https://www. ethnicity-facts-figures.service.gov.uk/education-skills-and-training/absence-and-exc lusions/permanent-exclusions/latest.

GOV.UK (2021c), *Universal Credit: Further Information for Couples*, https://www.gov.uk/government/publications/universal-credit-and-couples-an-introduction/universal-credit-further-information-for-couples#my-partner-wont-allow-me-access-to-any-of-the-payment.

Graham, K. (2016), 'The British School-to-Prison Pipeline', in K. Andrews and L. A. Palmer (eds), *Blackness in Britain*, 124–34, England: Routledge.

Hamilton, D. G. (2018), 'Too Hot to Handle: African Caribbean Pupils and Students as Toxic Consumers and Commodities in the Educational Market', *Race Ethnicity and Education*, 21 (5): 573–92, https://doi.org/10.1080/13613324.2017.1376635.

HMG (2000), *Immigration and Asylum Act 1999*, Stationery Office. Available at: https://www.legislation.gov.uk/ukpga/1999/33/contents. Accessed 6 August 2022.

HMG (2022), *Nationality and Borders Act 2022*, Stationery Office. Available at: https://www.legislation.gov.uk/ukpga/2022/36/contents/enacted. Accessed 6 August 2022.

Hunter, C. D., Case, A. D., & Harvey, I. S. (2019). Black college students' sense of belonging and racial identity. *International Journal of Inclusive Education*, 23 (9): 950–66.

Ibrahim, A. (2008), 'Operating under Erasure: Race/Language/Identity', *Comparative and International Education/Éducation Comparée et Internationale*, 37 (2): 56–76, https://doi.org/10.5206/cie-eci.v37i2.9119.

Jerome, L., and A. Elwick (2019), 'Identifying an Educational Response to the Prevent Policy: Student Perspectives on Learning about Terrorism, Extremism and Radicalisation', *British Journal of Educational Studies*, 67 (1): 97–114.

Joseph-Salisbury, R. (2020), *Runnymede Perspectives: Race and Racism in English Secondary Schools*, https://www.runnymedetrust.org/uploads/publications/pdfs/Runnymede Secondary Schools report FINAL.pdf.

Jun, M. (2019), 'Stigma and Shame Attached to Claiming Social Assistance Benefits: Understanding the Detrimental Impact on UK Lone Mothers' Social Relationships', *Journal of Family Studies*, 28 (1): 199–215, https://doi.org/10.1080/13229400.2019.1689840.

Kane, L. W. (2019), 'What Is a Family? Considerations on Purpose, Biology, and Sociality', *Public Affairs Quarterly*, 33 (1): 65–88, https://doi.org/10.2307/26910010.

Kapoor, N. (2013), 'The Advancement of Racial Neoliberalism in Britain', *Ethnic and Racial Studies*, 36 (6): 1028–46, https://doi.org/10.1080/01419870.2011.629002.

Kirton, D. (2018), 'Neoliberalism, "Race" and Child Welfare', *Critical and Radical Social Work*, 6 (3): 311–27, https://doi.org/10.1332/204986018X15388225078517.

Knight, M., K. Bunch, D. Tuffnell, R. Paterl, J. Shakespeare, R. Kotnis, S. Kenyon and J. J. Kurinczuk (2021), *Saving Lives, Improving Mothers' Care: Lessons Learned to Inform Maternity Care from the UK and Ireland Confidential Enquiries into Maternal Deaths and Morbidity 2017–19*, MBRRACE-UK, https://www.npeu.ox.ac.uk/assets/downloads/mbrrace-uk/reports/maternal-report-2021/MBRRACE-UK_Maternal_Report_2021_-_FINAL_-_WEB_VERSION.pdf.

80         *Reinventing the Family in Uncertain Times*

Lammy, D. (2017), *The Lammy Review: An Independent Review into the Treatment of, and Outcomes for, Black, Asian and Minority Ethnic Individuals in the Criminal Justice System*, HM Government, https://assets.publishing.service.gov.uk/governm ent/uploads/system/uploads/attachment_data/file/643001/lammy-review-final-rep ort.pdf.

Lorde, A. (1984), *Sister Outsider Essays and Speeches by Audre Lorde*, Berkeley: CA: Crossing Press.

Millar, J. (2019), 'Self-Responsibility and Activation for Lone Mothers in the United Kingdom', *American Behavioral Scientist*, 63 (1): 85–99, https://doi. org/10.1177/0002764218816804.

Office for National Statistics (2019), *Families and Households in the UK: 2019*, https:// www.ons.gov.uk/peoplepopulationandcommunity/birthsdeathsandmarriages/famil ies/bulletins/familiesandhouseholds/2019. Accessed 6 August 2022.

Office for National Statistics (2021), *Ethnic Group, National Identity and Religion*, https://www.ons.gov.uk/methodology/classificationsandstandards/measuringequal ity/ethnicgroupnationalidentityandreligion. Accessed 6 August 2022.

Okpokiri, C. (2020), 'Parenting in Fear: Child Welfare Micro Strategies of Nigerian Parents in Britain', *British Journal of Social Work*, 51: 427–44. https://doi. org/10.1093/bjsw/bcaa205.

Olson, L. C. (1998), 'Liabilities of Language: Audre Lorde Reclaiming Difference', *Quarterly Journal of Speech*, 84 (4): 448–70, https://doi.org/10.1080/0033563980 9384232.

Olusoga, D. (2019), 'I Was Born Black and Working Class. The Identities Need Not Be in Opposition', *The Guardian*, https://www.theguardian.com/commentisfree/2019/ apr/13/i-was-born-black-and-working-class-the-identities-need-not-be-in-opposit ion. Accessed 6 August 2022.

Rankin-Wright, A. J., K. Hylton and L. Norman (2020), 'Critical Race Theory and Black Feminist Insights into "Race" and Gender Equality', *Ethnic and Racial Studies*, 43 (7): 1111–29, https://doi.org/10.1080/01419870.2019.1640374.

Reynolds, T. (2003), 'Black to the Community: An Analysis of "Black" Community Parenting in Britain', *Community, Work & Family*, 6 (1): 29–45, https://doi. org/10.1080/1366880032000063888.

Reynolds, T. (2009), 'What Is Maternal Studies', *Studies in the Maternal*, 1 (1): 1–4. https://doi.org/10.16995/sim.162.

Reynolds, T. (2009), 'Exploring the Absent/Present Dilemma: Black Fathers, Family Relationships, and Social Capital in Britain', *The Annals of the American Academy of Political and Social Science*, 624 (1): 12–28, https://www.jstor.org/sta ble/40375950.

Reynolds, T. (2010), 'Don't Believe the Hype: Towards a Contextualised Understanding of Absent Black-Caribbean Fathers and Black Boys in Family Life. Response to Tony Sewell', in D. Weekes-Bernard (ed.), *Did They Get It Right?: A Re-examination of School Exclusions and Race Equality*, 18–19, Runnymede, https://www.runnyme

detrust.org/uploads/publications/pdfs/DidTheyGetItRight-2010.pdf. Accessed 6 August 2022.

Reynolds, T. (2020), 'Studies of the Maternal: Black Mothering 10 Years On', *Studies in the Maternal*, 13 (1): 1–10, https://doi.org/10.16995/sim.290.

Schmitz, R. M., and K. A. Tyler (2016), 'Growing Up before Their Time: The Early Adultification Experiences of Homeless Young People', *Children and Youth Services Review*, 64: 15–22, https://doi.org/10.1016/j.childyouth.2016.02.026.

Sear, R. (2021), 'The Male Breadwinner Nuclear Family Is Not the "Traditional" Human Family, and Promotion of This Myth May Have Adverse Health Consequences', *Philosophical Transactions of the Royal Society B*, 376 (1827): 20200020, https://doi.org/10.1098/rstb.2020.0020.

Solórzano, D. G., and T. J. Yosso (2002), 'Critical Race Methodology: Counter-Storytelling as an Analytical Framework for Education Research', *Qualitative Inquiry*, 8 (1): 23–44, https://doi.org/10.1177/107780040200800103.

Stop School Cuts (2020), *IFS: School Cuts Research Fairly Represents the Facts*, Stop School Cuts, https://schoolcuts.org.uk/story/funding-crisis-explained/.

Strand, S., and A. Lindorff (2021), 'Ethnic Disproportionality in the Identification of High-Incidence Special Educational Needs: A National Longitudinal Study Ages 5 to 11', *Exceptional Children*, 87 (3): 344–68. https://doi.org/10.1177/0014402921990895.

Sundhall, J. (2017), 'A Political Space for Children? The Age Order and Children's Right to Participation', *Social Inclusion*, 5 (3), 164–71, https://doi.org/10.17645/si.v5i3.969.

The Child Safeguarding Review Panel (2020), *It Was Hard to Escape*, The Child Safeguarding Review Panel, https://assets.publishing.service.gov.uk/government/uploads/system/uploads/attachment_data/file/870035/Safeguarding_children_at_risk_from_criminal_exploitation_review.pdf.

Timpson, E. (2019), *Timpson Review of School Exclusion*, Dandy Booksellers Limited, https://assets.publishing.service.gov.uk/government/uploads/system/uploads/attachment_data/file/807862/Timpson_review.pdf.

TUC (2012), *Youth Unemployment and Ethnicity*, TUC, https://www.tuc.org.uk/sites/default/files/BMEyouthunemployment.pdf.

Uhrig, N. (2016), *Black, Asian and Minority Ethnic Disproportionality in the Criminal Justice System in England and Wales*, Ministry of Justice London, https://assets.publishing.service.gov.uk/government/uploads/system/uploads/attachment_data/file/639261/bame-disproportionality-in-the-cjs.pdf. Accessed 6 August 2022.

Winter, C., and C. Mills (2020), 'The Psy-Security-Curriculum Ensemble: British Values Curriculum Policy in English Schools', *Journal of Education Policy*, 35 (1): 46–67, https://doi.org/10.1080/02680939.2018.1493621.

Women's Aid (2021), *Shadow Pandemic – Shining a Light on Domestic Abuse during COVID*, https://www.womensaid.org.uk/wp-content/uploads/2021/11/Shadow_Pandemic_Report_FINAL.pdf. Accessed 6 August 2022.

Yarrow, S. (2005), *The Experiences of Young Black Men as Victims of Crime*, Criminal Justice System Race Unit and Victims and Confidence Unit, http://library.college.pol

ice.uk/docs/homeoffice/Experiences-of-young-black-men-as-victims-of-crime.pdf. Accessed 6 August 2022.

Yıldız, Ü. (2021), 'An Anti-Racist Reading of the Notion of "Fundamental British Values". PRISM: Casting New Light on Learning', *Theory and Practice*, 3 (2): 91–107, https://doi.org/10.24377/prism.ljmu.0302206.

YMCA (2020), *Out of Service*, YMCA, https://www.ymca.org.uk/wp-content/uplo ads/2020/01/YMCA-Out-of-Service-report.pdf. Accessed 6 August 2022.

6

# Older Lesbians and Families of Friends

Catherine Lee

## Introduction

In the UK, lesbians in their fifties and sixties have lived through significant periods of challenge and an almost inconceivable level of sociopolitical change. Born into an era in which homosexuality in men was illegal and thought not to exist in women, they have endured invisibility and misrepresentation (Traies 2016). In many cases their relationships with their families of origin (or birth families) have been, and often still are, complex and necessarily disingenuous if they are not estranged from their families of origin all together (Wilkens 2016). The romantic relationships of older lesbians are likely to have been secret and only performed authentically within the confines of their homes. They are less likely to have children and are more likely to have relied on a small but enduring social network of other lesbians for support (Lottman and King 2020). These networks are often referred to as families of choice and become ever more important as lesbians grow older and make preparations for their own care (Dewaele et al. 2011).

This chapter draws on the experiences and perceptions of twelve lesbians eleven of whom were over the age of fifty, who have known each other over a period of approximately thirty years and live within twenty-five miles of one another in rural East Anglia in England. Drawing on social capital theory (Putnam 2000), the research deploys a semi-structured focus group discussion with the women to explore the social structures and relationships that connect these women and form their 'norms of reciprocity and trust' (Putnam 2000: 19).

Topics explored with the women include their relationships with their families of origin, childlessness, the role of the home, care for elderly parents and their own plans for receiving care in later life. The women are also invited to reflect on how key pieces of legislation such as the Equality Act (2010) and the Equal Marriage Act (2015) have affected them personally and collectively.

Social capital theory (Putman 2000) provides the theoretical framework for this chapter. The theory reasons that individuals gain advantage through their access to social relationships and networks with others (Putnam 2000). When applied to older lesbians, social capital theory argues that older lesbians form personal networks with each other that provide 'norms of reciprocity and trust' (Putnam 2000: 19), which create kinship and have a positive impact on their personal well-being. Conversely older lesbians without networks of peers are more likely to be lonely and isolated, which may lead to poorer health outcomes in the longer term (King 2016).

This chapter begins with a review of the literature related to the experiences of older lesbians before presenting the theoretical and methodological framework for the research. Next, the reflections of the twelve older lesbians, who took part in a focus group interview (Smithson 2000) and belong to a self-defined family of friends, are analysed before the salient issues are drawn together in a conclusion and recommendations for further research.

# Literature review

The number of lesbian and bisexual women in the UK over the age of fifty is estimated to be in the region of 750,000 (ONS 2018). The political and sociological landscape for lesbians in the UK has changed exponentially over the lifespan of these women. Since homosexuality (only ever recognized in men) was legalized in 1967, several key pieces of legislation have helped to provide lesbians with a degree of personal and professional security, similar to that enjoyed by their heterosexual peers (Traies 2016). The Equality Act (2010) identified lesbianism as a protected characteristic and prohibited discrimination in education, employment and access to goods and services. The Civil Partnership Act (2005) recognized same-sex unions for the first time, and the Equal Marriage Act a decade later allowed lesbian couples to marry and access the same benefits as heterosexual married couples.

Progressive developments in legislative protection have not necessarily translated into a greater sense of inclusion or belonging into local communities for lesbians, especially in rural or semi-rural locations, where attitudes to minority groups can remain stubbornly conservative (Lee 2019). Even where communities have latterly become more inclusive and welcoming, lesbians may continue to proceed warily as a legacy of their experiences during less tolerant times. Lesbians report being deeply affected by experiences of rejection and hostility during years of overt prejudice towards them in the last fifty years (Piggot 2004; Thompson-Lee 2017). Lesbians over fifty in the UK are likely to have hidden their relationship with their same-sex partner from their family of origin for the majority of their adult lives and are unlikely to have become a parent unless this involved bearing children in a heterosexual marriage (see also Gusmeroli and Trappolin, in this volume). According to Wallace (2011), one quarter of older lesbians live alone, compared to a fifth of older heterosexual women, and about half of older lesbians are married or living with a female partner, compared to two-thirds of older heterosexual women. According to Traies (2018), older lesbians suffer from marginalization and disempowerment and are largely invisible in UK society. Kehoe (1989) too described older lesbians as 'triply invisible' through a combination of sexism, ageism and heteronormativity.

Research by Dewaele, Cox and Berghe (2011) identifies a subtly insidious cultural climate towards older lesbians. Literature from the era in which these women were coming out for the first time shows that attitudes are, at best, only superficially tolerant. That tolerance is also contingent upon lesbians remaining largely invisible (Traies 2016) and never overtly displaying their lesbian identity. Clarke (1998) referred to this as the 'good homosexual'; in other words, a tolerance of lesbianism as long as it is not overtly displayed and provides no challenge to the heterosexual status quo. Epstein and Johnson (1998: 25) too identify requirements for negotiating an openly lesbian identity, noting that approval is conditional on a certain quietude and otherwise exemplary behaviour. They state that lesbians must leave unchallenged heterosexuality, marriage and male:female coupledom warning that 'where these are troubled, retribution is likely to follow' (25).

There is today greater acceptance of LGBTQ+ identities, and older lesbians have played an important part in challenging the heteronormative status quo. Those who were able, have lobbied for important rights for the LGBTQ+ community such as those afforded through the Equality Act 2010 and The Equal Marriage Act of 2015. However, homophobic climates live long in the memories of those experiencing them first-hand. Whilst there is today much greater acceptance of LGBTQ+ identities in mainstream British culture (Miles 2021), some older lesbians remain closeted, mistrusting and cautious, deeply scarred by events years ago (Laramie 2021).

Throughout the latter half of the twentieth century, the required quietude and a fear of homophobic hostility drove many lesbians to find support exclusively in the company of other lesbians (Mayfield 2001). As a result, many groups of older lesbians have developed a strong sense of unity, rooted in the shared experience of secrecy, stigma and discrimination across their life course. Traies (2016) also observes that the long-term shared experience of inequality binds older lesbian communities together.

The necessary concealment of lesbian identities and relationships has inevitably adversely affected the relationship between older lesbians and their families of origin. Older lesbians may have, for years, presented their life partner as a room-mate or friend to their own parents and siblings (Thompson-Lee 2017). Whilst lesbians may have wished to become parents, doing so would have necessitated a coming out to family members and an audacious challenge to the widely held belief at the time that children should not be raised by same-sex couples (Welsh 2011). Therefore, older lesbians tend to be childless and embrace aging without the support of adult children that some of their heterosexual counterparts get to rely on (Hadley, 2018; see also English, in this volume).

Whilst some research suggests that lesbians earn more than their female heterosexual peers (Drydakis 2014) other data point to what Martell (2019) describes as a lesbian earning penalty. Martell (2019) found that childless cohabiting lesbians earn approximately 11 per cent less than a childless married heterosexual couple.

The constraints placed upon lesbians in the UK over the past fifty years necessitated that they sought and achieved social capital in ways that are distinctive from their heterosexual peers. Bourdieu defines social capital as 'the sum of the actual or potential resources that are linked to the possession of a durable network of more or less institutionalised relationships of mutual acquaintance and recognition – in other words, to membership in a group' (Bourdieu 1986: 248). However, this chapter embraces the definition of Putnam, who popularized the concept of social capital and defined it as 'features of social organisation, such as trust, norms, and networks that can improve the efficiency of society by facilitating coordinated actions' (Puttnam 2002: 167). The creation of strong familial bonds and ties with other lesbians within an enduring and tight-knit group provides for lesbians a safe space in which to perform their identity and romantic relationships authentically (Slater 1995). The social support networks of older lesbians are exemplified by closer ties to friends in place of the reliance on their families of origin, the foundation of social support for most heterosexual older adults (Brennan-Ing et al. 2014). Over time, these distinctive relationships performed in safe spaces create intense bonds and ties that strengthen as the lesbians age and they begin to rely on the help of each other (Wilkens 2016).

## Families of choice

In 2011, Stonewall, the UK's LGBT lobbying group, commissioned YouGov, a British internet-based market research and data analytics firm, to survey a sample of 1,050 heterosexual and 1,036 lesbian, gay and bisexual people over the age of fifty-five across the UK. It found that whilst heterosexual respondents saw members of their family of origin either daily or more than once a week, only 28 per cent of lesbian, gay and bisexual respondents did so (Guasp, 2010). Braukmann and Schmauch (2007) describe friends as the backbone of the social support network for older lesbian and gay people. The term families of choice (Lottman and King 2020) refers to distinct kinship ties that for lesbians comprise of friends, partners and ex- partners. In cases where coming out as lesbian has caused the breakdown of relationships with families of origin or where lesbian identity is kept secret from parents and siblings, families of choice are mutually supportive networks that compensate for or replicate relationships most commonly associated with families of origin. According to Dewaele et al. (2011), families of choice create a place of safety in heteronormative environments uniting lesbians in spaces which allow them to embody their identities and intimate relationships authentically. Weeks (2005) describes families of choice as an act of resistance to normative family life, which can challenge heteronormativity and lead to collective recognition for those otherwise rendered invisible.

There is no particular way to perform families of choice. According to Dewaele et al. (2011), some lesbians create close bonds with other lesbians as the relationship with their biological family has broken down, whilst others integrate family and friendship networks together. The majority maintain some relationship with family of origin whilst having a separate family of friends, which compensates for the missing recognition of romantic relationships by family of origin members.

## Childlessness

Clarke et al. (2018) conducted research with childless and childfree lesbians in the UK and found that their discourses and performative practices of family were in stark contrast with those of their heterosexual peers. Drawing on Weeks, Heaphy and Donovan (2001), Clarke and others identified kin-like networks based on friendship and commitments that were emblematic of new ways of 'doing family'. In Clarke et al's study, older lesbians reported that if they sought contact with children they were able to get a parenting 'kid-fix' through regular contact with nieces, nephews and the children of heterosexual friends. This contrasts with the findings of Gillespie (1999), who found that her lesbian participants did not perceive their relationships with nieces and nephews as a substitute for mothering. Many older lesbians in her research lamented not becoming parents but noted that the social climate during their childbearing years was such that it was impossible to raise a child as a same-sex couple.

# Connecting in the pandemic

According to Guasp (2010), less than a quarter of lesbians saw members of their family of origin at least once a week compared to more than half of heterosexual people. One in eight lesbians see family members less than once a year compared to just one in twenty-five heterosexual people. Guasp (2011) showed that loneliness and isolation from others has a negative impact on the health and well-being of all older people, but older lesbians were twice as likely to have poor health outcomes linked to loneliness than heterosexual women. Fenge and Fanin (2009) concur that poor health and well-being are the consequences for older lesbians of social marginalization, an absence of intergenerational support, as well as fewer social networks and exclusion, resulting from protective adaptive responses to lifelong prejudice and discrimination.

The global Covid-19 pandemic, which began in 2020, resulted in national and local lockdowns prohibiting people from meeting other households. Westwood et al (2022) researched the physical and mental well-being, risk and protective factors among older lesbians/gay women in the UK during the initial Covid-19 lockdown of 2020. They found that lesbians reported feeling fearful of becoming ill with Covid-19 and no one being there to support them or even know they were ill. Westwood (2021) identified a lack of confidence in older lesbians of accessing health or social services often associated with the fear of coming out to strangers. Westwood reported that during lockdowns due to the pandemic, lesbians relied on mutually supportive social networks and created new non-cohabiting relationships with other lesbians. According to Bower et al. (2021), during the pandemic, lesbians, in common with the rest of the population, needed to demonstrate strong coping strategies and resilience to the environmental conditions imposed by the lockdown. Mock et al. (2020) observed extensive use of technologies by lesbians to foster and maintain contact with friends and families of choice. Westwood et al. (2020) called for ongoing work to support lesbians in developing robust and resilient social networks throughout their life course.

## Care requirements in later life

Traies (2018) found that older lesbians approach health and care services 'in ways that differ from younger lesbian women and from their heterosexual peers' (41). Older lesbians are, according to Traies, deeply mistrustful of services for the elderly due to the heterosexual assumptions made by those offering support. Almost half of the respondents in Traies's research said their doctor did not know they were a lesbian and 59 per cent said they did not feel able to discuss sexual matters with health professionals. Traies observed that older lesbians were the most likely group to need mental health and social care in the future, but were least likely to come out to these professionals. According to Traies, the resulting stress associated with secrecy and the inauthentic presentation to support services intensifies the isolation and disadvantage experienced by older lesbians. Traies also calls for more research to gain a greater understanding of the lives of older lesbians, in particular exploring their personal and community histories and the impact that years of oppression and concealment have had on them. According to Traies, health and social care professionals must avoid making heteronormative assumptions and create safe spaces in which older lesbians can present themselves authentically without fear.

## Theoretical framework

This research is underpinned by a theoretical foundation based on social capital theory (Putnam 2000). Social capital theory understands that strong social networks and relationships generate advantages for individuals whilst a lack of social capital can lead to isolation and poorer health and well-being outcomes, especially later in life (King 2016). Conceptualizations of social capital are however heteronormative (King 2016) in that social structures assume and privilege heterosexuality leaving lesbians (and gay men) othered and excluded. Over their lifetime, older lesbians have been shaped by an enduring climate of stigmatization, an absence of legal protection and a necessary culture of secrecy and often estrangement from their families of origin (Shiu, Muraco and Fredriksen-Goldsen 2016).

This chapter recognizes that lesbians can, however, use social capital in a distinctive way that can serve to disrupt its heteronormative foundations. Lesbians may create networks and relationships that are similar to the reciprocated kinship bonds formed in families of origin. These bonds form a wealth of functions, some of which serve to replace the ties that lesbians may lack in a heteronormative society. Over time, a new queer social capital emerges and gains strength as lesbians create bonds with their peers as a consequence of their common history and a need for mutual support.

# Methodology

This project sought to capture the experiences and perceptions of twelve lesbians eleven of whom were over fifty, who have known each other over a period of approximately thirty years and live within twenty-five miles of one another in rural East Anglia in England. It deployed a single focus group discussion with the women shaped by a series of prompts drawn from a review of the literature on the lived experience of older lesbians in the UK. Kitzinger (1994) states that it is valuable to conduct research with pre-existing groups of people because the groups offer a clear social context within which ideas are formed and decisions made. The women were known to the author, and it is important therefore to note that the methodological approach embraces subjectivity and celebrates a distinct collective lesbian group identity that has evolved from belonging to the same social group. Whilst this limits the onto-epistemological quality and rigour of the research, the relationship of the women to one another provides insight into the collective identity of the group and so presents an additional dimension not possible when recruiting individual older lesbians not previously known to one another.

The project utilized an exploratory case study (Yin 1993) within a social constructivist and interpretivist framework. This enabled the researcher to gain a rich picture of the way in which the lesbian participants perceived their membership of the group. Drawing on Bassey's (1999) 'fuzzy generalisations', the researcher let statements between the women emerge with a shared understanding and built-in uncertainty, which are possible in case study research without reducing its trustworthiness (Lincoln and Guba 1990).

The group discussion is a qualitative approach to learning about population subgroups with respect to sociocultural characteristics and processes (Basch 1987). Breen (2006) advocates the use of group discussions for the generation of new ideas formed within a social context, and recognizes the way in which group reflection can prompt recollection and deter or safeguard against distortion.

The researcher identifies as a lesbian, and is over the age of fifty. She is a peer of the lesbians and knows the women socially, sharing in many of their experiences. This researcher's insider positionality was advantageous in leading the conversation through the deployment of prompts. However, this also was a limitation of the research, as the researcher had a shared history with the women and so was able to draw on her prior knowledge of the women to help shape the group discussion.

The group discussion took place via Microsoft Teams and was recorded and transcribed in full by the researcher. Before analysis of the transcript took place, the women were invited to read the transcript and redact any comments made by them that they were not comfortable with. A balance of inductive and deductive coding was utilized, drawing on themes emerging from a review of the literature. The themes were grouped together according to the topic or general concept, and each group was then organized and ordered to create a structure ready for analysis.

Table 6.1 denotes descriptive details about the circumstances of the lesbians including their age, occupation and whether they have children. Pseudonyms are used throughout. The table also shows which of the friends is in a romantic relationship or married to another group member and also whether group members have been romantically involved in the past.

Before the group session commenced, the supportive nature of the relationships among the women was demonstrated. One member of the group, Eve, who often struggles with technology, was trying to access the video call on her computer and could only get in touch via the audio on her phone. Without comment, Denise, Eve's ex-partner's wife, left the house, travelled across the village green, walked into Eve's house unannounced and helped her to get online. She then returned home to join the group discussion. The act conducted with almost no comment demonstrated the ease with which the women naturally supported each other.

## Forming the group

Once the discussion commenced, the lesbians were asked to recall how their group was formed. Membership of the group was loosely based around a hockey

**Table 6.1** Sample description

| Name | Age | Occupation | Partner | Length of relationship | Marital status | Previous partners in the group | Children |
|---|---|---|---|---|---|---|---|
| Anna | 59 | Retired teacher | Bette | 20 years | Yes | Gerry, Eve, Isobel | No |
| Bette | 53 | Painter and decorator | Anna | 20 years | Yes | – | No |
| Chloe | 65 | Retired senior leader HE | Denise | 15 years | Yes | Eve | No |
| Denise | 56 | Banking | Chloe | 15 years | Yes | – | No |
| Eve | 69 | Retired senior manager NHS | Single | – | – | Chloe, Anna | No |
| Fran | 46 | Senior manager energy supplier | Gerry | 7 years | No | – | No |
| Gerry | 55 | Administrator artist | Fran | 7 years | No | Anna | No |
| Helen | 53 | HE | Isobel | 25 years | Yes | – | No |
| Isobel | 56 | Senior manager customer service | Helen | 25 years | Yes | Anna | No |
| Jane | 66 | Retired radio broadcasting | Kate | 8 years | No | Married to a man | 2 daughters |
| Kate | 59 | Retired police | Jane | 8 years | No | Married to a man | 2 sons and a daughter |

Note: Table 6.1 provides some information about the research participants, including their pseudonym, age, occupation, partner's pseudonym, length of current relationship, marital status, previous partners in the group and children.

club in the main county town and evolved from friendships and previous romantic interactions. Anna, who had been romantically involved with four of the group, noted 'We wouldn't be together as a group if we hadn't stayed friends with our exes … that's the lesbian way.' Over their thirty years together, the group had survived the break-up of several romantic partnerships. Anna noted 'when a relationship breaks up, there's a period of time when you don't see that person, or you don't see much of them, or there [is] a level of animosity, depending on who dumped who. But at some point that all gets resolved. Everybody moves on, and you go back to the group'. Lottman and King (2020) state that relationships with ex-partners play a particularly important role in the lives of lesbians, particularly in provincial or rural areas. They observe that there are simply not enough lesbian social groups to support the breaking of ties with an entire network of lesbian friends. For these women, locally at least, there was an absence of other lesbian networks of women the same age, and so even when romantic relationships came to an end with members of the group, they remained together as friends. Anna observed that despite some tumultuous times when romantic relationships ended, the lesbians found a way to make the group work and valued membership of it over any hurt feelings through romantic relationship breakdown.

Humour was identified by group members as being a key facet of their enduring friendship. Anna said, 'we love being together. And we laugh a lot … we're all very different. But actually, we've got a common bond and things that we laugh about are each other and our characteristics.' The group acknowledged that they teased one another mercilessly with acerbic banter that had endured for years. In this regard, the women resembled siblings rather than friends, especially with all acknowledged feeling safe within the group, and having absolute trust in each other. The women attributed their feelings of safety to having a shared past, something Kate, the newest member of the group and in her first lesbian relationship, lamented not being part of. Kate said, 'I know I'm the new one and I wished I had known you all sooner especially when you're talking about all the things that you've gone through together.' Kate went on to indicate that she might not have stayed in her heterosexual marriage for as long as she did, had she been aware that there was a network of other lesbians she could turn to for support. According to Dewaele et al. (2011) lesbians and gay men most often turn to lesbian and gay friends when confronted with problems related to their sexual orientation. Friends offer emotional support, foster a sense of unity and act as role models, leading to strong bonds based on shared experiences, especially during periods of adversity.

94        *Reinventing the Family in Uncertain Times*

Next the group were asked to describe, and if possible name, what they were to each other. Clarke et al. (2018) found that lesbians conceptualized family and intimate relationships in ways that diverged from traditional, heteronormative values and rhetoric. The women in Clarke et al.'s study had close relationships for which they felt there was no language, especially when describing them to heterosexual others.

As the women seemed unable to name what the group was, I posited family of choice as a suggestion. This was quickly rejected by Gerry, who said 'I don't think family of choice is the right expression because I think it sounds like we're choosing friends over family. I think for me it's another family.' Denise suggested 'rainbow family', referencing the rainbow that symbolizes LGBTQ+ identities, before Gerry and several others mused that they did consider the group their family but would not want their family of origin to know this in case it was upsetting. Kate mentioned that her parents referred to the group as her family despite her having children and a grandchild of her own from her heterosexual marriage. After further deliberation, the group agreed that 'family of friends' was the most fitting descriptor.

## Relationships with families of origin

The relationships that each group member had with their family of origin differed considerably. Some members had recently lost parents and some had caring responsibilities for elderly parents. Despite a history of secrecy and rejection from family members in the past, all lesbians in the group were understanding, respectful and generous in evaluating the less-than-favourable ways in which their families had behaved towards them previously. The lesbians generally agreed that their relationships with their siblings had generally improved over the years as they had over time gradually got used to having a lesbian sister. Chloe mused that she thought her heterosexual sister was envious of her family of friends. She said of her sister,

> She's quite envious of the closeness of us all. She calls you all 'my girls', 'my lesbian friends', 'my gay friends', 'my gay family', if you like. She knows that we have our Christmas dinner, she knows that we get together on a regular basis … she would love to have a group of girlfriends like I have.

Kate also noted that her heterosexual sister was envious of the friendship bonds in the group, especially of the Christmas get-togethers, which take place the weekend before Christmas but are commonly referred to by the group as their 'real Christmas day'. Kate said, 'I tell my sister about our group and our Christmas meals ... how Chloe is playing the piano ... and she's so envious. She wants to be there as well.'

Eve, the oldest member of the group at sixty-nine, comes from a Methodist Christian family and for her entire adult life has hidden her lesbian identity from her parents (now deceased) and siblings. Eve said 'I don't talk openly about being gay with my family ... because it's one of those things that I've never done, so it almost seems as if, why should I do it now?' Anna recognized the dilemma facing Eve and stressed that there was a sense of deceit and betrayal in coming out to one's family of origin in later life. Instead it felt easier to continue the pretence, especially with very elderly parents. Eve agreed and pointed to the religious views held by her family stating:

> My brother is quite religious and [so is] my sister in law, and I'm not sure how me being gay sort of fits with [their] religious ideas. When my parents were alive, [it was] exactly the same for them as well. I didn't really want to put them through it.

Eve's comment, that she did not want to put her parents through it, is evidence of the way in which the religious ideals of her family were at odds with her lesbian identity. Implicit in Eve's comment was an acknowledgement that being gay was not acceptable and there was no attempt to suggest that her family of origin was wrong for not providing her with the space or opportunity to be herself. Eve recognized that because she continued to hide her sexual identity from her family of origin, it had become hard to spend more than brief amounts of time with them. Instead, she said that the group was the family she preferred to spend her time with and where she was most herself. Dewaele et al. (2011) found that within the intimate social network of lesbians, friendship networks served to compensate when primary kinship ties were absent or strained.

Anna had recently lost both her parents and discussed the way in which group members had rallied when her parents were ill. With only male siblings, Anna found that the group brought a femininity to the nature of the support offered, noting she felt moved when Chloe wrote to Anna's parents. Since losing her parents, Anna recognized the group as her 'closest family members'. Like Anna, Denise had brothers and similarly favoured the group over the siblings with whom she declared she had nothing in common. Neither of Denise's brothers attended her wedding to Chloe, and it was unclear whether they knew that she was gay.

When group members explored their relationships with their families of origin, all agreed that they had been adversely affected by years of secrecy in which romantic relationships were disguised as friendships. This secrecy had taken place in an era in which feelings were rarely discussed especially for Anna and Gerry raised in northern or working-class family environments in which emotion was discouraged. Anna said, 'Well, I was of an era where nobody talked about anything … In Yorkshire, we didn't talk about feelings at all, let along being gay.' Anna's relationship with her brothers improved when she married Bette, and several others who had come out to siblings in later life also described recent repaired and fortified relationships with siblings.

# Children

Two members of the group were in their first lesbian relationship with each other, having previously been married to men. Both had adult children and grandchildren from their former marriages. The rest of the group had not entered motherhood, and there were a variety of reasons for this. Anna and Chloe were happy not to have become mothers and doubted that they would have been 'good enough' parents. Anna expressed enjoyment in being the 'fun auntie' to her nieces but acknowledged that the social climate during the years she was able to bear children prevented motherhood being an option for her. Fran, the youngest member of the group, had tried to conceive through fertility treatment but had been unsuccessful. Whilst this was obviously very painful, she had relinquished further plans for motherhood, instead spending extensive time looking after the child of a heterosexual friend. Eve described how well into her twenties, and despite several lesbian relationships, she still expected to 'wake up one day and get married and have babies and not be gay anymore'. She added that it took years to come to terms with the fact that her lesbianism was not just a phase. Once she came to terms with not being a parent, she described how all broodiness subsided. Helen described a strong desire to have children in her late twenties during the 1990s, but did not pursue fertility treatment through fear that her becoming a parent in a lesbian relationship would cause shame for her family of origin. Becoming a teacher initially satisfied Helen's maternal instincts but later Helen found that being with children each day compounded her feelings of loss and ultimately led to resentment. Consequently, Helen left teaching. In common with this study, Clarke et al's (2018) lesbians were not lacking exposure to children but their romantic relationships differed from those of their heterosexual peers as they were not underpinned by reproductive decision-making.

Jane and Kate as parents of now adult children from heterosexual marriages discussed coming out to their children and described fears that their children regarded them as dishonest. Very little seemed to have been said in their families of origin about their lesbian relationship, and Kate and Jane hoped that their children were getting support from their peers and discussing it amongst their friends. After staying in heterosexual marriages, in large part to ensure stability for their children, Jane and Kate, felt that they were entitled in later life to live in the way they had always wanted to. Both acknowledged, however, that their lives had been easy when compared to that of the other group members. Kate lamented the lack of a shared history with the group during more challenging times and observed that the shared homophobia and heterosexism had created an enduring bond for some members of the group, which Kate and Jane did not share.

## Lesbian visibility

The families of choice or families of friends in which older lesbians seek mutual support and social capital perform the function of providing older lesbians with reflections of themselves that are almost completely absent in the media. There are still almost no depictions of older lesbians in the media, and when they are depicted fleetingly in films, dramas or soap operas, they are usually represented unfavourably, meeting some unfortunate end or being eventually revealed as being the perpetrator of a crime (Cowan and Valentine 2006). The lesbians acknowledged that the group provided them with a mirror of sorts, enabling them to compare themselves with others, creating much needed reference points of how to present themselves, what to wear and as a means of gaining validation for their opinions and ideas. Chloe stated that despite several recent depictions of young feminine lesbians in advertisements, she still felt utterly invisible. She added,

> There are no programmes on the television … I can't even think of a drama let alone a soap or anything … that I can vaguely relate to in terms of my own life or my lifestyle. I mean, all the soaps now have got young lesbian characters in them but they're all girly lesbians … A butch lesbian is still a no no … I guess for the camera they are too unattractive … I don't have anyone that I identify with other than you guys.

Traies (2018) states that representations of older lesbians are rare in the media. Older lesbian women are not physically attractive to heterosexual men, who control the majority of media organizations, and so older lesbians suffer from a combination of ageism, sexism and heterosexism.

Jane agreed with Chloe and added that there were no magazines, rarely any books and few older lesbians depicted in any media sources generally. Traies (2018) states that the discourses which underpin older lesbians' cultural invisibility originate from heterosexist assumptions that depict older women in relation to their position within a family, that is, married and usually a mother. A woman who is neither of these is, according to Traies, likely to invoke dismissive cultural stereotypes of the old maid or spinster.

Denise, Gerry and Chloe discussed frequently speculating that women in the media might be lesbian, hoping to find figures to whom they could relate. They cited the late comedian Victoria Wood and chef Monica Galletti as examples. Kate, Chloe and Helen stated that older lesbian invisibility extended to shopping, especially for clothes. Chloe admitted always heading straight to the men's clothing department with others acknowledging the strange stares they received walking around menswear departments and the impossibility of trying men's clothes on in store.

## Coping in the pandemic

Westwood et al. (2022) identified that during Covid-19 lockdowns, lesbians and gay men were resourceful and resilient. As a consequence of the Covid-19 pandemic, the group had maintained regular contact online with a regular quiz, a life-drawing activity, Easter Egg gifts by post and regular group chats over drinks. Denise, Chloe and Chloe's ex-partner Eve formed a family bubble together so that Eve was not left alone for days on end. All acknowledged that calls over the internet had been important but the group dynamic differed to that which existed in person, as only one conversation was possible at any one time. The banter and teasing had suffered through the needs to take it in turns when talking. All agreed that the calls had been a poor substitute for face-to-face socializing.

In contrast, the pandemic and the use of technologies to keep in touch had, in some cases, strengthened relationships between the women and their families of origin. Eve said, 'I've had more zoom calls, and seen more of my family in lockdown than usual because we have a zoom call every week … the technology has been brilliant in helping me keep in touch for short bursts.'

Eve was the only single group member, and those in couples described the way in which their romantic relationships had been affected when the couple was required to remain at home. Fran and Gerry who had been together seven years described walking together every day and still learning things about each other during their conversations. Chloe and Denise felt fortunate to have space in the house to be alone if needed and expressed concern for heterosexual families with young children and an absence of space. All agreed that due in large part to their rural locations, the lockdown had only limited impact and that technology had aided group contact immeasurably.

## Planning for later life

Finally, the group were asked to consider their plans for later life and the role the family of friends would play in this. Westwood et al. (2022) found that many older lesbians and gay men avoided formal social care, even if much needed, due to fears about prejudice and discrimination by care providers (Willis et al. 2020). Denise recognized that the family of friends supported each other periods of health and cited examples of practical and emotional support offered by the group to the patient and the patient's partner. She added that this requirement for support had always been temporary, and so she wondered how any longer-term need for additional support would sit amongst members of the group who were in large part fiercely independent. Denise said

> We don't make demands on each other on a day-to-day basis for practical support. I will be interested to see what happens when as we get older, whether or not we feel safe enough to call on one another in the longer term. If anyone has a crisis in the group, of course we'd all be there short term, but what happens when things are permanent. I mean, who will check if Eve is still breathing every day?

Denise's joke at Eve's expense curtailed further consideration of care plans for later life but Jane and Kate were asked whether they felt reassured that as parents, their children would care for them when required. Neither wished their children to become their carers but did stress that they did not expect their children to put them in a home. Heaphy et al. (2004) suggest that for older lesbians, romantic partners are the main source of help and support if care is needed. They add that relationships to siblings, nieces and nephews often fail as a source of help and support as a result of secrecy and estrangement. Lesbians and gay men in later life are at an elevated risk of developing poor physical and mental health and depression (Fredriksen-Goldsen et al. 2013). Access to social capital is important for resilience and a good quality of life, and amongst older lesbians depressive symptoms positively correlate with a small social network, living alone without a partner and low emotional support (Traies 2018).

Denise stressed that she thought the family of friends would step in if anyone was faced with being placed in a care home. Whilst no one expected to provide intimate care for other members, there was broad agreement that the friends would finance carers should they be required, enabling individuals to remain in their own homes. Denise said 'I think we'd step into that role, not of physically caring, but of financially putting things into place for each other.' Guasp (2011) found that lesbians and gay men are up to four times more likely to turn to a friend if they are ill or need help than heterosexual people. Traies (2018) states that a distrust of health and social services professionals by lesbians is a legacy of a long-standing experience of institutionalized discrimination, and is often reinforced by unsympathetic practice by professionals who make heterosexist assumptions and fail to recognize that the care needs of lesbians are distinct from those of heterosexual women.

The family of friends began to explore the feasibility of purchasing a large plot of land or a large house for the entire group, and employing live-in carers which everyone could share. All agreed that this was preferable to going into a care home but noted the complications of separating their estates after a group member dies. According to Westwood et al. (2022), the friends on which older lesbians and gay men depend are not usually given decision-making powers in palliative and end-of-life care. Older lesbians and gay men who have remained closeted all their lives are thought to experience isolation when a partner dies. According to Doka (2002) this occurs when the loss is not acknowledged or validated by society, denying the griever the right to grieve. At its most extreme, some older lesbians find themselves excluded by families of origin from the funerals of loved ones, because families of origin are not aware of the relationship, or they prefer not to acknowledge it.

Lottman and King (2020) found that fears about discrimination in retirement housing and care homes affected how older lesbian and gay people view their future housing needs and especially who they think they would turn to for help and support. The heteronormative nature of care homes seemed to be of most concern to the family of friends and all agreed that a lesbian care home, similar to those emerging in the United States, might be acceptable. Chloe captured the views of the majority, stating

*Older Lesbians and Families of Friends*

> I feel very comfortable with other lesbians, even if I don't know them, and so I imagine a lesbian home would be great. There would be banter immediately. I think there is a business opportunity for homes for lesbians.

Care services which are truly inclusive are still, unfortunately, rare (Almack and Simpson 2014), and there is still a need to build professional practice which allows every older lesbian to feel valued and validated by those who care for her. Despite an estimated population of 120,000 lesbians and gay men over the age of sixty in the UK, there are currently only LGBTQ+ specific sheltered housing places for seventy-four people (Lewis 2021). It is crucial therefore that health and social care services recognize the way in which lesbians do family differently and provide resources for them that are inclusive and respect the way in which they wish to be supported in later life.

## Conclusion

This research has explored the reflections of a single group of older lesbians living in rural East Anglia in the UK. Through a semi-structured group discussion, it has demonstrated the way in which the self-described family of friends has created strong bonds of kinship and mutual support. By reflecting on the origins of the group's formation, their shared history, their relationships with families of origin and plans for elderly care, the research has shown that the lesbians have queered social capital disrupting its heteronormative foundations. This lesbian family of friends perform a wealth of functions which serve to replace the social capital that lesbians may lack through their invisibility in heteronormative society. An enduring climate of intolerance to lesbian identities has had a profound impact on the women. None were able to have children except as part of a heterosexual marriage and several of the group kept long-standing romantic relationships secret from their families of origin. As they grow older, they increasingly look to one another for care arrangements in later life, mistrusting health and social services that they perceive as heteronormative and 'not for them'.

Future research is needed to understand the care requirements of older lesbians. Professionals in geriatric health and social care must recognize the importance of families of choice and families of friends to the lesbian community and ensure that provision is inclusive and respectful of the diverse ways in which older lesbians create enduring kinship with their peers.

## References

Almack, K., and P. Simpson (2014), 'Care Home Survey: Knowledge, Attitudes and Practices Concerning LGBT Residents' (unpublished report), Nottingham, England: University of Nottingham.

Basch, C. E. (1987), 'Focus Group Interview: An Underutilized Research Technique for Improving Theory and Practice in Health Education', *Health Education Quarterly*, 14 (4): 411–48.

Bourdieu, P. (1986), 'The Force of Law: Toward a Sociology of the Juridical Field', *Hastings Law Journal*, 38: 805.

Bower, K. L., D. C. Lewis, J. M. Bermúdez and A. A. Singh (2021), 'Narratives of Generativity and Resilience among LGBT Older Adults: Leaving Positive Legacies despite Social Stigma and Collective Trauma', *Journal of Homosexuality*, 68 (2): 230–51.

Braukmann, S., and U. Schmauch (2007), 'Lesbische Frauen im Alter – ihre Lebenssituation und ihre spezifischen Bedürfnisse für ein altengerechtes Leben', *Forschungsbericht des gFFZ, Frankfurt a. M.*

Breen, R. L. (2006), 'A Practical Guide to Focus-Group Research', *Journal of Geography in Higher Education*, 30 (3): 463–75.

Brennan-Ing, M., L. Seidel, B. Larson and S. E. Karpiak (2014), 'Social Care Networks and Older LGBT Adults: Challenges for the Future', *Journal of Homosexuality*, 61 (1): 21–52.

Clarke, G. (1998), 'Queering the Pitch and Coming Out to Play: Lesbians in Physical Education and Sport', *Sport, Education and Society*, 3 (2): 145–60.

Clarke, V., C. Kitzinger and J. Potter (2008), '"Kids Are Just Cruel Anyway": Lesbian and Gay Parents Talk about Homophobic Bullying', *British Journal of Social Psychology*, 43 (4): 531–50.

Dewaele, A., N. Cox, W. Van den Berghe and J. Vincke (2011), 'Families of Choice? Exploring the Supportive Networks of Lesbians, Gay Men, and Bisexuals', *Journal of Applied Social Psychology*, 41 (2): 312–31.

Doka, K. J. (2002), *Disenfranchised Grief: New Directions, Challenges, and Strategies for Practice*, Champaign, IL: Research PressPub.

Drydakis, N. (2014), 'Bullying at School and Labour Market Outcomes', *International Journal of Manpower*.

Epstein, D., and R. Johnson (1998), *Schooling Sexualities*, Irvine, CA: McGraw-Hill Education.

Fenge, L. A., and A. Fannin (2009), 'Sexuality and Bereavement: Implications for Practice with Older Lesbians and Gay Men', *Practice: Social Work in Action*, 21 (1): 35–46.

Fredriksen-Goldsen, K. I., H. J. Kim., S. E. Barkan, A. Muraco and C. P. Hoy-Ellis (2013), 'Health Disparities among Lesbian, Gay, and Bisexual Older Adults: Results from a Population-Based Study', *American Journal of Public Health*, 103 (10): 1802–9.

Gillespie, R. (1999), 'Voluntary Childlessness in the United Kingdom', *Reproductive Health Matters*, 7 (13): 43–53.

Hadley, R. A. (2018), 'Ageing without Children, Gender and Social Justice', in *Ageing, Diversity and Equality: Social Justice Perspectives*, 66–81, London: Routledge.

King, A. (2016), *Older Lesbian, Gay and Bisexual Adults: Identities, Intersections and Institutions*, London: Routledge.

Laramie, J. A. (2021), 'Issues in the Lives of Older Lesbian, Gay, Bisexual, Transgender, and/or Queer Women', *Clinics in Geriatric Medicine*, 37 (4): 579–91.

Lee, C. (2019), 'Fifteen Years On: The Legacy of Section 28 for LGBT+ Teachers in English Schools', *Sex Education*, 19 (6): 675–90.

Lincoln, Y. S., and E. G. Guba (1990), 'Judging the Quality of Case Study Reports', *International Journal of Qualitative Studies in Education*, 3 (1): 53–9.

Lottmann, R., and A. King (2020), 'Who Can I turn To? Social Networks and the Housing, Care and Support Preferences of Older Lesbian and Gay People in the UK', *Sexualities*, 259(1–2): 9–24.

Martell, M. E. (2019), 'Age and the New Lesbian Earnings Penalty', *International Journal of Manpower*, 41 (6): 649–70.

Mayfield, W. (2001), 'The Development of an Internalized Homonegativity Inventory for Gay Men', *Journal of Homosexuality*, 41 (2): 53–76.

Miles, S. (2021), 'Let's (Not) Go Outside: Grindr, Hybrid Space, and Digital Queer Neighborhoods', in *The Life and Afterlife of Gay Neighborhoods*, 203–20, Berlin, Germany: Springer.

Mock, S. E., E. P. Walker, A. M. Humble, B. de Vries, G. Gutman, J. Gahagan, L. Chamberland, P. Aubert and J. Fast (2020), 'The Role of Information and Communication Technology in End-of-Life Planning among a Sample of Canadian LGBT Older Adults', *Journal of Applied Gerontology*, 39 (5): 536–44.

Office for National Statistics. 'Sanders 2018 Sexual Orientation UK 2018 Sexual orientation', ons.gov.uk. Accessed 6 August 2022.

Piggot, M. (2004), 'Double Jeopardy: Lesbians and the Legacy of Multiple Stigmatized Identities' (unpublished thesis), Psychology Strand at Swinburne University of Technology, Australia.

Putnam, R. D. (2000), 'Bowling Alone: "America's Declining Social Capital"', in *Culture and Politics*, 223–34, New York: Palgrave Macmillan.

Puttnam, R. (2002). *The Role of Social Capital in Development: An Empirical Assessment*, England: Cambridge University Press.

Shiu, C., A. Muraco and K. Fredriksen-Goldsen (2016), 'Invisible Care: Friend and Partner Care among Older Lesbian, Gay, Bisexual, and Transgender (LGBT) Adults', *Journal of the Society for Social Work and Research*, 7 (3): 527–46.

Slater, S. (1995), *The Lesbian Family Life Cycle*, Champaign: University of Illinois Press.

Smithson, J. (2000). Using and Analysing Focus Groups: Limitations and Possibilities. *International Journal of Social Research Methodology*, 3 (2): 103–19.

Thompson-Lee, C. (2017), *Heteronormativity in a Rural School Community: An Autoethnography*, Berlin: Springer.

Traies, J. (2016), *The Lives of Older Lesbians: Sexuality, Identity & the Life Course*, Berlin: Springer.

Traies, J. (2018), 'Older Lesbians, Ageing and Equality', in *Ageing, Diversity and Equality: Social Justice Perspectives*, 101–13, London: Routledge.

Weeks, J. (2005), 'Elective Families: Lesbian and Gay Life Experiments', in *Analysing Families*, 238–48, London: Routledge.

Weeks, J., B. Heaphy and C. Donovan (2001), *Same Sex Intimacies: Families of Choice and Other Life Experiments*, New York: Routledge.

Welsh, M. G. (2011), 'Growing Up in a Same-Sex Parented Family: The Adolescent Voice of Experience', *Journal of GLBT Family Studies*, 7 (1–2): 49–71.

Westwood, S., T. Hafford-Letchfield and M. Toze (2022), 'Physical and Mental Well-Being, Risk and Protective Factors among Older Lesbians/Gay Women in the United Kingdom during the Initial COVID-19 2020 lockdown', *Journal of Women & Aging*, 34 (4): 501–22.

Wilkens, J. (2016), 'The Significance of Affinity Groups and Safe Spaces for Older Lesbians and Bisexual Women: Creating Support Networks and Resisting Heteronormativity in Older Age', *Quality in Ageing and Older Adults*, 17 (1): 26–35.

Yin, R. (1993), *Applications of Case Study Research*, Beverly Hills, CA: Sage Publishing.

7

# Queering Familialism? Lesbian and Gay Claims of Parenthood and the Transformation of Intimate Citizenship in Italy

Paolo Gusmeroli and Luca Trappolin

## Introduction

By the end of the twentieth century, same-sex families – including those with children – imposed themselves as a 'new frontier' in family research and fostered a 'rapid growth industry' in social sciences (Allen and Demo 1995; Stacey and Biblarz 2001). Since then, various socio-anthropological and queer reflections – like those of Kath Weston (1991) or Judith Butler (2002), to name a few – have been questioning how lesbian and gay families affect the conventional understanding of kinship. On the one hand, studies like the one conducted by Catherine Donovan, Brian Heaphy and Jeffrey Weeks (2003) showed how same-sex partners and parents challenge (hetero)normative definitions of kinship, building relatedness and solidarity beyond 'blood' and legal ties. On the other hand, Kath Weston (1991) herself warned researchers of the risk of reifying a rigid boundary between families of 'blood' and 'choice'.

In addition to the ways family choices of lesbian and gay people challenge heteronormativity, the relevance of normative systems of kinship seems particularly crucial when investigating familialist countries such as Italy.[1] Here, queer experiences of relatedness and parenthood are far from being included in citizenship. However, kinship alliance and intergenerational moral obligations still provide non-heterosexual people with symbolic resources and practical support.

Chiara Bertone and Maria Pallotta-Chiarolli (2014), among others, valued the relevance of the kinship system for LGBTQ people and claimed the need of 'putting families of origin into the queer picture'. In this sense, the role of the families where lesbians and gay men have grown up is not relegated to the reactions in front of the coming out of sons and daughters.

In the next pages we follow this direction. Drawing on data and narratives from two groups of Italian lesbian and gay parents, we aim to understand how they define *what counts as family* when facing – although in different ways – their exclusion from the institutional and relational (hetero)normative system of kinship. The results highlight the intersection between transformation and reproduction that qualifies the queer experiences of family life.

## Research samples of Italian lesbian and gay parents

Our analysis is supported by two mix-method studies of Italian lesbian and gay parents recruited through LGBTQ organizations. The studies addressed divergent research aims and covered topics outside the scope of this essay. The first study involved intentional lesbian and gay parents (ILGPs) – that is, women and men who had children within same-sex couples through sperm/egg donors and surrogate mothers – to investigate the normalization of their transition to parenthood and the organization of households (Tiano and Trappolin 2019). The second study addressed lesbian and gay parents with children from heterosexual marriages or relationships, usually called post-heterosexual lesbian and gay parents (PHLGPs). In this case, the analysis focused on the fight against internalized homophobia and social hostility during – and after – their transition outside heterosexuality (Gusmeroli and Trappolin 2021a). The two studies have not been compared yet. Here, we rely on how ILGPs and PHLGPs negotiate their relationships with parents and relatives to set a common ground for analysis.

Between 2015 and 2016, we collected eighty-eight standardized online questionnaires (sixty-eight women and twenty men) from ILGPs of *Famiglie Arcobaleno* (Rainbow Families). Then, sixteen women and eleven men in the self-selected sample agreed to be interviewed face to face. Established in 2005, *Famiglie Arcobaleno* is the first Italian organization composed of queer parents – mainly lesbian mothers and gay fathers – and prospective parents. Currently, it has more than three thousand members from all over Italy. Since its founding, *Famiglie Arcobaleno* has rapidly become a reference point for a new generation of 'out and proud' lesbian and gay parents who achieved parenthood outside heterosexuality and for lesbians and gay men who are willing to follow their paths. A substantial majority (fifty-nine out of eighty-eight) of the parents we interviewed had never been married at the time of the research or had married abroad with a same-sex partner.[2] Only seven respondents were separated or divorced from their different-sex spouses. All participants declared that they had become parents through assisted reproductive technology (ART) and surrogacy.[3] As with similar organizations in Western countries, *Famiglie Arcobaleno* succeeded in representing ILGPs as a cultural and political vanguard in national public debate and social research on queer parenthood (Grilli and Parisi 2016; Gusmeroli and Trappolin 2021a; Trappolin 2017).

In the following pages, we analyse ILGPs for how they relate to the pathways towards filiation. Their practical choices for achieving and managing parenthood highlight the relevant challenges to the traditional understanding of kinship and, at the same time, the processes of relational and symbolic relatedness with their families of origin.

The younger and smaller organization *Rete Genitori Rainbow* helped us collect sixty-three standardized online questionnaires (thirty-one women and thirty-two men) from PHLGPs between 2019 and 2020.[4] Of the sample, thirteen women and nine men agreed to engage in an in-depth interview using voice-over internet protocol technologies. This organization was established in 2011 by PHLGPs, who attempted to resist the marginalization of their experience produced by the organizations they initially turned to, such as *Famiglie Arcobaleno* or 'friendly' groups of divorced parents. The majority of our respondents were women and men who married their different-sex partners with whom they had children. Only seven (out of sixty-three) became parents within a non-marital heterosexual relationship. In most cases, their marriages ended before or after coming out. Only three divorced parents decided to regularize the relationship with their new same-sex partners through civil union.[5] The PHLGPs in our study are undoubtedly among the most socially visible people in the population addressed by *Rete Genitori Rainbow*. That group potentially includes all those parents who hide their homoerotic attitudes and are 'silently suffering in a mix-orientation marriage' (Mishra 2020: 791).

In this chapter, we analyse narratives and features of PHLGPs to relate their coming-out choices and family practices to their multiple family belongings. Focusing on their willingness to preserve those family bonds – institutionalized by marriage and filiation – that they deem relevant, we bring to light the constraints of the 'old' family alliances. However, this is only one side of the story. The other side is the way PHLGPs seek social recognition of their same-sex families from their kinship system.

## ILGPs and PHLGPs in familialist Italy

The familialist features of intimate networks, welfare state provisions and the Italian legal system represent key topics for national research, as well as inescapable rationalizations for scholars from abroad (Ginsborg 2003: 68). The subsidiarity of the state in relation to extended family solidarity – where members hold responsibilities of care and support according to their gender – have been typically related by Italian scholars to the reproduction of gender inequalities, the drop in birth rate, the length of dependence of youngsters from the family and the lack of social mobility (Saraceno 2004, 2017; Sgritta 1988).

Notwithstanding cultural and institutional barriers, the family practices of the Italian population show widespread patterns of detraditionalization. Significant indicators of current transformations include reduced marriage rates, increased marital instability, the diffusion of premarital cohabitation and the increasing number of unmarried cohabitant couples in which neither partner comes from a previous marriage (see Ferrera 2005; Saraceno 2017).

Another indicator is the 'growing visibility of … LGBT parenting' (Naldini and Long 2017: 94). In the population census of 2011, the Italian National Statistical Institute interviewed 7,513 same-sex cohabitating couples, including 529 with children. The institute considered these findings as largely underestimated. Years later, official data on civil unions in Italy showed that between the approval of the law (May 2016) and the beginning of the Covid-19 pandemic, less than 12,000 unions had been celebrated, representing 1.5 per cent of all marriages during the same period (2016–19). Members of civil unions – to which only same-sex couples have access – are primarily gay men and lesbian women who are not immersed within heteronormativity. In fact, only 15 per cent of all unions involve at least one member who was previously in a heterosexual marriage. Unfortunately, official data on the presence of children in civil unions are not currently available.

The prevalence of lesbian and gay parents and same-sex households with children has been estimated by some national and international surveys with self-selected samples of the Italian LGBTQ community. For example, in 2014, the European Union Agency for Fundamental Rights found that Italian lesbian mothers and gay fathers represented 15 per cent and 5 per cent, respectively, of a little less than 11,000 respondents. Moreover, data showed that 12 per cent of same-sex cohabitating couples lived with children. In 2016, the *Italian Rainbow Families' Census* (see Girasole and Roberti 2020) intercepted 1,390 LGBTQI households, including almost 400 households with children (28 per cent).[6] Data showed that children of non-heterosexual parents were primarily raised in nuclear families, with a considerable predominance of lesbian couples. Furthermore, due to the higher visibility of ILGPs, this survey found that 80 per cent of children were born using assisted reproductive techniques, including surrogacy.

It is well known that transformations in family practices are not matched by comparable changes in Italian civil law and welfare state arrangements. Therefore, according to Italian scholars Bernini (2008) and Saraceno (2015), the involvement in untraditional family trajectories leaves individuals in a state of uncertainty that is frequently faced – especially during times of crisis (see Bà 2020) – by turning to intergenerational solidarity and family alliances.

Lesbian and gay people are particularly subjected to institutional uncertainty. They have been directly involved in some significant issues that Stefania Bernini identifies in the contemporary Italian political debate on the family: the regulation of the access to ART and the recognition of non-married cohabiting couples (Bernini 2008: 306). Both topics have been targeted by the Italian 'anti-gender' movement that, since the beginning of the 2010s, has emerged to oppose the advancement of LGBTQ rights in the reproductive and family domains (Gusmeroli and Trappolin 2021b; Trappolin 2022).

Whereas surrogacy practices in the country are prohibited by law 40/2004 for all citizens, access to ART in Italian clinics is allowed only for heterosexual couples. Consistently, if lesbians do not consider co-parenting with male friends, they are forced to engage in cross-border reproductive journeys – mainly in Spain, Denmark and the Netherlands – to become mothers. Recently, Italian courts and the European Court of Human Rights have supported ILGPs by affirming the legitimacy of cross-border reproductive care as being in the best interest of the child. Moreover, the crime of false declaration when registering in Italy the birth of a child born abroad from a surrogate mother has been rejected by the national courts (Naldini and Long 2017). The decision to ask for recognition before the court (which is very selective) and court decisions (that are often unpredictable) cannot mitigate the uncertainty produced by how the legal system frames lesbian and gay parenthood.

As for the recognition of non-married cohabiting couples, the 2016 law on civil unions extended to same-sex couples most of the rights enjoyed by heterosexual married couples (Lasio and Serri 2019). Nevertheless, the law does not create kinship ties between the relatives of the two partners, and same-sex partners who officially register their relationship remain excluded from ART and adoption. The legal recognition of non-biological parenthood

110    *Reinventing the Family in Uncertain Times*

can be achieved only through unpredictable court decisions related to stepchild adoption. However, it has to be remembered that if the social parents succeeded in adopting their stepchildren, the stepchildren would not be legally tied to the relatives of the adoptive parent. In recent years, publications like those by Giunti and Fioravanti (2017), Gusmano and Motterle (2019), Franchi and Selmi (2020) have helped renew the scientific debate on the link between lesbian and gay families and the above-mentioned familialist features of Italian society. Besides testifying to the inventiveness of families of choice that challenges heteronormative understandings of kinship, the authors showed that symbolic relatedness and interdependence bond queer parents, their families of origin and (ex)relatives. In other words, there is a growing awareness of how the innovation produced by non-heterosexual women and men does not automatically imply migration from traditional kinship.

In the following sections, we rely on our research findings to deepen the understanding of tensions and alliances between different ideas of family and kinship.

## ILGPs within heterosexual kinship

In this section, we consider survey data and narratives of ILGPs that refer to family practices in the context of structural marginalization, focusing on how they negotiate inclusion into extended kinship networks.

To achieve parenthood, same-sex couples must engage in cross-national reproductive journeys and face some practical decisions from which heterosexuals are most often exempt. For example, they must determine who, in the couple, would be the biological – and, supposedly, for the Italian law, the sole legal – parent. Acknowledging how pathways to parenthood are deeply gendered, we consider lesbian and gay narratives separately.

In lesbian couples, the first decision is about who will be the mother *di pancia*.[7] When both partners share the same desire for motherhood through pregnancy, choosing the biological/legal mother requires sensitive negotiations. The position of the non-biological mother is made particularly vulnerable by Italian law, not only for the child but also in her relationship with the partner.[8] Moreover, even if a strict biological definition of parenthood is abandoned in favour of an intentional one, pregnancy is socially related to a privileged intimate bond with the child. Other (gendered) moral rationalities link this decision to the meaning motherhood will have in the eyes of respective families of origin. The intentional mother who is not biologically or legally linked to the child risks not being recognized as such by her parents or her partner's parents. Also, children can be unwillingly included in the kinship, suffering further forms of marginalization. The decision to have more than one child, at different times, represents – when available – a strategy adopted to overcome the asymmetry between the lesbian partners reinforced by law. Among the sixty lesbian households in our sample, we found nine households composed of two women who experienced pregnancy at different times.[9]

To solve the dilemma by safeguarding symmetrical relations, negotiation between partners tends to focus on criteria to promote the success of the pregnancy (such as age and health conditions) and access to welfare benefits (such as conditions of employment).

Deciding who will be the biological/legal parent is not easier in gay couples. As for the lesbian couples, this choice introduces a relevant legal asymmetry between the partners and before the child.[10] Negotiations are accounted for by referring to criteria similar to those expressed by women. However, for men, criteria aimed at meeting the patrilineal expectations of respective families of origin also play a role. Here, the biological dimension of parenthood is deemed relevant because it symbolically marks the continuity of the family lineage. The same logic informs even altruistic choices taken by those who leave the partner the opportunity of being the biological (as well as legal) parent by stressing how important it might be to give a grandchild to grandparents who do not yet have one.

Once the decision is made, lesbian and gay couples enter their distinct pathways towards parenthood in equally different destinations. Women are involved in a potentially long and exhausting process of fertilization and pregnancy, which, in some cases, implies strong medicalization. As with most heterosexuals, lesbian couples usually resort to anonymous sperm donors to affirm the centrality of the couple's project and legitimize the exclusive bond of both partners with the newborn. By stressing intentionality and welcoming the baby's arrival as the result of fusional commitment, lesbian partners normalize social parenthood in the eyes of their families of origin. But their intelligibility as a two-parent family remains potentially limited, at least to a heteronormative gaze. In this sense, somatic correspondence between the social parent and the sperm donor is considered playing a sensitive, although ambivalent, role. On the one hand, opting for similarity would contradict the assumption that 'love' and not 'biology' makes a family. On the other hand, assimilation to the traditional, heteronormative and racialized codes of filiation respond to worries about the children's well-being in the society in which they are assumed to grow.

For gay couples, the attempt to depersonalize the surrogate mother's role is more complicated. Indeed, fathers' ideas of a 'virtuous' surrogacy process imply maintaining relations with the surrogate. Her availability to be contacted after birth is identified as a crucial criterion for selection, as well as her willingness to engage in periodic meetings with the new family. However, the relationship with the surrogate mother is expected to involve the two fathers rather than the child/children. This relationship implies a sensitive relational and symbolic effort focused on two primary needs. The first need is the possibility of disclosing to children the existence of the woman from whom they came to life. Together with two cohabiting fathers, this possibility allows designing a plausible family story that children may understand and explain to their peers. The second need relates to displaying the (nuclear) family boundaries and the kinship system in which the child is included. The lack of a genetic bond between surrogate and child, assured resorting to oocyte donors, allows to individualize the contribution of the surrogate by detaching it from her biological genealogy.

Men are also more explicit in stating the importance of the phenotypic similarity between the social parent and the woman from whom the oocytes come. By pursuing the resemblance with the child – identifying a compatible oocyte donor – gay couples try to facilitate the recognition of their parental status and the child's inclusion in the broader family genealogy.

Once the child is born, negotiations with the family of origin become somehow unavoidable. Both gay and lesbian parents are aware of how the (future) grandparents would no longer be able to hide – or circumscribe – the sexual identity of their respective children. Family respectability is a shared capital, and all members – lesbian and gay men included – are held implicitly responsible for it. Thanks to the newborn's arrival, grandparents and other relatives are called to overcome their possible hostility against homosexuality and support the narrative strategies adopted by same-sex parents, beginning with the linguistic labels they use to define their family and roles in front of the child.

The legitimation of social parenthood is also logically claimed as crucial for the well-being of children. When lesbian and gay parents preserve relations with their family of origin, relatives are warmly invited – although they may refuse – to take part in this 'daily coming out'. When these expectations are disregarded, the results of the negotiations with families of origin oscillate between welcoming of the child and 'strategies of silence' (Poulos 2009). In other situations, open hostility translates into expulsion from family networks.[11] On the contrary, when requests of recognition made by lesbian and gay parents are met, relatives are explicitly invested in a political role. In these cases, they are narrated not just as sources of care and support but as protagonists of social change. For lesbians and gay men, to be legitimized as parents by their family of origin enhances intimate citizenship in front of the broader social and legal misrecognition. The effects are not only symbolic: intergenerational bonds of solidarity play a crucial role in countries like Italy, where economic and care resources are expected to come from family networks. It is very telling, for example, that fifty-seven of seventy-eight households in our sample are settled near the families of origin of lesbian and gay parents. In these cases, mutual support can be shared daily, although it does not mean full recognition of the new family arrangement.

Despite the relevance of family networks in daily arrangements, the exclusion of same-sex families from kinship alliances – reaffirmed by the Italian law on civil unions – often goes unnoticed, even if it jeopardizes relevant intergenerational and (gendered) mutual exchanges of care and material support.

## Negotiating precarious family belongings as PHLGPs

The family life of PHLGPs presents specific and usually less visible challenges to normative ideals of heterosexual family. In contrast to intentional lesbian and gay social parents, PHLGPs usually claim 'to have the rights': meaning that their parental status is legally preserved and generally not put under scrutiny by the courts. However, as already stressed in the literature (see Berger 2000), they experience multiple forms of stigmatization – both as homosexuals and separated parents – which occur within one's family, the extended family network and the broader social context.

This section discusses PHLGPs' transition to same-sex intimacies in the background of past and present family networks through which they move. We focus on how their 'betweenness' (Fortier 2001) into heteronormative family norms translates into both sources of uncertainty and resources for social recognition and practical support. Coming out strategies, redefined intimacies, parental practices and family display are the topics of the following analysis.

Scholars have already shown that PHLGPs experience their transition to homosexuality differently from those who identify as lesbians and gay men without – or before – having children (Berkowitz 2009; Clarke and Earley 2021; Rickards and McLeod 2016). Given the family obligations and constraints they are subject to, coming out tends to be managed as a 'group process'. In other words, to come out is perceived as a risky move and, at the same time, a precious strategy whose meaning goes far beyond individual emancipation. What is at stake is also the possibility to (re)negotiate new family and parental status and relationships. Furthermore, PHLGPs' transition to a new sexual identity is strongly marked by uncertainty related to the loss of (heterosexual) parental and family respectability. Even if coming out can occur at different times during or after a heterosexual marriage/union, suspicions of deceit and assumptions about their 'past inauthenticity' or 'double life' can make them valued as less deserving than 'out and proud' lesbian and gay parents (see Dunne 2001).[12] Other sources of uncertainty are related to the marginalization suffered within LGBTQ organizations, as both their family practices and individual trajectories are barely perceived as queerly intelligible.

Simply put, PHLGPs' experience of exclusion is only partially assimilable to that of any (heterosexual) separated/divorced couple with children (Buxton 2005). Coming out not only produces the breakdown of the marital relationship but also causes the breakdown of the heteronormative belief system shared until that moment by the same individuals who come out and their family members.

Worries about the well-being of children are narratively crucial when accounting for coming out strategies and (post)separation arrangements. Of course, the children's age makes a difference. Child-centred narratives of family life are, however, very ambivalent. On the one hand, they might trigger further stigmatization by hostile or homophobic relatives and former in-laws. On the other hand, they might open areas of negotiation concerning new family boundaries, intimate networks and chains of support. The two opposite effects often converge. For example, even the most hostile (ex)partners can be expected to support the changes that the one who came out is crossing, not as former intimates, but as part of their parental duty.

It would be misleading to situate PHLGPs' family troubles on a fixed background of immutability projected onto straight (and hostile) families and kinship. It is not rare, for example, that uncertainty and personal grief are partially relieved by the (sometimes unexpected) support received from heterosexual (ex)partners. Their help can relate to emotional work, the negotiated timing of coming out to children or the legal arrangement to be adopted for managing separation or divorce. In any case, strong, trusting relationships and intimate norms based on authenticity make the expectations of this kind of support more common than it might be expected. For some, the (ex)partner's support is even deemed as equally valuable as the one they receive from experts or community networks.

As anticipated, when it comes to PHLGPs' belongings or family display, a simple schema of inclusion/exclusion from family is not applicable: hostility from family of origin can pair with forms of support received in pragmatic daily arrangements. Indeed, survey data show a frequent geographical and social proximity with first-marriage family networks. In forty-one of sixty-three cases, PHLGPs live in the same municipality or province as their parents (and children's grandparents). In thirty-three cases, they also live near their (ex) parents-in-law. Furthermore, survey data and interviews pointed to the strong involvement of both ex-partners (and their respective intergenerational ties) in childcare. These arrangements result from shared post-separation parenting obligations, which define a structural intertwining between heterosexual and queer family practices.

As for any couple with children, post-separation arrangements also mean new pragmatic parenting, usually involving more than two adults despite and beyond legal parenthood. As individuals, PHLGPs tend to follow well-established, if not traditional, gendered trajectories. Data from the survey show that twenty-four of twenty-seven women live with their children, versus only fourteen men out of thirty-two. The shared custody of children – agreed in the course of separation – seems, therefore, to combine with a prevalence of mothers as primary residential parents.

The gender distinction in PHLGPs' post-separation trajectories also emerges when the household compositions are concerned. Gay fathers, whose children usually live with their mothers or are independent, tend to live alone or be involved in 'living apart together' relationships. Instead, it is common for women to create same-sex households with children. It is also not unusual for them to build so-called extra-blended families where both partners bring their children from previous relationships into the new household.[13]

These gendered family patterns are connected with different experiences, in which challenged parenthood (in our case, more often told by gay fathers) is distinguished from authenticating new parenting arrangements (in our case, more frequently told by mothers). In other words, as the new partners of the ex-wives may reside with their children, fathers are more typically exposed to new competing parental figures. One of the gay fathers said that he had to come to terms 'with the fact that next to my daughter's mother there is another man behaving like a father'. Moreover, when coming out involves children who are young adults, fathers are likely to consider it more as a strategy to reaffirm their own parenthood on a more 'authentic' basis than as a strategy to authenticate new (same-sex) family arrangements.

Mothers in lesbian stepfamilies tend to tell a different story about the relationship between coming out and new parenting. When children are still young and cohabiting with their mother's new partner, self-disclosure tends to be described as a daily process that 'happens more with behaviours than with words'. It is also less focused on the individual identity as it is on the display of a loving same-sex couple. More importantly, authenticating the couple in front of the children implies explaining and giving a name to the intertwining of old and new parental figures. When asked about who counts as a parent, a mother living with her partner and children (of both) says that their children have two mothers and one father. However, she is aware that the bond with her partner's children does not have any legal protection.

When negotiating between competing ideas of family belongings beyond legal definitions, a relevant variable is represented by time. Sharing significant time together can transform the new household into the 'real' family in their members' eyes. In other cases, family members' time (and troubles) define boundaries of belonging, which entitles those established by heterosexual filiation and marriage, keeping new partners on the margins. Outcomes and arrangements are very diversified. In all cases, adopting a strict distinction between 'chosen' and 'blood' family ties or between 'social' and 'biological' parenthood would mean oversimplifying the issue.

Some of these dynamics and uncertainties can be assimilated with those encountered by any stepfamily as they present the same conflicts between parental and couple subsystems. For example, family membership partially loses its self-evidence and fixity, and can be defined differently by family members, children included. But the fact that these family dynamics involve same-sex relationships defines specific degrees of (un)intelligibility and (in)visibility. For example, the child-centred narratives of family life, together with widespread norms of respectability, play a relevant role in making first-marriage heterosexual kinship much visible and binding. Needless to say, the non-heteronormative character of new relationships makes new families even more invisible and difficult to authenticate. Closeness with in-laws and families of origin, moreover, implies negotiations among competing and overlapping family displays. Some are recognized by law and culture; others are not. Lesbian and gay parents and their children tend to inhabit different social spaces adopting different family self-representations. They may take part in 'traditional' intergenerational family events but also march 'out and proud' in an LGBTQ parade presenting themselves as a 'rainbow' family.

Some mothers' narratives clearly show how their ongoing inclusion in families of origin may mirror their assimilation into an 'out of date' family display. In these cases, relatives may behave 'as if nothing had changed'. However, condescending to fictional family unity is interpreted as an ambivalent relational

*Intimate Citizenship in Italy*

work. On the one hand, it allows maintaining family material and care support, allowing children to keep enjoying a proper family-like atmosphere. On the other hand, it is a form of respect towards old (grand)parents who are deemed unable to understand, or endure, separation and coming out. Therefore, even when lesbian and gay identities and relationships are made visible, usually due to a long and difficult pathway, emancipation from the previous intergenerational family display may not be an easy task (see also Lee, in this volume). Who to invite to family events, such as Christmas celebrations or birthdays, and how to name new partners (not 'friends') and new families (not just 'cohabitations'), become symbolic battlefields. What is at stake is the negotiation of old and new family meanings and belongings.

## Final remarks

From the point of view of their intimate lives, Italian ILGPs and PHLGPs are bonded differently with heteronormative family norms and dynamics, showing distinct elements of 'outsiderness' (Patton-Imani 2020), 'betweenness' (Fortier 2001) and family life (un)intelligibility.

The experiences of ILGPs have been translated into political claims focusing on a specific set of missing rights to be achieved: from the legal recognition of non-biological parents to the access to ART and adoption. These demands for social justice mirror the emergence of new definitions of family, filiation and parenthood that cross heteronormative and familial boundaries. Though they emerge from negotiations within the perimeter of the traditional kinship, the family forms created by ILGPs are made vulnerable by the legal system. It is hilarious only at first glance that – as an activist reported – the legal recognition of social parenthood is easier when a civil union splits up and a court decision is needed for the custody of the child.

The political claims of PHLGPs are much less visible in Italian public debate and within LGBTQ activism since their social experience is often referred to as typical of an 'old' generation of lesbian and gay subjects with fewer resources of emancipation. However, their individual trajectories also mirror important patterns of detraditionalization of their family contexts. In this sense, they expand the debate on lesbian and gay families and parenthood by adding further complexity already acknowledged in research on stepfamilies. For example, PHLGPs can help promote a debate on multi-parenting that in Italy is still not considered even when it refers to heterosexual stepfamilies.

In addition to their respective distinctions, ILGPs and PHLGPs share some features that bring to light ambivalent mechanisms of innovation and reproduction. For example, the child-centred orientation of their family choices strengthens their inclusion in the heteronormative system of family alliances. Struggling with constraints and (legal) uncertainties, lesbian and gay parents can mobilize the support of their family of origin – as well as those coming from their (ex)spouses – in the name of safeguarding the (grand)children. Of course, this is easier when they succeed in queering their kin to be fully recognized as a same-sex family. But it can also happen when they are subjected to different forms of misrecognition.

On the one hand, the social and spatial proximity with the family of origin exposes lesbian and gay parents to extended family expectations of normalization into 'narrowly defined, gendered and (hetero) sexualised family models' (Kim and Friedman 2021: 461). On the other hand, intergenerational relatedness represents a valuable material and symbolic resource to build intimate citizenship outside legal protection.

The choice to put the heteronormative kinship system into the queer picture – to recall Chiara Bertone and Maria Pallotta-Chiarulli (2014) – has allowed us to achieve fruitful insights to explain how Italian lesbian and gay parents transform intimate citizenship. However, we assume that innovation and reproduction are always interwoven, not only in national contexts – like Italy – where cultural and institutional uncertainty surrounds anti-normative family patterns. Whatever the context, we claim that following this approach helps avoid the naïve idea that patterns of detraditionalization brought about by lesbian and gay families stand out of a fixed and immutable scenario of heterosexual family life.

# Notes

1 Following scholars like Chiara Saraceno (2016) and Sigrid Leitner (2003), familialism refers to heavy reliance – in ethical and pragmatic terms – on forms of gendered solidarity based on legally recognized kinship relationships. Since its emergence (see Esping-Andersen 1999), this concept has been used to define a specific characteristic of Southern European countries.

2 The fieldwork ended a few weeks after the approval of the law on civil unions that passed in May 2016.

3 On the whole, lesbian mothers declared to have eighty-three children living with them, whereas gay fathers spoke of thirty-one children. In both cases, parenthood was managed mainly within same-sex households.

4  In English, *Rainbow Parents' Network*. Currently, this organization has around one hundred members, although its activities include a larger number of parents (see Gusmeroli and Trappolin 2021a).

5  On the whole, PHLGPs involved in our study have ninety-two children born in heterosexual marriages or relationships.

6  Among the 1,390 households, only 2 per cent included at least one transgender person.

7  *Mamma di pancia*, literally *belly mommy* (see Gamson 2013), is a label used to overshadow the biological meaning of having a baby, while recognizing the bodily experience.

8  This misrecognition becomes exceptionally violent in light of two events: if the biological mother dies, and if the couple separates. In both cases the social parent must rely on the benevolence of the child's legal family to maintain her relations with the child.

9  In these cases, if stepchild adoption is not achieved – and notwithstanding the cohabiting children are socially raised as brothers or sisters – each woman of the couple is legally bounded only with the child she brought to life.

10  Potentially, the decision about who is going to be biologically linked to the child – resorting to a surrogate mother – could be separate from who will be designated as the legal parent under Italian law. Significantly, this distinction is not considered in the narratives collected.

11  By answering a question about the invisible forms of discrimination intercepted by *Famiglie Arcobaleno*, an activist affirmed that 'what is invisible may be the relationship with families of origin. Some people have distanced themselves from their family of origin, changed city, then embarked on a parental path. Others no longer have relations with one of the couple's parents'.

12  In only one case, among those collected, the coming out does not produce a couple break-up. One of the gay fathers negotiates with his wife the refusal of a fracture deemed too painful for the couple and the daughters.

13  These differences cannot be generalized, as sub-samples of mothers and fathers are different in terms of their age and, most importantly in this case, the age of their children. Nevertheless, the collected narratives reflect the significant role of gender in structuring their choices, possible strategies and constraints.

# References

Allen, K. R., and D. H. Demo (1995), 'The Families of Lesbian and Gay Men: A New Frontier in Family Research', *Journal of Marriage and the Family*, 57 (1): 111–27.

Bà, S. (2020), 'Precarity and Family Life in Italy and Great Britain. Job Insecurity as Commodification of Labour', *Journal of Contemporary European Studies*, 28 (4): 544–55.

Berger, R. (2000), 'Gay Stepfamilies: A Triple-Stigmatized Group', *Families in Society: A Journal of Contemporary Human Services*, 81 (5): 504–16.

Berkowitz, D. (2009), 'Theorizing Lesbian and Gay Parenting: Past, Present, and Future Scholarship', *Journal of Family Theory & Review*, 1/2009: 117–32.

Bernini, S. (2008), 'Family Politics: Political Rhetoric and the Transformation of Family Life in the Italian Second Republic', *Journal of Italian Modern Studies*, 13 (3): 305–24.

Bertone, C., and M. Pallotta-Chiarolli (2014), 'Putting Families of Origin into the Queer Picture: Introducing This Special Issue', *Journal of GLBT Family Studies*, 10 (1–2): 1–14.

Butler, J. (2002), 'Is Kinship always already Heterosexual?', *Differences*, 13 (1): 14–44.

Buxton, A. P. (2005), 'A Family Matter. When a Spouse Comes Out as Gay, Lesbian, or Bisexual', *Journal of GLBT Family Studies*, 1 (2): 49–70.

Clarke, V., and E. Earley (2021), '"I Was Just Fed up of Not Being Myself": Coming Out Experiences of White British Divorced and Separated Gay Fathers', *Journal of GLBT Family Studies*, 17 (3): 251–72.

Donovan, C., B. Heaphy and J. Weeks (2003), *Same Sex Intimacies. Families of Choice and Other Life Experiments*, London: Routledge.

Dunne, G. A. (2001), 'The Lady Vanishes? Reflections on the Experiences of Married and Divorced Non-Heterosexual Fathers', *Sociological Research Online*, 6 (3): 1–17.

Esping-Andersen, G. (1999), *Social Foundations of Postindustrial Economies*, Oxford: Oxford University Press.

Ferrera, M. (ed.) (2005), *Welfare State Reform in Southern Europe. Fighting Poverty and Social Exclusion in Italy, Spain, Portugal and Greece*, London: Routledge.

Fortier, A.-M. (2001), '"Coming Home" Queer Migrations and Multiple Evocations of Home', *European Journal of Cultural Studies*, 4 (4): 405–24.

Franchi, M., and G. Selmi (2020), 'Same-Sex Parents Negotiating the Law in Italy: Between Claims of Recognition and Practices of Exclusion', in M. Digoix (ed.), *Same-Sex Families and Legal Recognition in Europe*, 73–93, Cham: Springer.

Gamson, J. (2013), 'The Belly Mommy and the Fetus Sitter: The Reproductive Marketplace and Family Intimacies', in A. Frank, P. Clough and S. Seidman (eds), *Intimacies. A New World of Relational Life*, 146–62, London: Routledge.

Ginsborg, P. (2003), *Italy and Its Discontents. Family, Civil Society, State, 1980–2001*, New York: Palgrave Macmillan.

Girasole, L., and V. Roberti (2020), 'Dal progetto #Contiamoci! Una fotografia delle famiglie LGBTQI', in F. De Cordova, G. Selmi, C. Sità (eds), *Legami possibili. Ricerche e strumenti per l'inclusione delle famiglie LGB*, 109–26, Pisa: Edizioni ETS.

Giunti, D., and G. Fioravanti (2017), 'Gay Men and Lesbian Women Who Become Parents in the Context of a Former Heterosexual Relationship: An Explorative Study in Italy', *Journal of Homosexuality*, 64 (4): 523–37.

Grilli, S., and R. Parisi (2016), 'New Family Relationships: Between Bio-genetic and Kinship Rarefaction Scenarios', *Antropologia*, 3 (11): 29–51.

Gusmano, B., and T. Motterle (2019), 'The Micropolitics of Choice in Italy: How the Law Affects Lesbian and Bisexual Women's Daily Life', *Journal of Lesbian Studies*, 23 (3): 336–56.

Gusmeroli, P., and L. Trappolin (2021a), 'Family Practices of Italian Lesbian and Gay Parents with Children from Heterosexual Relationships. Identity Transition and Pragmatic Bricolage', *Rassegna Italiana di Sociologia*, 4/2021: 879–904.

Gusmeroli, P., and L. Trappolin (2021b), 'Narratives of Catholic Women against "Gender Ideology" in Italian Schools: Defending Childhood, Struggling with Pluralism', *European Societies*, 23 (4): 513–32.

Kim, S. K., and S. L. Friedman (2021), 'Productive Encounters: Kinship, Gender, and Family Laws in East Asia', *Positions*, 29 (3): 453–68.

Lasio, D., and F. Serri (2019), 'The Italian Public Debate on Same-Sex Civil Unions and Gay and Lesbian Parenting', *Sexualities*, 22 (4): 691–709.

Leitner, S. (2003), 'Varieties of Familialism. The Caring Function of the Family in Comparative Perspective', *European Societies*, 5 (4): 353–75.

Mishra, J. (2020), 'Understanding Re-partnership in Non-normative Conjugality: Narratives of Gay Men in Odisha, India', *Journal of Family Issues* 41 (7): 789–809.

Naldini, M., and J. Long (2017), 'Geographies of Families in the European Union: A Legal and Social Policy Analysis', *International Journal of Law, Policy and the Family*, 31: 194–213.

Patton-Imani, S. (2020), *Queering Family Trees. Race, Reproductive Justice, and Lesbian Motherhood*, New York: New York University Press.

Poulos, C. N. (2009), *Accidental Ethnography: An Inquiry into Family Secrecy*, Walnut Creek, CA: Left Coast Press.

Rickards, T., and D. McLeod (2016), 'Authenticating Family: A Grounded Theory Explaining the Process of Re/claiming Legitimacy by Lesbian Stepfamilies', *The Family Journal: Counseling and Therapy for Couples and Families*, 24 (2): 122–31.

Saraceno, C. (2004), 'The Italian Family from the 1960s to the Present', *Modern Italy*, 9 (1): 47–57.

Saraceno, C. (2015), 'Trends and Tensions within the Italian Family', in E. Jones and G. Pasquino (eds), *The Oxford Handbook of Italian Politics*, 465–77, Oxford: Oxford University Press.

Saraceno, C. (2016), 'Varieties of Familialism: Comparing Four Southern European and East Asian Welfare Regimes', *Journal of European Social Policy*, 26 (4): 314–26.

Saraceno, C. (2017), 'Southern European Welfare Regimes: From Differentiation to Reconvergence?', in P. Kennett and N. Lendvai-Bainton (eds), *Handbook of European Social Policy*, 218–29, Cheltenham: Edward Elgar Publishing.

Sgritta, G. B. (1988), 'The Italian Family: Tradition and Change', *Journal of Family Issues*, 9: 372–97.

Stacey, J., and T. J. Biblarz (2001), '(How) Does the Sexual Orientation of Parents Matter?', *American Sociological Review*, 66 (2): 159–83.

Tiano, A., and L. Trappolin (2019), *Diventare genitori, diventare famiglia. Madri lesbiche e padri gay in Italia tra innovazione e desiderio di normalità*, Milano: Wolters Kluwer.

Trappolin, L. (2017), 'Pictures of Lesbian and Gay Parenthood in Italian Sociology. A Critical Analysis of 30 Years of Research', *Italian Sociological Review*, 7 (3): 301–23.

Trappolin, L. (2022), 'Right-Wing Sexual Politics and Anti-Gender Mobilization in Italy: Key Features and Latest Developments', in C. Möser, J. Ramme and J. Takács (eds), *Paradoxical Right-Wing Sexual Politics in Europe*, 119–43, London: Palgrave Macmillan.

Weston, K. (1991), *Families We Choose: Lesbians, Gays, Kinship*, New York: Columbia University Press.

8

# Kithship: Protective Aspects of a Family of Choice for Older Transgender Persons

Sara J. English

Humans are relational creatures. Social connections and relationships are predictors of well-being, and the emotional connections created through early experiences with caregivers create the foundation for social relationships across the whole of the life course. Social connections are built upon the interaction(s) one has with others, a relating *to* and *with*. These connections can be deep or superficial, meaningful or thoughtless, satisfying or servicing. Relationship is the manifest action of the desire for meaningful belonging. Yet, as Bandura (1989) noted, this 'is not a monolithic process'. How persons experience family and relationships is unique, tied to specific experiences within space (the social environments where one lives, works, plays, strives and survives) and place (the roles one fills within particular social environments). The relationships one experiences and the social support one receives from those relationships influence the development of the infrastructure of one's physical and psychosocial well-being and has been described as being fundamental to the development of one's resiliency (Hauser and Allen 2006). Indeed, over half a century ago Perlman (1968) noted that *persona* – the essence of the self – is rooted in the idea of connection to – and with – others.

Family is the primary source of safety, security and social support. Definitions have historically framed *family* as a group of persons sharing a biological or legally recognized relationship, often within a common space (Carmona 2017; Health Resources and Services Administration 2017; World Health Organization 2021). For more than half a century, the World Health Organization (1978) has identified *family* as the primary social institution that promotes well-being through the minimization of risks and the promotion of protections, explaining that 'life within a family is an inter-active, dynamic process, the individual and the group constantly reacting in covert and in overt ways'.

Primary relationships with one's family of origin (or caregiving others) influences a person throughout the thread of life, forming the weft and weave of the personal self (Hauser and Allen 2006; Perlman 1968). Imprints from early experiences help to establish one's personal social infrastructure and resilience, thus, contributing to one's ability to adapt and adjust to adversity (George and West 2011; Hauser and Allen 2006). The quality of social support a person receives from relationships influences one's physical and psychosocial well-being. Yet, relationships with one's family of origin – one's *kin* – are not always constant or comforting. A study by Gonzales et al. (2020) found that almost half of the respondents to a survey examining mental health needs of LGBTQ+ youth reported that immediate family members did not support their sexual identity. Brown and colleagues (2020) explored the association between family relationships and health, noting that persons who identify as being gender or sexually diverse experience more challenges to health and wellness, when compared to cisgendered peers; however, gender and sexually diverse youth with strong familial ties experience higher outcomes of health and wellness than those who report familial strains or estrangement.

Indeed, von Doussa, Power and Riggs (2017) noted that familial relationships are a primary indicator of psychosocial wellness for persons who identify as transgender. Though strong families provide support for gender and sexual minorities, revelations about sexuality and transitioning are often seen as a disruption of family expectations and may further fracture frail relationships (von Doussa, Power and Riggs 2017).

The term *transgender* is relatively new, having been coined in the 1960s, to describe persons who expressed a gender identity different from one's initially assigned gender. Though the term *transgender* casts a wide net over a diverse group of persons (persons who have completed gender affirmation surgery; persons who have partially completed gender affirmation surgery; persons who have received hormonal treatment to suppress secondary sex characteristics, associated with an assigned gender; persons who have received hormone-blocking treatments to delay adolescence; persons contemplating or engaging in some form of transitional process; persons who experience and/or express a fluidity of gender identity), Boza and Nicholson Perry (2014) noted that the term *transgender* may also describe gender-diverse individuals who are androgenous, intersex, bi-gendered or genderqueer. Additionally, the term may be used to encompass transfeminine, transmasculine and twin-spirited or two-spirit persons as well. Broadly, *transgender* describes persons who express and/or present as a member of a gender class that does not align with the biological sex assigned at one's birth. Individuals who identify as transgender, gender-expansive or as a gender minority often face multiple and intersecting challenges, including lower levels of education, lower rates of employment, lower socio-economic status and lower health outcomes (Boza and Nicholson Perry 2014; Carpenter, Eppink and Gonzales 2020; Quinn et al. 2017). These intersecting challenges may result in long-lasting unacknowledged or unrecognized trauma for individuals that leaves emotions and relationships in a labile state, triggering heightened experiences of anxiety, depression or uncertainty, especially in times of unrest and unpredictability (Bhalla and Agarwal 2021).

As Fleishman (2020) noted, despite some recent and focused studies, research has often historically overlooked the experiences of gender minorities. An inclusive examination of *family* must embrace a consideration of persons who live outside tidy definitions. Regardless of age, health, race, socio-economic status, experience or political stance, persons are influenced by primary social groups (Amati et al. 2018). Perhaps, persons are especially influenced when they face difficulties within those primary social groups, which may manifest as disorganized patterns of attachment, uncertainty about one's place within a familial group and maladaptive behaviours. A longitudinal study from the Pew Research Center found that while awareness and acceptance of gender minorities has risen, about 40 per cent of LGBTQ+ persons reported ostracism from family members (Minkin and Brown 2021). Further, transgender persons are twice as likely to experience bullying and social ostracism (Heino, Ellonen and Kaltiala 2021).

Vulnerabilities compound as persons age. Although it is unknown how many older persons are members of the transgender community worldwide, findings reported by the Advocacy and Services for LGBTQ+ Elders (SAGE) (2022) established that many older persons who identify as gender and sexual minorities face several barriers to healthy ageing, including social isolation and ageing without partners. Ongoing data collection from SAGE (2022) also shared that LGBTQ+ elders are 'twice as likely to be single and live alone; four times less likely to have children; far more likely to have faced discrimination and social stigma; more likely, therefore, to face poverty and homelessness, and to have poor health'. Additionally, the large number of members of the LGBTQ+ community ageing without children is distressing, as adult children are often tasked with filling gaps of care. For example, Ageing Without Children reported that in the UK, 92 per cent of unpaid care is provided by family (Hadley (2018)).

This chapter examines contemporary and extant literature and introduces a conceptual model of the reciprocal protective process of *kithship* for persons who experience frail, fragmented or fractured relationships with one's family of origin. (see also Lee, in this volume) It also shares qualitative statements from an ongoing study of older transgender persons (sixty-five years of age and older) that examines non-familial social ties, illuminating some of the key ways non-traditional familial relationships provide protective aspects for transgender persons, across the lifespan.

## What is a family, anyway?

Traditional definitions of *family* are based on generationalized expectations of behaviour and expression, arising from dominant social groups within a social environment (see also Gusmeroli and Trapollin, in this volume). These standards reflect a patriarchal social structure. Persons who fail to fit into a category based upon a gendered binary have historically been pathologized and *othered*, with transgender persons 'framed as a threat to cisgendered people and, therefore, must be denied autonomy, dignity, and freedom to live authentically' (Proctor 2021). This extends beyond family relationships.

## Legal considerations

The aspect of *transgender* as a protected class is not universally respected. For example, in the United States, President Barack Obama signed an executive order in 2014, establishing gender and sexual identity as a protected class, but this definition is increasingly challenged by legislation in some states. Support waffles, according to whatever political party seems to hold the most sway, with 'the current state of political uncertainty threatening' rollbacks and hard-won rights (English 2020; Fleishman 2020). For example, transgender rights that had been earlier secured were threatened under the administration of Donald Trump; however, these rights were reaffirmed by executive order under President Joseph Biden. A narrowing of rights has been documented in other countries, as well, including the 'defacto criminalization of trans people under laws' (Wareham 2020). Though the United Nations outlined rights of transgender persons in 2017, less than one-sixth of member countries of the United Nations legally support the rights of transgender individuals (United Nations 2017). The understanding of *protected class* is dynamic and dependent upon the political wind. As a result, transgender persons who voice their identity may risk the loss of socially determined, gender-based privilege or fall short of gendered expectations regarding power and control. Boza and Nicholson Perry (2014) found education about gender is necessary, but not a sufficient approach to achieving equity, as merely broadening acceptance and understanding about the complexity of identity does not eliminate endemic social and systemic barriers. Gender non-conforming persons challenge familial and social expectations, and those who do not conform to expectations may experience lower levels of support and higher incidents of marginalization from both the broader social environment and traditional family structures that may fail to affirm their gender identity, resulting in lower health and overall well-being (Quinn et al. 2017; von Doussa, Power and Riggs 2017).

## Family, defined

A *family* is a unit of social structure; however, the definition of *family* varies, according to social norms and expectations. Sharma (2013) explained that definitions of family as 'an integrated and functional social structure' commonly understood to be 'all persons living in one household', fail to capture the rich diversity of family structures, which vary according to circumstance and social norms. Sharma (2013) posited that the term *family* is complex, uniquely defined and cannot be captured without a consideration of composition, location, marriage type and the social structure of authority. Further, Gavriel-Fried, Shilo and Cohen (2012) argued that the commonly held idea of family as a social unit involving children fails to reflect unique experiences and perceptions. Indeed, traditional definitions of *family* do not adequately encompass the full and dynamic meaning of the term and current laws often lack a clear explanation of what it means to be in, or of, a family (Degtyareva 2012).

In a publication regarding standards of practice, The US-based National Association of Social Workers (2013) reported that *family* is personally and 'uniquely defined by each individual'. Though there is variance in type, size and situation, the family is often seen as the seat of the habitus of human relationship. Alletta (2009) noted some common qualities of positive family functioning, with one fundamental quality of family functioning being that of *promise*: the implied and understood agreement that the interactions and experiences one has with another will be trustworthy and reliable (Lincoln et al. 2010; Ma, Meng and Shen 2015).

128        *Reinventing the Family in Uncertain Times*

Though not all familial connections are universally healthy, bonds of caring and love protect individuals, teaching persons to positively function within the social environment. Reciprocal regard from persons outside of the family of origin is important for persons, especially for those who experience estrangement and stigma, including gender and sexual diversity (von Doussa, Power and Riggs 2017).

## Family estrangement

The family is commonly described as 'the fundamental unit of society', with a primary purpose to offset risk and promote resilience (Carmona 2017); yet, traditional definitions of *family* fail to encapsulate the rich diversity of familial human relationships. Carmona (2017) noted that a more contemporary definition that better aligns with the promotion of human dignity and human rights, allowing for an interpretation 'in the light of present-day conditions' to reflect 'the legal and social developments that have occurred regarding the family over time'. In short, *family* is a unit of *promise*, where persons share a commitment and mutual care. Certainly, many persons experience strong and secure family. Not all do.

Human beings can construct families in different forms, with a family as a function of either chance or choice: *Kin* – the family of chance – encompasses relationships of blood, primary caregivers and the fictive kin that are connected by social ties to our *kin,* as well as *Kith* – the Family of Choice, which is curated and formed through intentional, reciprocal relationships.

Family estrangement is the loss of a bond between *kin*. Disagreements and emotional distance can cause a change in bonds, creating relationships that may become progressively frailer, fragmented or fractured. Frail relationships involve connections of persistent tension, especially when there is disagreement about one's personal expression of behaviours, gender, lifestyle or partnership. The labile nature of frail relationships may result in difficulty anticipating reactions from *kin*. Conflict – both emotional and physical – may bubble up, as persons project behaviour upon others. Frail relationships are lived expressions of *I don't think I know you, anymore*!

Fragmented relationships can occur when interpersonal difficulty and physical distance become more pervasive. Individuals may intentionally keep distance, preferring absence to presence. Persons may remain emotionally connected, especially due to feelings of relationship or responsibility; however, feelings of rejection, the absence of coping skills and limited experiences of enjoyable time together influence perceptions about family ties and the desire to maintain them (Brown et al. 2020). Under these conditions, conflict arising from personal expressions may be less, as individuals acknowledge the conflict, but avoid direct interaction or discussion. Fragmented relationships are lived expressions of *I don't think I want to know you, anymore!*

Fractured relationships involve emotional and/or physical cut-off. These insecure relationships result from experiences where family members may drift away from one another or have initiated a dramatic end to the relationship. Katz-Wise, Rosaris and Tsappis (2017) described fractured relationships as estrangement, often involving dismissal, othering, rejection or emotional/ physical abuse. Fractured relationships are expressions of *I do not know you and I do not want to know you, anymore!*

Family systems that fail to provide the physical, material, emotional and psychosocial needs of its members are often described as dysfunctional. Yet, it is important to remember that these types of families do, indeed, function. Family functioning is often subject to a dichotomous definition, but family functioning is fluid, existing not as one thing or another, but along a sliding scale. The family which includes abusive members, functions. The family which includes indulgent members, functions. So, too, does the family that includes members who are absent, distant, negligent, manipulative, unaware or uninvolved. Families who include members living with mental illness and/ or substance use are, also, functional. Families may not function well, but they all function, and within their functioning, lessons are learned within the family unit. Dysfunctional families do not fail to function; rather, they fail to function within the commonly accepted social norms as understood within a particular social environment (Aletta 2009). Families that experience conflict and instability function, but they function in an inadequate, impaired and often rigid manner (Hayaki et al. 2016).

Negative experiences within family structures are associated with lower psychosocial wellness and increased tension (Lincoln et al. 2010). Emotional disorders, such as anxiety, depression, dysthymia and obsessive compulsive disorder have been linked with in-family conflict (Hayaki et al. 2016; Kessler et al. 1998). Additionally, negative familial relationships may be associated with increased social isolation (Lubben et al. 2017), which escalates the vulnerability of individuals who experience friction with *kin*.

Repeated negative familial experiences erode the infrastructure of the self and damage the way in which persons respond to, and interact with, the environment in which one lives; even sporadic negative interactions are associated with lower rates of emotional well-being across the lifespan (Krause 2005). Yet, regardless of experience or situation, each person is endowed with the opportunity to have two families: Chance and Choice.

## Kin

The Family of Chance – one's *kin* – is a Family of Chance and includes non-professional caregivers; primarily, persons to whom one is related to by blood or legal bonds. For most persons, the Family of Chance is the collective of persons to which one is born or the social unit that provides primary caregiving during infancy. This group also provides one's introduction to the social world, within the context of that particular environment (George and West 2011). Members of the Family of Chance are bound by social expectations and the understood *promise* to create and maintain relationships that are trustworthy and reliable (Ma, Meng and Shen 2015). This Family of Chance is bestowed upon us, with additions and deletions made through adoption, birth, death, divorce, marriage or formally recognized association or estrangement.

Brofenbrenner first explained the family as a system in 1979, finding that one's *kin* created a microsystem of interconnected individuals that influence – and are influenced by – each other. This influence extends across the lifespan and even beyond death, where *kinship* and familial norms influence the way persons relate to others and home individuals cope with change and challenge.

## Fictive kin

Fictive kin are extensions of the Family of Chance and are defined as persons who are not blood relatives, but are presented as such, connected and presented as part of the familial group (Nelson 2014). While fictive kin have been described as invented relationships of 'play children, Godchildren, or foster children' (Nelson 2014), they are often close family friends or residual persons whose complex social ties were created through marriage or other relationships. Ex-spouses, boyfriends, girlfriends, co-workers, *othermothers*, sorority sisters, fraternity brothers or other persons who were once significant partners of a family member may also be seen as fictive kin (Ibsen and Klobus 1972; Spruill et al. 2014). Fictive kin are sometimes viewed as chosen family; however, this definition does not meet the criteria for inclusion in one's Family of Choice, as fictive kin are bestowed. One does not agentically choose who is or who is

*Protective Aspects of a Family of Choice* 131

not considered to be *kin* or fictive kin by the social unit. Regardless of whether the members of one's Family of Chance are blood or fictive relations, the roles these persons play have been determined by others, as fictive kin are connected through kin. One's Family of Chance is provided, not produced.

## Kithship

The intentional curation of a Family of Choice – one's *kith* – allows one to intentionally form familial bonds with non-*kin*. This process is beyond the mere social support that may be found through colleagues (Ackerman 1961; Krause 2005). Though friends are certainly important components of one's Family of Choice and kindred persons may be folded into the group as well, the establishment of *kith* is an agentic, intentional, purposeful and reciprocal process that offers protections promoting resilience, especially for persons experiencing frail, fragmented or fractured relationships with *kin*. The creation of intentional and reciprocal relationships benefits persons who have difficult or disruptive familial relationships, often punctuated through past trauma and unexpected events.

A Family of Choice provides purposeful 'closeness, joining, or intimacy' (Barnhill 1979), establishing bonds that incorporate the positive qualities of family functioning (respect, emotionally safe environments, resilient foundations etc.) that are social expectations of healthy *kin* relationships (Aletta 2009). The protective aspect offered by *kithship* empowers individuals and lowers rates of risk for vulnerable persons across multiple arenas, including in the personal, the communal and the broader social environment (Substance Abuse and Mental Health Services Administration 2019).

The intentional mutuality of reciprocity can be beneficial to all persons, but may be especially beneficial for persons who have experienced strains with *kin* relationships, including transgender persons who may experience estrangement and emotional cut-off from parents and other members of the Family of Chance. As Brown et al. (2020) noted, the *kin* relationships that remain are often toxically strained. For persons who do not experience supportive *kin*, *kith* relationships offer benefits for persons across the lifespan.

## Support and kith

Social support helps affirm and offset marginalization experienced by persons who are *othered*. Trujillo et al. (2017) noted non-familial social support as strongly associated with emotional well-being among transgender persons who may experience harassment and rejection from their Family of Chance. They looked at the role of social support among the transgender community and surmised that support was essential for well-being, noting it as 'especially important for reducing the effects on mental health and suicidal ideation' in this vulnerable population.

A 2021 report by Trans PULSE Canada outlined the importance of social support for transgender and non-binary persons, noting supportive family as being a primary factor in well-being. Among the participants ($n = 2873$), 58 per cent reported supportive relationships with family, noting that positive family relationships were tied to positive physical and emotional well-being. This was especially true for younger participants (under the age of twenty-five), who reported kin as the primary source of social support. Respondents older than twenty-five years of age reported non-kin as the primary source of social support, offering protection 'against mental health issues, even in the face of discrimination and stigma'. Boza and Nicholson Perry (2014) found that these supportive benefits are present whether support is tangible or perceived, with support providing an essential promotion of well-being that can offset harm, whether at the hands of others or oneself.

In essence, a Family of Choice provides a means to build the social support and opportunities that create stronger emotional structures to develop greater resilience. Bonds built upon reciprocity and trust allow for what Bandura (1989) noted as social *bi-directionality*, where persons create opportunities for transformational connections with persons and social environments. Such bonds may help develop better problem-solving skills and provide the support that allows individuals to manage emotional residue, which may be present for those who have survived earlier trauma.

A Family of Choice does not serve as surrogates for blood relations. Rather, *kithship* – one's chosen family – may be viewed not as substitutes, but as an intentional family of non-kin, who purposefully provide ongoing, reciprocal emotional support through strong and trusting bonds.

## Space, place and context

Ideas about families and family function are generally based on contextual experiences that are framed by social norms. The ecological perspective explains the influence upon social ties with persons, both inside and outside of the immediate family unit (Barnhill 1979; Bowen Center 2016). The roles individuals play within groups serve to build bridges – or barriers – for group cohesion.

Family Systems Theory (FST) examines the family as an interconnected system, with the roles of the individual family members and the interactions between the individuals influencing the whole (Martin and Martin 2000). Individuals are connected, one to another, within the family. Murray Bowen developed FST in an effort to clarify the dynamics of the family whole, illustrating these dynamics through pictorial representation (Bowen Center 2016). Bowen further explained that *how* people were linked within the family was associated with positive or negative family functioning. Familial connections may be close, conflicted, distant, estranged, fused, poor or some combination of these and other factors.

While much research has examined the ways children relate to primary caregivers, Waters, Hamilton and Weinfield (2000) emphasized additional factors as fundamental for positive relationships across the lifespan, noting that although childhood attachment type (secure, avoidant, ambivalent, disorganized) influences the interpersonal relationships and attachments in later life, individual experiences, including changes in parent–child relationships (separation, abandonment, divorce or death), create opportunities for attachments to others. Individual agency also determines one's ability (or inability) to positively form attachments to others throughout the entire life cycle and was noted by George and West (2011) to influence 'general human bonding, including coworkers or others not specified by human biology'.

The Social Exchange Framework (SEF) is based upon several perspectives from economic and behavioural schools of thought, explaining interactions as based upon an analysis of costs and benefits, with relationships being established, maintained or severed according to the emotional and psychosocial balance between what an individual gives and what an individual receives within a given relationship.

The *promise* of reward drives persons to seek out exchanges with others. This emotional trading is similar to an economic transaction. It is a construction, with relationships seen as investments in one's emotional future (Winek 2010). These investments may be defined as desire for acceptance: the want for human connection and alliance and the hope for emotional, psychosocial and physical safety.

Cumulative negative interactions experienced within one's Family of Chance can influence persons to abandon costly negative relationships in exchange for the *promise* of a more profitable emotional return through relationships of choice. The economy of social exchange is 'one we use every moment of our lives'

(Houmans 1958) and this distributive form of social interaction is based upon justice and reciprocity. Relationships involving social exchange are:

- Characterized by interdependence in which the benefits received are contingent upon the benefits one is able to provide;
- Regulated by social norms of the social environment;
- Based upon a foundation of trust and commitment;
- Emergent and dynamic relationships, which change over time.

The process of entering new relationships is a leap of faith, based upon a cost–benefits analysis. Primarily, the intentional curation of one's *kith* aligns with Promise Theory, which was originally developed by computer scientist Mark Burgess (2014) to explain how individual agents cooperate with one another, in a repeated fashion, to create a desirable new outcome. Originally designed to explain how humans and machines interact systemically, Promise Theory can be adapted as a Social Theory of Promise, illustrating protective aspects created by 'repeatable processes that keep promises through tailored relationships' (Burgess 2014).

# Kithship in the transgender community

## Transgender persons and ageing

### History

Though the first reported gender affirmation surgery took place in 1931, transgender persons have been present across cultures and history. Though many indigenous cultures embrace *two-spirit* persons as tribal leaders, the transgender community has been long maligned and misunderstood, experiencing familial and social ostracism, including overt and covert bias and discrimination, social exclusion and microaggressions (Beemyn 2022; Fleishman 2020; Jain 2021; Stinchcombe, Kortes-Miller and Wilson 2016; Wesselmann et al. 2021). Yet, this community has a rich history of support, some of which arose in Victorian times, as heteronormative expectations of sexuality became dominant in most cultures, as presented in legislation that criminalized and pathologized less-dominant sexual behaviour and expression. More recently, this support has been well-illustrated in the ballroom and bar culture, especially in house culture that emerged in the early twentieth century, where appointed *mothers* and *fathers* looked after the *house children*, providing guidance, protection and support

Protective Aspects of a Family of Choice

for young transgender persons of colour, who experienced social and family pressures (Fernández et al 2020; Fleishman 2020).

Spizzirri et al. (2021) estimated that less than 1 per cent of the total world population is known to be transgender. Data suggested that one in 250 persons in the United States are transgender (Meerwijk and Sevelius 2017). Regardless of how one defines the term, *trans* refers to the *movement towards* or the *evolution of* an identity of self and the meaning about where one is on the path to being and embracing one's identity, which may vary considerably from the expectations of kin and social environments (Beemyn 2022; Thorne et al. 2019).

## Discrimination in old age

Older persons often face ageism and discrimination, but such marginalization is often a lifelong experience. Older transgender persons live with a heavier intersection of vulnerability, which may be especially keen for persons who have limited social relationships. If an older transgender person requires care assistance, the intersection becomes even heavier. Though legislation now supports same-sex marriage and opportunities to partner and parent, many older members of the LGBTQ+ community did not enjoy these same options in their youth. Sue Lister, the founder of the Aging without Children network, reported that a survey of members found about 90 per cent of older members of the LGBTQ+ community have no children and most live alone (S. Lister, personal communication, November 2021). These findings echo census data outlining the burgeoning number of older persons who are ageing without support of adult children (United States Census Bureau 2021). Though many may have ties to relationships beyond children (in-laws, nieces, nephews and other relations), data from the Behavioral Risk Factor Surveillance System survey indicated that those who experienced disconnection with kin will likely continue to face multiple intersections of disadvantage (Brown et al. 2020; Pharr 2021). The lack of a familial person to advocate, represent or serve as one's medical proxy may cause an individual to become fully dependent upon the hoped-for kindness of strangers. Advocacy groups, such as the International Lesbian, Gay, Bisexual, Trans and Intersex Association (ILGA), the Advocacy & Services for LGBTW+ Elders (SAGE) and the National Center for Transgender Equality, work with communities to address bias and improve the life experiences of older transgender persons, responding to the need for education and training for providers of health and housing. This is especially true if older transgender persons enter more formalized social care settings, where they may encounter bias and prejudice from uncaring or uneducated healthcare staff, who receive limited training regarding person-centred and culturally competent care.

Strong non-*kin* relationships – or *kithships* – can help offset challenges experienced by older transgender persons, including isolation, poverty and the lack of informal support, including assistance with care and transportation. White et al. (2015) noted strong non-*kin* relationships as contributing to *mattering* among older LGBTQ+ persons, which is rooted in feelings of being wanted and valued by persons on whom one can depend.

## Youth and emerging adults

Older transgender persons can express feelings of isolation and a lack of connection to others, which often originated in their earlier years and extend across the lifespan. There is a paucity of research devoted to social relationships among younger transgender persons; however, some scholarship outlines the vital support that social relationships provide for youth who are negotiating the complex time between adolescence and adulthood. Adolescents who identify as a gender minority reported greater rates of substance use, self-harm and suicidality than their cisgender peers (Rimes et al. 2019). Potvin, Ragan and Root (2021) noted that 'the majority of trans youth are often no safer in their own homes than they are anywhere else. Many parents do not understand what it means to be transgender, think it is a rebellious stage their child is going through, or otherwise refuse to support them.'

Non-familial supportive relationships can offer gender-affirming social support that aligns and may be absent in *kin* relationships. Close friends and supportive others, who refer to individuals by their preferred name and pronouns, support one's choice of expression and provide feedback about efforts towards social transition and provide positive regard that may be absent from *kin*. Even younger children, who express gender outside of a heteronormative binary, may seek and receive security from accepting others (Carlile 2020). Meyer (2003) noted the results of both passive and purposeful hostility that may be directed towards minorities, with sexual minorities experiencing high rates of *minority stress*, which he described as a comprehensive experience that is unique, chronic and socially based. Carlile (2020) also noted that 'experiences of the transgender and non-binary children … demonstrate the negative impact on their mental and physical health of the "minority stress" they experience'. The

Protective Aspects of a Family of Choice

creation of reciprocal, supportive relationships outside the family of origin may serve as a long-term offset to trauma.

A current study is in the process of data collection from an exploratory survey on the perceptions of social support among older transgender persons. The importance and longevity of some *kithships* was expressed by a seventy-year-old transgender woman, who noted the importance of her curated and intentional relationships:

> I have let a lot of people go, but the ones that I have kept have really helped me heal from my early years. I could never be myself with my parents. I was never good enough and I was always going to hell, as far as they were concerned.
>
> But I stayed with them. The day my mother died was one of the happiest days of my life, also the saddest. I wasted a lot of time listening to her and trying to be something I knew I wasn't. I met Billie and Max when my mom kicked me out.
>
> That was a lifetime ago. They're still there. They are my family.

## Allostatic load

Allostatic load refers to the burden of cumulated stress experienced over one's lifetime and aligns closely to Meyer's exploration of the chronic nature of minority stress. Experiences of disparity and marginalization contribute to one's allostatic load, which influences outcomes of health and wellness. Persons who experience intersections of vulnerabilities, including implicit and explicit biases, prejudice or covert microaggressions live with a disproportionate and imbalanced burden of stress, leading to an allostatic overload. McEwan and Steller (1993) introduced this concept to explain the mental, physical and social costs of persons who lived with prolonged levels of elevated stress and unrecognized trauma, exacerbated by abuse, discrimination, injuries, insults, marginalization, microaggression, neglect, prejudice, social ostracism and unpredictable traumatic events.

Though wear and tear from allostatic load negatively impacts health and wellness, Juster et al. (2019) noted that strong relationships can offset negative outcomes and provide 'pathways toward resilience'. Such pathways are created through socially supportive and trustworthy relationships, and lead to a clarification of how one defines the self (Newen 2018).

Acceptance of gender minorities is present in many communities of today and most countries recognize marriages and legal partnerships between LGBTQ+ persons. Yet, the recognition of the rights of gender minorities is fairly recent and some recent legislative debates, such as limitations of transgender athletes to compete in sporting events, illuminates a troubling possibility of reversal. Older persons who do not conform to heteronormative expectations have many years of encountering bias, hostility and legal supports. Further, internalized stigmatization contributes to poor outcomes among transgender seniors. Negative experiences and mindsets may affect levels of trust among older transgender persons, limiting support of this ageing demographic. Issues relating social determinants of health, such as age, race and socio-economic status are made more complex for older transgender persons.

## Alone, not lonely

Fleishman (2020) noted that *kithships* offer protective factors for transgender persons by offsetting discrimination and disparities. Older transgender and gender non-conforming seniors live along or beyond the traditional frameworks provided by *kin* and may be well supported through the purposeful and intentional curation and editing of non-familial relationships that are useful, helpful and supportive (Ibsen and Klobus 1972; Pharr 2021; White et al. 2015).

*Kithship* may be especially significant in the lives of persons who may be ageing without the benefit of the support of children, providing protective aspects and a resilient life-path for transgender persons, across the lifespan. Reciprocal bonds with *kith* offset trauma and offer the promise of familial connection, between two or more persons, who intentionally interact to create a Family of Chance – *Kith*.

## Methods of the current study

To explore perceptions of social support of *kith* among transgender persons, aged sixty-five and older, a mixed methods study was developed, which included an original survey instrument that was distributed to older transgender persons, using social media and organizational Listservs. Built relationships with trans-friendly organizations proved to be an important bridge between researchers and participants, with response rates to survey invitations being a more successful form of recruitment than social media blasts. Potential participants were invited to complete a short online survey, which collected demographic information and scaled perceptions of social support based upon a five-point Likert scale.

To capture perceptions regarding lived experiences, two open-ended questions were included in the survey. Participants were invited to share the survey link and a majority of responses were a result of this snowball recruitment. Collection of survey responses is, currently, open and will be collected for a period of one year, with data analysed on an ongoing basis. All responses are analysed through cross tabulation, which allows for the analysis of relationships between and across demographic and other variables. Qualitative responses are analysed to reveal patterns and themes. Additionally, respondents are selected through a systematic random sample of participants to participate in one-on-one interviews via telephone or Zoom. These one-on-one interviews follow a semi-guided protocol of four questions and last approximately one hour. Data collection is ongoing; however, collected qualitative data support the protective aspects of kith for older transgender persons. For example, in response to the survey about perceptions of social support, a 68-year-old transgender man noted the purposeful curation of kith, noting the desire to be rid of persons who fail to be supportive:

> If they aren't there to help, they can go and be disruptive elsewhere.
>
> They don't belong in my life.

## Hypothesis and conceptual model – Social Theory of Promise

Human beings construct meaning through interactions with others, within the social environment. Shared experiences and intentional engagement create *promise* between individuals who may use intentional and reciprocal interactions to create and maintain a Family of Choice. The proposed model for a Social Theory of Promise illustrates how *kith* provides supportive and protective families for older transgender persons.

As shown in Figure 8.1, there are two main components of the reciprocal process – the individual and individual(s) identified as one's *kith*. The establishment of *kith* is an intentional and purposeful curation, where individuals work together in a cooperative way to create a new Family of Choice, which is based on *promise* made and *promise* fulfilled. The relationship between individuals is secondary to the intensity and strength provided by secure attachment. Indeed, the moderating variable of secure attachment is essential to the development of *kithships*, influencing the direction, intensity and strength of the relationship.

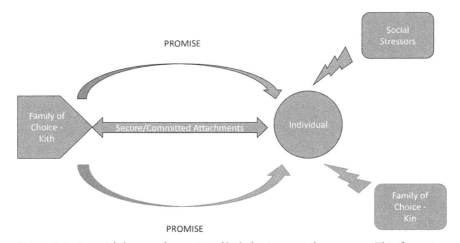

**Figure 8.1** A social theory of promise of kith for transgender persons. This figure is a representation of a social theory of promise of kith for transgender persons.
Note: This model is a visual representation of factors in the continuous, reciprocal creation and recreation of *promise* between the individual and other(s). This agentic process provides support and protection to offset stress and trauma arising from social stressors and familial *kin*.

A secure and committed attachment between the individual and select others helps to move the relationship beyond that of friendly cohorts. Without secure and committed attachment, *kithship* is not possible. Older transgender persons experiencing emotional or physical estrangement with the Family of Chance benefit from this process. This collaborative process provides protective aspects across the lifespan, including financial, physical and psychosocial support.

Social ties with *kith* provide opportunities for members of one's Family of Chance to extend *promise* – the implied and expressed expectancy of commitment and care.

Another survey participant who works as a clinical social worker, and who is the female spouse of a transgender woman, described it this way:

> With gender and sexual minorities, the support of chosen family is definitely a protective factor. When we come out, often it feels like the love of our blood family becomes conditional and contentious. Whereas with chosen family, acceptance is often unspoken but simply known. It feels safer and we will reciprocate that support back.

People are intertwined within a social environment, with social expectations and norms influencing life experiences. When conflict occurs between expression and expectation, individuals can become ostracized and outcast.

This may affect the way persons experience interpersonal relationships with *kin*, creating environmental and relational stress. The establishment of *kithship* promotes and protects individuals, through an agentic and ongoing process, where individuals, who have established secure and committed relationships, engage in reciprocal exchanges to intentionally create and maintain non-sanguineous familial connections.

## Youth and emerging adults

Older transgender persons express feelings of isolation and a lack of representation, which often originated in their earlier years (Advocacy & Services for LGBTQ+ Elders 2015; Fleishman 2021; Stinchcombe, Kortes-Miller and Wilson 2016). Recent scholarship outlined the vital support that social relationships provide for youth who are negotiating the complex time between adolescence and adulthood. Adolescents who identify as a gender minority reported greater rates of substance use, self-harm and suicidality than their cisgender peers (Rimes et al. 2019). Behaviours of self-harm are frequently responses to hostile environmental stressors. A generation past, Mallon and DeCrescenzo (2006) found that gender-expansive children experience alarming rates of abuse, stigma and violence within their social environments; however, affirming social relationships with others buffer the impacts of these experiences.

Indeed, the creation of reciprocal, supportive relationships – the Family of Choice – which lies beyond the social bubble of *kin*, may serve as a long-term offset to trauma, both past and prescient.

## Kithship, forward

The conceptual model of the Social Theory of Promise has implications for persons who experience allostatic overload due to emotional, environmental and relational stressors. The intentional curation of a Family of Choice empowers individuals through the process of identifying, promoting and sustaining relationships. All persons have moments of vulnerability and all persons are valuable. *Kithships* illustrate the centrality and importance of human relationships (National Association of Social Workers 2021; United Nations 1948) and address the Grand Challenge of Social Isolation (Lubben et al. 2017), which is exacerbated by change and challenge, including disasters, emergencies and the current and ongoing Covid-19 pandemic.

Social justice is a product of just practice, which identifies and moves to dismantle the entrenched barriers and barricades faced by persons who may live along the margins. Older persons, gender minorities and persons who experience additional intersections of disadvantage are often seen as *other*. This othering is seated within social environments and may be experienced both formally and informally. Identifying, promoting and supporting the non-familial *kith* relationships of transgender persons helps to defend and empower individuals who may have been, heretofore, dismissed.

# Conclusion

Though familial relationships are broadly seen as the primary source of social support, transgender persons can receive acceptance and affirmation through the creation and curation of a Family of Choice, promoting protective social connections and social well-being. These *kith* relationships can bridge the gap that occurs with family estrangement, as persons form intentional and reciprocal bonds with secure and committed others. One's connection with family is an actionable embodiment of the self. Amati and colleagues (2018) noted that one's personal network is both a source and product of social support. Newen (2018) posited that one's self cannot be seen as separate from one's social world, with the self as 'an integration of an embodied, basic affective flow with an intentional object'. In the case of *kith*, the intentional object is one's Family of Choice and the connecting ties between kith, satisfaction, wellness and well-being (Amati et al. 2018).

Though these *kith* relationships provide protection for older transgender persons, they also provide a means to create important trusting connections among all persons who experience frail, fragmented or fractured relationships with members of the Families of Chance or the broader social world. Indeed, the power of *kith* illustrates the centrality, importance and primacy of familial social connections, whether those connections be chance or choice. As one member of Aging Without Children noted the importance of kith in the form of a handwritten note, written along the margins of a survey:

> There aren't a lot of people I trust, but the ones I do, are pure gold, pure family.
> That is what I – what we all – need most.

# References

Ackerman, N. (1961), 'Symptom, Defense, and Growth in Group Process', *International Journal of Group Psychotherapy*, 11 (2): 131–42.

Advocacy & Services for LGBTW+ Elders (2015), *Transgender Aging: What's Different?*, 18 November, https://www.liebertpub.com/doi/abs/10.1089/lgbt.2021.0009?journalCode=lgbt. Accessed 1 July 2022.

Advocacy & Services for LGBTQ+ Elders (2022), *Your Rights and Resources: LGBTQ+ Aging Facts*, https://www.sageusa.org/your-rights-resources/.

Aletta, E. G. (2009), *What Makes a Family Functional vs. Dysfunctional?*, 15 December, http://psychcentral.com/blog/archives/2009/12/15/what-makes-a-family-functional-vs-dysfunctional/.

Amati, V., S. Meggiolaro, G. Rivellini and S. Zaccarin (2018), 'Social Relations and Life Satisfaction: The Role of Friends', *Journal of Population Studies*, 74 (7): 1–18.

Bandura, A. (1989), 'Social Cognitive Theory', in R. Vasta (ed.), *Annals of Child Development. Vol. 6. Six Theories of Child Development*, 1–60, London: JAI Press.

Barnhill, L. R. (1979), 'Healthy Family Systems', *The Family Coordinator*, 28 (1): 94–100.

Beemyn, G. (2022), 'Transgender History in the United States', in L. Erickso-Schroth (ed.), *Trans Bodies, Trans Selves: A Resource by and for Transgender Communities*, Oxford: Oxford University Press, https://www.umass.edu/stonewall/sites/default/files/Infoforandabout/transpeople/genny_beemyn_transgender_history_in_the_united_states.pdf.

Bhalla, R., and S. Agarwal (2021), 'Life in a Pandemic: Intersectional Approach Exploring Experiences of LGBTQ during COVID-19', *International Journal of Spa and Wellness*, 4 (1): 53–68.

Bowen Center (2016), *Eight Concepts*, http://www.thebowencenter.org/theory/eight-concepts/.

Boza, C., and K. Nicholson Perry (2014), 'Gender-Related Victimization, Perceived Social Support, and Predictors of Depression among Transgender Australians', *International Journal of Transgenderism*, 15: 25–52.

Brown, C., C. M. Porta, M. E. Eisenberg, B. J. McMorris and R. E. Sieving (2020), 'Family Relationships and the Health and Well-Being of Transgender and Gender-Diverse Youth: A Critical Review', *LGBT Health*, 7 (8): 407–19.

Burgess, M. (n.d.), 'Frequently Asked Questions about Promise Theory', http://markburgess.org/promiseFAQ.html. Accessed 1 July 2022.

Burgess, M. (2014). Promise Theory – What Is It? *Linux Journal*, 2014(244): 3.

Burgess, M. (2015), *Thinking in Promises*, Sebastopol, CA: O'Reilly Media.

Carlile, A. (2020), 'The Experiences of Transgender and Non-binary Children and Young People and Their Parents in Healthcare Settings in England, UK: Interviews with Members of a Family Support Group', *International Journal of Transgender Health*, 21 (1): 16–32.

Carmona, M. S. (2017), 'A Contemporary View of "Family" in International Human Rights Law and Implications for the Sustainable Development Goals (SDGs)', New York: UN Women.

Carpenter, C. S., S. T. Eppink and G. Gonzales (2020), 'Transgender Status, Gender Identity, and Socioeconomic Outcomes in the United States', *International Law Review – Cornell University*, 73 (3): 573–99.

Degtyareva, V. (2012), 'Defining Family in Immigration Law: Accounting for Nontraditional Families in Citizenship by Descent', *The Yale Law Journal*, 120 (4): 862–908.

Fernández-Rouco, N., R. J. Carcedo and T. Yeadon-Lee (2020), 'Transgender Identities, Pressures, and Social Policy: A Study Carried Out in Spain', *Journal of Homosexuality*, 67 (5): 620–38.

Fleishman, J. (2020), *The Stonewall Generation: LGBTQ Elders on Sex, Activism & Aging*, Skinner House Books.

Gavriel-Fried, B., G. Shilo and O. Cohen (2012), 'How Do Social Workers Define the Concept of Family?', *British Journal of Social Work*, 44 (4): 992–1010.

George, C., and M. West (2011), 'The Adult Attachment Projective Picture System: Integrating Attachment into Clinical Assessment', *Journal of Personality Assessment*, 93 (5): 407–16.

Gonzales, G., E. L. de Mola, K. A. Gavulic, T. McKay and C. Purcell (2020), 'Mental Health Needs among Lesbian, Gay, Bisexual, and Transgender College Students during the COVID-19 Pandemic', *Journal of Adolescent Health*, 67 (5): 645–8.

Hadley, R. A. (2018), Ageing without Children, Gender and Social Justice', in *Ageing, Diversity and Equality: Social Justice Perspectives*, 66–81, London: Routledge.

Hauser, S. T., and J. P. Allen (2006), 'Overcoming Adversity in Adolescence: Narratives of Resilience', *Psychoanalytic Inquiry*, 26 (4): 546–76.

Hayaki, C., K. Anno, M. Shibata, R. Iwaki, H. Kawata, N. Sudo and M. Hosoi (2016), 'Family Dysfunction', *Medicine*, 95 (49): e5495.

Health Resources and Services Administration (2017), *Definition of Family*, https://www.hrsa.gov/get-health-care/affordable/hill-burton/family.html.

Heino, E., N. Ellonen and R. Kaltiala (2021), 'Transgender Identity Is Associated with Bullying Involvement among Finish Adolescents', *Frontiers in Psychology: Gender, Sex and Sexualities*, 8 January, https://doi.org/10.3389.fpsyg.2020.612424.

Houmans, G. C. (1958), 'Social Behavior as Exchange', *American Journal of Sociology*, 63 (6): 597–606.

Ibsen, C. A., and P. Klobus (1972), 'Fictive Kin Term Use and Social Relationships: Alternative Interpretations', *Journal of Marriage and Family*, 34 (4): 615–20.

Jain, R. (2021), 'The Life of Transgender's Is Characterized by Pain, Atrocities, Discrimination, Stigma, State of Being Ostracized Opines Transgender Rights Activist Laxmi Narayan Tripathi', *Socio Story*, https://www.sociostory.org/impact-stories/the-life-of-transgenders-is-characterized-by-pain-atrocities-discriminat ion-stigma-state-of-being-ostracized-opines-transgender-rights-activist-laxmi-nara yan-tripathi. Accessed 15 April 2023.

Juster, R. P., M. B. de Torre, P. Kerr, S. Kheloui, M. Rossi and O. Bourdon (2019), 'Sex Differences and Gender Diversity in Stress Responses and Allostatic Load among Workers and LGBT People', *Current Psychiatry Reports*, 21 (11): 110.

Katz-Wise, S. L., M. Rosario and M. Tsappis (2017), 'LGBT Youth and Family Acceptance', *Pediatric Clinics of North America*, 63 (6): 1011–25.

Kessler, R. C., G. Andrews, D. Mrockel, T. B. Ustanand H. U. Wittchen (1998), 'The World Health Organization Composite International Diagnostic Interview', Summary, http://www.hcp.med.harvard.edu/wmhcidi/ftpdir_public/KesslerUstu n_WMHCIDI_IJMPR%202004.pdf.

Krause, N. (2005), 'Negative Interaction and Heart Disease in Late Life: Exploring Variations by Socioeconomic Status', *Journal of Aging Health*, 17: 28–55.

Lincoln, K. D., R. J. Taylor, K. M. Bullard, L. M. Chatters, J. A. Himle, A. T. Woodward and J. S. Jackson (2010), 'Emotional Support, Negative Interaction and DSM IV Lifetime Disorders among Older African Americans: Findings from the National Survey of American Life (NSAL)', *International Journal of Geriatric Psychiatry*, 25 (6): 612–21.

Lubben, J., M. Gironda, E. Sabbath, J. Kong and C. Johnson (2017), 'Social Isolation Presents a Grand Challenge for Social Work', *American Academy of Social Work and Social Welfare*, https://grandchallengesforsocialwork.org/wp-content/uplo ads/2015/12/WP7-with-cover.pdf.

Ma, Q., L. Meng and Q. Shen (2015), 'You Have My Word: Reciprocity Expectation Modulates Feedback-Related Negativity in the Trust Game', *PLOS ONE*, 10 (2): 1–10.

McEwen, B. S., and E. Stellar (1993), 'Stress and the Individual Mechanisms Leading to Disease', *Archives of Internal Medicine*, 153: 2093–101.

Mallon, G. P., and T. DeCrescenzo (2006), *Transgender Children and Youth: A Child Welfare Practice Perspective*, Child Welfare League of America, http://itgl.lu/wp-cont ent/uploads/2015/04/mallon_transgender_adolesents.pdf.

Martin, D., and M. Martin (2000), 'Understanding Dysfunctional and Functional Family Behaviors for the At-Risk Adolescent', *Adolescence*, 35 (140): 785–92.

Meerwijk, E. L., and J. M. Sevelius (2017), 'Transgender Population Size in the United States: A Meta-Regression of Population-Based Probability Samples', *American Journal of Public Health*, 107 (2): e1–e8.

Meyer, I. H. (2003), 'Prejudice, Social Stress, and Mental Health in Lesbian, Gay, and Bisexual Populations: Conceptual Issues and Research Evidence', *Psychological Bulletin*, 129 (5): 674.

Minkin, R., and A. Brown (2021), 'Rising Shares of US Adults Know Someone Who Is Transgender or Goes by Gender-Neutral Pronouns', *Pew Research Center*, 27.

National Association of Social Workers (2013), *Case Management Standards*, New York: National Association of Social Workers.

National Association of Social Workers (2021), *Code of Ethics*, New York: National Association of Social Workers.

Nelson, M. K. (2014), 'Whither Fictive Kin? Or, What's in a Name?', *Journal of Family Issues*, 35 (2): 201–22.

Newen, A. (2018), 'The Embodied Self, the Pattern Theory of Self, and the Predictive Mind', *Frontiers in Psychology*, 9 (2270).

Perlman, H. H. (1968), *Persona: Social Role and Personality*, Chicago: University of Chicago Press.

Pharr, J. R. (2021), 'Health Disparities among Lesbian, Gay, Bisexual, Transgender, and Nonbinary Adults 50 Years Old and Older in the United States', *LGBT Health*, 8 (7), published online, https://www.liebertpub.com/doi/abs/10.1089/lgbt.2021.0009?jour nalCode=lgbt. Accessed 1 July 2022.

Potvin, L., C. Ragan and E. Root (2021), '"My Whole Life Has Been Coming Out of One Closet or Another": Narratives of Transgender Youth in Cape Breton Regional Municipality', in K. Carter and J. Brunton (eds), *Transnarratives. Scholarly and Creative Works on Transgender Experience*, 13–24, London: Women's Press.

Proctor, J. (2021), 'Anti-transgender Legislation and the Politics of Patriarchy. The Gender Policy Report', University of Michigan, https://genderpolicyreport.umn.edu/ anti-transgender-legislation-and-the-politics-of-patriarchy/. Accessed 1 July 2022.

Quinn, V. P., R. Nash, E. Hunkeler, R. Contreras, L. Cromwell, T. A. Becerra-Culqui, D. Getahun, S. Giammettei, T. Lash, A. Millman, B. Robinson, D. Roblin, M. J. Silverberg, J. Slovis, V. Tangpricha, D. Tolsma, C. Valentine, K. Ward, S. Winter and M. Goodman (2017), 'Cohort Profile: Study of Transition, Outcomes and Gender (STRONG) to Assess Health Status of Transgender People', *BMJ Open*, 7 (12): 18–21.

Rimes, K. A., N. Goodship, G. Ussher, D. Baker and E. West (2019), 'Non-binary and Binary Transgender Youth: Comparison of Mental Health, Self-Harm, Suicidality, Substance Use and Victimization Experiences', *International Journal of Transgenderism*, 20 (2–3): 230–40.

Sharma, R. (2013), 'The Family and Family Structure Classification Redefined for the Current Times', *Journal of Family Medicine and Primary Care*, 2 (4): 306–10.

Spirzzirri, G., R. Eufásio, M. C. P. Lima, H. de Carvalho Nunes, B. P. C. Kruekels, T. D. Steensma and C. H. Najjar Abdo (2021), 'Proportion of People Identified as Transgender and Non-binary Gender in Brazil', *Scientific Reports*, 11 (2240), https:// doi.org/10.1038/s41598-021-81411-4.

Stinchcombe, A., K. Kortes-Miller and K. Wilson (2016), 'Support Needs of Lesbian, Gay, Bisexual, and Transgender Older Adults in the Health and Social Environment', *Counseling et spiritualité/Counselling and Spirituality*, 35 (1): 13–29.

Substance Abuse and Mental Health Services Administration (2019), *Risk and Protective Factors*, https://www.samhsa.gov/sites/default/files/20190718-samhsa-risk-protect ive-factors.pdf.

Thorne, N., A. Kam-Tuck, W. P. Bouman, E. Marshall and J. Arcelus (2019), 'The Terminology of Identities between, Outside, and beyond the Gender

Binary – A Systematic Review', *International Journal of Transgenderism*, 20 (2–3): 138–54.

Trujillo, M. A., P. B. Perrin, M. Sutter, A. Tabaac and E. G. Benotsch (2017), 'The Buffering Role of Social Support on the Associations among Discrimination, Mental Health, and Suicidality in a Transgender Sample', *The International Journal of Transgenderism*, 18 (1): 39–52.

United States Census Bureau (2021), *First Ever Census Report Highlights Growing Childless Older Adult Population*, 31 August, https://www.census.gov/newsroom/press-releases/2021/childless-olderadultpopulation.html#:~:text=Of%20all%20adults%20ages%2055,those%2075%20years%20and%20older.&text=About%2022.1%20million%20adults%2055,whom%206.1%20million%20were%20childless.

United Nations (1948), *The Universal Declaration of Human Rights*, Author.

United Nations (2017), *Basic Facts about the United Nations* (42nd ed.), Author.

United Nations (2017), *Free & Equal. Transgender*, https://www.unfe.org/wp-content/uploads/2017/05/UNFE-Transgender.pdf.

Von Doussa, H., J. Power and D. W. Riggs (2017), 'Family Matters: Transgender and Gender Diverse Peoples' Experiences with Family When They Transition', *Journal of Family Studies*, 26 (2): 1–14.

Wareham, J. (2020), 'New Report Shows Where It's Illegal to Be Transgender in 2020', 30 September, *Forbes*.

Waters, E., C. E. Hamilton and N. S. Weinfield (2000), 'The Stability of Attachment Security from Infancy to Adolescence to Early Adulthood: General Introduction', *Child Development*, 71 (3): 678–83.

Wesselmann, E. D., E. R. DeSouza, S. AuBuchon, C. Bebel and L. Parris (2021), 'Investigating Microaggressions against Transgender Individuals as a Form of Social Exclusion', *Psychology of Sexual Orientation and Gender Diversity*, Advance Online Publication, https://doi.org/10.1037/sgd0000513.

White, R. G., A. J. LeBlanc, I. H. Meyer and F. A. Harig (2015), 'Internalized Gay Ageism, Mattering, and Depressive Symptoms among Midlife and Older Gay-Identified Men', *Social Science and Medicine*, 147: 200–8.

Winek, J. L. (2010), *Systemic Family Therapy: From Theory to Practice*, Thousand Oaks, CA: Sage Publications.

World Health Organization (1978), 'Health and Family. Studies on the Demography of Family Life Cycles', *World Health Organization*, https://apps.who.int/iris/bitstream/handle/10665/40336/16937_eng.pdf?sequence=1.

World Health Organization (2021), *Family and Community Practices That Support Child Survival, Growth and Development* (ISBN: 9241591501).

9

# Family Practices and Strategies of Middle-class Teachers in Argentina in the Context of Covid-19: Transformations and Discomforts in the Face of Care Processes and Labour Relations

Leila M. Passerino and Denise Zenklusen

## Introduction

The Covid-19 pandemic that apparently started in December 2019 in Wuhan, China, and spread quickly to every continent, resulted in the most significant global disruptive episode of the twenty-first century up to its inception. The pandemic impacted every aspect of society including economic, social, cultural, health and family; it consequently exposed the various underlying influences in political decision-making. In the Argentine context, the first measures taken by the national government date back to July 2020. By December 2020, the mandatory lockdown was decreed (ASPO – by its Spanish acronym) to prevent the circulation and spread of the virus. By means of the decree in July 2020, everyone was required to remain in their usual residences, abstain from going to their places of work and from moving through public roads, ways and spaces. However, it was necessary to create a category of *emergency* services, tasks or functions that were exempted from the said lockdown. Some of these services or emergency tasks were: health personnel, security forces, armed forces, higher authorities of the national, provincial, municipal governments, personnel of the justice services on duty, persons who assist others with disabilities including family members in need of assistance; personnel working in communication services, wholesale and retail supermarkets and retail stores, pharmacies, workers who maintain basic services such as water, electricity, gas, communications and so on; and essential services including: security, cleaning and guard services, public transportation, home delivery of food, medicines, hygiene products, cleaning products and other necessary supplies.

The lockdown period was also marked by different moments. Initially, there was *Stage 1 – Strict lockdown* when there was borders and trade closure and restrictions such as movement control. All entertainment, sports, cultural, religious and political events were cancelled, and in-person classes were suspended in schools all over the country. From 12 to 26 April 2020, *Stage 2 – Administrative lockdown* started, during which, although lockdown was still in place, more tasks were exempted from the obligation of remaining at home. In this second stage, the provincial governments could implement new exemptions, within the framework of their territorial competence, under the recommendations of the provincial health authority and according to the epidemiological and sanitary situation.

During these phases, education was not acknowledged as an essential activity, and it was one of the most affected sectors because of the closure of schools, institutes and universities. Nevertheless, this did not necessarily imply the suspension of educational and teaching activities. This unprecedented situation required adjusting teaching processes, making decisions in each institution, creating resources and enabling non-extended or unusual modalities so that children, young people and students could continue with the learning process. Undoubtedly, there were numerous situations and difficulties that arose during the course of this process, in terms of pedagogy, access and inequalities that marked the context. The absence of workspaces in homes was one of the difficulties encountered as well as access, management and planning for other teaching modalities (Becher 2020; Gluz et al. 2021; Pavesio 2020).

The situation of teachers in the context of the pandemic also had a strong impact and acquired different characteristics throughout the development of the stages. This, in turn, is a product of the dispositions and decisions of each educational institution. In this scenario, it is important to recover some data from the National Survey 'Health and Teacher's Working Conditions during the Covid-19 Sanitary Emergency' carried out by the Confederation of Education Workers of the Argentine Republic (CTERA, by its Spanish acronym) during May–June 2020. The goal of the survey was to acknowledge and show the teachers' perspective regarding their working conditions in the context of world sanitary emergency and of social lockdown at a national level and provide some data about it. The sample covered a total of 15,634 teachers of all levels and modalities of the twenty-four jurisdictions of the country. Results showed that 80 per cent of the teachers claimed to have devoted more time to work than when they delivered in-person classes. Likewise, 65 per cent of the total number of interviewees lived with children or teenagers in their care (CTERA 2020). This shows that the pandemic context did not only lead to an increase in the tasks and time allocated, but that these also joined, overlapped and demanded specific strategies to articulate paid teaching work with unpaid or care work, with transformations in family dynamics and arrangements.

After a year of ASPO, and because the epidemiological situation was heterogeneous in the national territory, the state introduced a new modality for the management of the pandemic that considered: the different impact on the dynamics of virus transmission; the geographic, socio-economic and demographic diversity of each jurisdiction in the country, linked to the increased autonomy regarding the decisions taken in each of them. On 13 March 2021, almost a year after ASPO, Decree 168/2021 ruled the Social, Preventive and Mandatory Distancing (DISPO, by its Spanish acronym), whose main goal was to recover the social and economic functioning, especially in those areas where there was no virus transmission.

In this new stage, the Federal Council of Education (organism of concertation, agreement and coordination of the Argentine national education policy) passed, in February 2021, resolutions No. 386 and No. 387 that defined the general guidelines for the in-person return to school for the 2021 school cycle. Specifically, in the province of Santa Fe, the Ministry of Education allowed a model of *full in-person classes*, as long as the security measures contemplated in the protocol could be met and *combined in-person classes* with virtual classes when classrooms did not have enough space (due to social distancing).

Santa Fe is one of the twenty-three provinces that are part of the Argentine republic. It is located in the north-west, and it borders to the north with Chaco, to the east with the Paraná River that separates it from Corrientes and Entre Ríos, to the south with the province of Buenos Aires and to the west with the provinces of Córdoba and Santiago del Estero. With around 3,195,000 inhabitants in 2010, it is the third most populated jurisdiction – after the provinces of Buenos Aires and Córdoba.

The return to in-person classes forced the provincial state to consider education workers as *strategic*, that is, to position teachers as people who perform important and necessary management functions for the executive branch and have an increased risk of exposure in their in-person tasks (Resolution 712/2021, Ministry of Health of the Nation). This, in turn, had an impact on the sanitary decisions regarding priorities, for example, related to the vaccination scheme. In Santa Fe, education workers (kindergarten, elementary and secondary levels) constituted a strategic group prioritized for vaccinations, followed by health personnel and adults older than seventy years.

Having introduced some contextual aspects that contribute to understanding how the teaching activity is positioned in the period marked by the emergence of ASPO and the continuity of DISPO until December 2021, this chapter investigates the family practices and strategies of female education workers, particularly teachers in the province of Santa Fe in Argentina.

This research is based on a qualitative fieldwork based on a corpus of five in-depth interviews and fifteen semi-structured interviews with middle-class heterosexual female teachers of different marital status (married, separated, cohabiting with their partners), with children under twelve years of age in the province of Santa Fe, Argentina. The choice of heterosexual women seeks to reflect on a family model that continues to be the hegemonic one, although other possible dynamics and links are not ignored. In the next section, we will cover some points in this regard.

At the time of the fieldwork, all the women interviewed had formal jobs in public or private educational institutions, which allowed for a certain economic stability during the first stage of isolation and in some cases the support of family life in the case of single mothers or partners who lost their jobs. Teleworking as a predominant modality in teaching was also a way to guarantee the care of children who remained in confinement, given that many of interviewed women partners were considered 'essential' due their occupations and this necessarily implied 'leaving' their homes. In other cases, the presence of other family members, such as grandparents, made it possible to share or lessen the burden of care. However, it should be noted that this figure was also controversial and a matter of debate within each of the families, as the elderly were considered to be at risk, which is why for many of them 'care' implied their confinement, and the impossibility of delegating care tasks.

The fieldwork was conducted during the ASPO and DISPO stage (2020–21). This implied a series of methodological challenges linked, fundamentally, to the restrictions on the mobility of people. That is, the conditions to produce scientific knowledge were different from those prior to the pandemic. For example, we could not meet *face to face* with the people being interviewed. This led to the creation and use of a series of tools – linked to the use of technology – that we were not aware of or did not contemplate until then. For this work we adopted two strategies. On the one hand, the semi-structured interviews were conducted by WhatsApp during the height of the pandemic (ASPO), which coincided with the start of classes and the readaptation to remote teaching by teachers. During this stage, women with whom we worked encountered some difficulties – such as lack of time and space – to have a 'calm' video call. Based on the elaboration of a script, we shared through WhatsApp messages a series of questions that were answered via voice messages. This made it easier for them to answer at any time of the day, whenever they considered it appropriate and even while doing other activities related to their work or care work.

As a second strategy, for the in-depth interviews we arranged video calls made via the Meet platform. These interviews, which required synchronous time and sought to capture some sentiments and feelings about the experience, were conducted during the DISPO stage, when many of the women had already returned to their jobs in person, which implied a different use of time and space. The video calls allowed time to listen, to exchange and dialogue with the women, to observe their gestures and even to get to know the spaces in their houses and their distribution in relation to the workspaces. With the informants' permission, the interviews were recorded for transcription and subsequent analysis.

The exchanges were developed using the 'snowball' method; it was the key informants who engaged other women. From the empirical material collected, we favoured a methodological strategy and an analysis that would allow us to identify the diversity of experiences and practices developed by women teachers during the pandemic.

We have mostly based our testimonies on women, since they represent the highest percentage of people devoted to teaching tasks, variable according to the level. At the same time, the care of the households, children, the sick, the disabled or the elderly had fallen to a greater extent on the women of each family. As expressed in some reports, women in charge of children under twelve years of age were the most affected by the fall in economic activity due to the increase in caregiving tasks, as a consequence of health measures in response to the pandemic (ELA 2022). For this reason, in the first section we make reference to gender inequalities, limitations for work development and the worries and discomforts that mediate the experiences lived in the context of the pandemic crisis and that appear in the normative construction of the family. In the second stage, we focus more specifically on the practices, feelings and family strategies developed to sustain teaching activities, as well as care and family dynamics. We delve into the transformations and the ways in which they assumed the movements and vicissitudes that occurred in the health, institutional and teaching context both at national and provincial levels. In order to do so, we took up the family's own experiences, strategies and mechanisms, discomforts and difficulties that were reported during that period.

## Family, care relations and professional practices. Theoretical approaches

The experience initiated in the Covid-19 context in Argentina entailed transformations in the working relations and in the processes of care, which provoked disruptions and changes in the family practices. As a starting point, it is also necessary to mention that the pandemic context deepened the unequal distribution of care tasks inside families (Rosas 2020), with repercussions and consequences mainly for women, thus our interest in this aspect.

In the education field, teaching has been challenging due to the tensions and the (over)demands of paid and unpaid work. It was an activity that, having exposed the gender division of domestic and care work, now appeared with greater intensity with the consequences of the pandemic impacting the family arrangements themselves.

Teaching in Argentina is a highly feminized profession. According to Morgade (2020), the female presence in kindergartens is almost total, representing 99 per cent of the professionals; it is very strong in the elementary level, where it represents 90 per cent of the teaching staff and it is reduced in the secondary level, where two out of three teachers are women. These data can be related to other information, considering the already mentioned survey (CTERA 2020), in which it is expressed that 84 per cent are in charge of family and domestic work. Those who are in charge of children and teenagers, 65 per cent of the total, expressed that the combination with household and family tasks was *problematic*.

The numerical expression makes visible more than a quantitative distribution and gives us some clues to understand why the main consequences of the pandemic have had a strong impact on women in at least two dimensions. On the one hand, there are difficulties in combining teaching work with domestic and family chores and demands, on the other, difficulties are expressed in their personal working conditions (Duhalde et al. 2021), not only regarding the lack of technological equipment – which constituted a material aspect that reproduces evident inequality – but also regarding their personal working conditions, the performance of the tasks, considering spaces and time, inside the households.

The issue of continuity in the education sphere has had various consequences, but, as Morgade rightfully states: 'The pedagogical continuity promoted as a policy during the lock-down has been, then, a feminized task' (2020: 54), related to the responsibilities of catering, recognizing others, caring. This imperative of 'continuity', somewhat empty with respect to what, how and under what assumptions it is constructed, was associated, as described by Dussel (2020), to another slogan referring to 'not losing the school year'. The initial tendency was to distribute tasks to occupy the workday and also to be protected against criticism of teacher neglect (Dussel 2020). During the pandemic education process, there were changes and decisions *along the way*, according to the national measures and the international echoes. What emerged was the difficulty in creating conditions remotely for the appropriation of the school curriculum, the rhythms, the manners, the differences that are part of this subjective and collective construction. These aspects, as they appeared in our fieldwork, were often toned down and denied by the excessive emphasis placed on technology and the lack of access to it. In the words of Zelmanovich (2020), this constituted a political answer to the *great hole* we had to experience as a society, with paradoxical effects. Thus, *pedagogical continuity* overlapped with *continuity in the family*, resulting in an imperative hard to conciliate, where 'the moving to the domestic would not be a change in the sociocultural hierarchies, but a reproduction' (Dussel 2020: 6).

In this instance it is important to make some theoretical disquisitions regarding how to understand the interrelations between family, care relationships and professional teaching practices, so as to denature and problematize some implications of these bonds that will be shown and analysed in the next section.

The family is conceptualized by Jelin's (2005) study as a social organization, a micro cosmos of production relations, reproduction and distribution, with its own structure of power and components of ideological and affective order, within a gender relations system. Although there is no single family model and the heterosexual model is only one way of thinking about possible links, it has prevailed as a sexist system of care (Jelin 2021). Hence, the need to analyse it in order to transform in light of the claims made by feminist and sexual diversity discourses.

It is important here to stress several issues. First, the productive-reproductive component is important to understand how the domestic and care work within the families articulates capitalism and patriarchy because it is a method – most of the times internalized and made invisible – that guarantees the support of the family organization itself and the economic activity as a productive dimension. Located in a stratum of scarce social recognition, the reproductive aspect is characterized by the feminization and control over women's lives. However, the emotional plot has proved to be an extremely powerful way of ordering and assuming greater margins of responsibility. As Jelin emphasizes, 'in the occidental modern paradigm, the social expectation is that family bonds are based on affection and mutual care' (2005: 41).

The family, particularly in the hegemonic heterosexual model, is sustained on a system of gender relations and their expressions. It is never an isolated institution, reduced to the sphere of what is private/domestic, but it shares political and cultural patterns that support it. This applies to introducing the dimension of care in sustaining family life and the link with female participation in the labour force, two aspects that are problematic. Although it is not the subject of this chapter, it is worth mentioning that in single-parent families with dependent children, the drop in labour activity during the pandemic was 70 per cent greater than that of other women (Tuchin 2021).

Since the 1980s, the fight for equality with men has been taking place in a context of growing social inequality; income polarization, privileges on the one side, more misery and marginality on the other and effects of a crisis that affects both genders, although in an unequal way. Caring for others is not unrelated to the opportunities and to the personal development and access to the professional framework for women, but they adapt to wider contexts and structural inequalities, none more so than during the pandemic.

During the beginning of the pandemic in Argentina, care took a central place in the public and communicational agenda, by directly appealing to the instruction to 'stay home' and related to 'we take care of each other'. It assumed a central place and inevitably brought a drastic change in people's daily life within the family framework, as well as in the local space and in the neighbourhood (Passerino and Trupa 2020). Given the exceptional situation, the first period of 'stay home' was a 'trial' for many of the interviewed families, who, through necessity, created new ways of relating to one another. There are many testimonies of those first moments when the difficulties of carrying out care in the context of lockdown with little children were shown to be considerable.

In Tronto's terms, care constitutes a ubiquitous element in human life; 'the set of activities by which we act to organize our world, so that we can live in it the best way possible' (2009: 14). This central and omnipresent activity, as the author mentions, assumed during the pandemic a place with higher visibility, though that is not necessarily translated into an assessment of its implications and the costs or consequences on human bodies. During non-pandemic times many of the familiar obligations and responsibilities were undertaken by people who did not necessarily share the home, especially in highly privileged households, where those obligations and responsibilities were given over to paid caregivers such as nannies or cleaners.

The family and domestic organization was a central element mainly assumed by women. If we also look at structural data, women are the ones who mostly perform this task. The 2014 survey of the National Institute of Statistics and Census of Argentina (INDEC, by its Spanish acronym) published the 'Survey on Unpaid Work and Use of Time', which concluded that women in Argentina devote an average of almost 6 hours a day to unpaid care work – including household chores, care of dependent people and school support – against 2 hours that men devote to these tasks each day. So, 'if during "normality" women carry out most of the unpaid domestic chores – 76% according to this survey – it is not surprising that when the health crisis forces us to retire into the domestic space, the unequal structure becomes evident and accentuated' (Passerino and Trupa 2020: 137). Furthermore, if we focus on the existing literature (Batthyány 2020; O'Reilly 2020; Rosseau 2020), women with children have faced, during the pandemic, a double if not triple work increase. Confinement has not been a solution for the already inexistent inequalities; on the contrary, it has reinforced them.

The care dimension, however, is not isolated but closely related to the transformations at a working level. This is an aspect that has intensified in families in the context of the pandemic. Although women have increased their resources and their cultural capital, these work patterns related to gender were not accompanied by meaningful changes in the domestic and care spheres: 'There aren't major "domestic revolutions" that imply shared domestic responsibilities' (Jelin 2005: 51). These aspects have generated more gender inequalities during the pandemic in heterosexual families.

## Family practices and strategies of female education workers

As we have mentioned, the family practices and strategies are part of larger contexts. The pandemic has worked in this direction as a peculiar instance, altering and changing routines, restructuring and producing transformations in the pre-existent dynamics. In this section we focus on these aspects that could be reconstructed from the testimony of the women teachers interviewed. We considered the space and temporal dimensions, as turning points that allow us to notice the transformations that take place and mediate the working relationships with the care dynamics and family arrangements. Thus, we refer to: (1) The blurring between domestic space and workspace and (2) the transformations in the teaching organization and conditions.

## (1) Blurring between domestic space and workspace

The pandemic has brought with it a 'blurring' of borders between the education or paid workspace and the domestic one, which manifested in difficulties for the self-development of teaching tasks. Housing conditions were among the first aspects taken into consideration. Most of the people interviewed did not have houses with spaces suitable for professional work specifically. Mercedes states 'and now we are here, and also with my partner working full time, there is a kind of struggle for the spaces, the timetable, that at the beginning was a bit chaotic' (Mercedes, thirty-four years old, with a two-year-old child, secretary and teacher at a tertiary institute).

Also, the fact that teaching tasks were carried out at their own homes also represented an intrusion, somehow: 'Video-conferences from home are a window to our private life, a space that used to belong to our strict intimacy' (Orsini 2020). This blurring of borders brought with it discomfort for the development of the activity itself, such as Victoria mentioned:

> The first month we didn't see anyone, they [her daughters] were used to spending time with their grandparents a lot and it was difficult. The youngest one interrupted the scheduled classes a lot. For me it was embarrassing listening to her shouting 'teat, teat' so I breastfed her. Always making sure it did not appear on camera. I was afraid of being recorded. During those first months, there wasn't much of a schedule, we did what we could (Victoria, thirty-one years old, two children, four and two years old, middle-level and university teacher).

Facing an uncertain horizon, educational institutions at every level required that space in the house should be transformed into an improvised office, and the timetable became a fragmented function that often overlapped with the household chores. The combination itself of teaching work with caregiving, assistance and presence of family members generated numerous difficulties in the attempt to 'reconcile' this overlap. Soledad said:

> You can't work, honestly, you can't work because they demand a lot of time from you, and you need someone to look at them and to take care of them. Or you have to stop working, one of those options, I don't know … That is my main difficulty, who is taking care of her, who is looking at her. (Soledad, thirty-four years old, elementary-level teacher, four-month-old daughter)

As teaching became located in the domestic domain, teachers looked for corners, times and working routines in unprepared, shared and disputed spaces. The resulting difficulties are observed in countless of our interviewees' stories:

# Strategies of Middle-Class Teachers

I live with my husband who has to work from home, in the living-room. The day is hard, if I have to define it. Although we are both at home, we have to deal with many situations, and every day or in our daily life we delegate those tasks. In my case I have to assist my children, cook, clean, plan the classes, correct papers, continue planning, and, on top of that, collaborate with our parents who are old. (Agustina, thirty-four years old, secondary-level teacher, children five-year-old and twenty-month-old)

It can be said that the continuity between family and school reinforces the need and importance of separating spaces. Zelmanovich (2020) explained why institutions are important and the need to have rules such as spatio-temporal delimitations. In her words, knowing the difficulties, discomforts and dilemmas they represent, they are also the boundaries from where to carry out, delimit and set, at least up to a certain point, professional practices. The presence of the institutions is a border between home and work that divides not only space, but also time, the time devoted to teaching. Many of our interviewees pointed out that this issue interferes in a harmful way with their disposition to care and to be present for their children, in this case, under their charge:

The days I'm working from home are a problem because, my house is my home, I don't bring work tasks home. My house is my family's temple. So, I refuse to let my children to be involved with certain things that belong to the world of adults. Besides, they do not understand that you are there, but you are not there *for them*. (Clarisa, thirty-six years old, secondary-level teacher, children five and two years old)

The presence of the institutions also acts as an organizing and facilitating center for the exchange among colleagues. Sharing time and spaces contributes to collectively channel the emerging issues that in the domestic setting have remained, in many cases, individualized, subject to the individual possibilities and scope for their resolution. In this process, they have also been depoliticized and left at the mercy of the teacher's 'goodwill' or personal circumstances.

Finally, the 'blurring' between the workplace and home has resulted in feelings of discomfort, alongside the pressures and abrupt transformations in the routines and ways of living, as well as the distress associated with the possible consequences of Covid-19 in people's health. Anxieties and fears about the health of family members exacerbated the strain placed on family dynamics.

There were significant consequences where the borders between work and the domestic environment disappeared. Our interviewees reported that men assumed a 'helping' role at home, but most stopped short of assuming full responsibility for caregiving, as Dani states:

> Fortunately, Dani helps a lot at home. He has no problem tidying up, putting things in order, taking care of the children. He is at a pause at work, but … he is always doing something, he gets entertained. (Valeria, thirty-four years old, elementary-level teacher, children six and three years old)

It is worth mentioning that in separated or single-parent families, this situation has worsened for women, who more often than not assume full responsibility for caregiving and increase the number of hours invested in it.

## (2) Transformations in the teaching organization and conditions

As we saw in the previous section, the transformation of the physical space produced a blurring of the border between the domestic space and the workspace. Simultaneously, there was a change in the use of time. The intensification of the school 'workday' exponentially increased the hours devoted to teaching. As Dussel points out: 'These are exhausting times, of permanent connection, work intensification, constant fatigue' (Dussel 2020: 342). In the interviews, participants observed that time assumed a new dimension that crossed the everyday family and working life:

> The worst part is having to be available all day long, in different ways, whether by phone or in the various media platforms, or on the computer. We have found ourselves answering work stuff at strange times. During atypical days: holidays, weekends. (Manuela, thirty-seven years old, university professor, four-year-old son)
>
> As for work, what I have noticed is that the time limits are erased. I work when I can, where I can. … From 8 am up to 11 pm I receive messages from students, projects, homework, questions, requests to explain the assignments again. There are no Saturdays, there are no Sundays, there are no holidays. (Agustina, thirty-four years old, secondary-level teacher, children five years old and twenty months old)

The interviewees pointed out that they had to sustain long working days to ensure teaching; this situation blurred the boundaries between working time and rest time. Many of them found themselves answering messages at any moment of the day, participating in multiple virtual meetings – even in holidays – planning activities and taking training courses online to handle

Strategies of Middle-Class Teachers          161

virtual platforms, preparing specific material for the new format. It was a time of permanent connectivity when the new ways of technological subjection exposed the consequences of teleworking without legislation and the strong impact it had in the teaching practice.

> I believe now more than ever we, teachers, are putting our bodies into it. The hours demanded by planning, evaluating, correcting through virtual schooling are not the same as the ones demanded by in-person classes. I think that this has to do mainly with the fact that we were not ready to face a situation like this. (Amelia, thirty-six years old, secondary-level teacher, four-year-old daughter and pregnant)

> During the first day I thought I was going to explode, I couldn't deal with *that* much! Then I adjusted: I set apart two specific days a week for communicating with my students and I handed out corrections the following week. I would send the activities through the parents' WhatsApp group, and I would answer questions only at the time we used to have classes in person. Otherwise, it was crazy! Parents don't look at a clock, and they ask about homework at 11 pm. (Paula, thirty years old, elementary-level teacher, one-year-old daughter)

In view of this situation, some teachers – as we can see in Paula's comments – deployed strategies – such as setting timetables – that, in the end, aimed at redefining that border, establishing a certain order in an overwhelming context.

Another dimension that arises along with the usage of time are the material working conditions. Some teachers pointed out that at home they only had one computer that they had to share with their partners or children. That implied having to work at different times, sometimes, at night or in the early hours of the morning, which meant higher weariness or fewer hours of rest. As Mercedes said: 'For a lot of work, I had to get organized and work during the early hours of the day. Everything is chaos, the family organization is upside-down, so, trying to figure out how to cope' (Mercedes, thirty-four years old, secretary and teacher at a tertiary institute, two-year-old daughter).

Finally, the interviewees expressed concern that there were new challenges and new responsibilities related to work. Those who worked at schools that serve breakfast, tea or *cups of milk* (the term for establishments that provide food for children in need) said that they had to go to the institutions to deliver the bags of food every fifteen days. In addition, teachers visited students from low-income families to deliver or take school material. As Mara's testimony shows, it was an effort sustaining the bond between the teacher and the student, especially with no in-person classes:

> The same thing happens to us as teachers, we try to generate that contention, but since we do not have experience and all the virtual world moves us from our working comfort zone, because our work is more related to presence learning, that is also hard. But yes, in my opinion there was an over-demand. (Mara, forty-three years old, tertiary- and secondary-levels teacher, four-year-old son)

As we have said, this time management in the pandemic increased the number of hours devoted to caring tasks for women, which is not proportional to the case of men (Faur 2020). This situation was intensified in the cases of couples where, for example, one of its members takes on an 'essential' task and is required to attend the workplace. As testimonies express:

> My husband works a lot of hours a day, he is a doctor, essential worker, and is never here to help me with the girl's things, or to cook for her, to take care of her ... In my case my husband continues working out of the house, he is not teleworking, so I am alone with her every day 24/7 and that is remarkable, I cannot replace it, I cannot be at video conferences because it is very hard for me to organize the time schedules now that she is not at school or nursery, or with her grandmas who are the ones that would normally help me when I have to go to work ... . I see that there are much more obstacles than advantages in working at home. (Amelia, thirty-six years old, secondary-level teacher, four-year-old daughter and pregnant)

In short, working organization and conditions were affected by gender-based inequalities in the case of women teachers. Sustaining the commitment to teach alongside new caring responsibilities, rhythms and demands in the home have had repercussions on women's bodies. Tiredness, stress, exhaustion and discomfort had, prior to the pandemic, been confined to a private domain within the family dynamics. It is worth politicizing and making these situations visible since, far from being exceptional, they are part of sociocultural processes, updated and intensified in pandemic contexts.

## Conclusions

The pandemic in Argentina highlighted the existent gender inequalities related to, in our case, responsibilities at home. In particular, the state did not acknowledge the teaching practice as an essential activity, although it represented one of the most affected sectors by the measures taken. In view of the closing of educational institutions, and with the aim of guaranteeing education, teaching was performed in a virtual learning modality and tasks, contents and resources had to be adapted. In this context, we emphasize that teaching did not accept discontinuities and was sustained within the homes simultaneously alongside family life.

From the field work with teachers in the province of Santa Fe (Argentina) we identified that the time and space dimensions were central to understand the way in which heterosexual women had to combine and sustain the professional practice with caregiving and reproducing the family life during lockdown. These combinations of tasks and responsibilities implied a spatial blurring that intensified one of the hardest and most invisible sides of inequality referred to the function of caregiving performed, mainly, by women.

From a more time-based perspective, there was a transformation in the teaching organization and conditions: increase in the hours devoted to work, demand for permanent connection, training for virtual learning and new responsibilities. This made the working conditions precarious and left the women who had to guarantee education, sustain the care and education of their children and perform the housework – all at the same time – fatigued.

The analysis of teachers' work in combination with the family dimension during the pandemic contributed here to evidence gender inequalities linked to certain limitations for work development, as well as the imperatives, concerns and discomforts that mediate the experiences initiated in the pandemic frame of reference. As we have expressed, the family is never an isolated institution, but it is sustained on a system of gender relations, under sociocultural and political patterns. Therefore, shared normative constructs are produced with a differential impact on heterosexual women that, far from contributing to more equitable family relationships and arrangements, have intensified and strengthened a sex division of unequal work based – particularly in a crisis moment such as the sanitary emergency – on the bodies of women in ways not always explicit.

In this sense, we take the proposal of Segato (2020) who, in one of her public interventions during the pandemic, warned that the power dispute will be over the narrative (Zelmanovich 2020). The performativity of narratives creates realities and views on processes. Here lies our interest in recovering testimonies and in making visible some of the ways in which inequalities and overload on women, teaching workers, have appeared and actively participated, not only in sustaining the education activity as a feminized practice, but also as caring support in the family dynamics and arrangements.

## Additional information

### Funding

This research was supported by (1) Research Project *Escolarización secundaria y ejercicio de la ciudadanía. Producciones escolares y prácticas de subjetivación docente en dos escuelas secundarias de la ciudad de Rafaela* (Ruling 438/2020, SITT-UNRaf); (2) Research Project *Pandemia, Pos-pandemia y vida cotidiana. Una aproximación etnográfica a las transformaciones sociales vividas en Rafaela y la región* (Ruling 449/2020, SITT-UNRaf) and (3) *Migrantes del sistema educativo: trayectorias académicas y relaciones con el(los) saber(es) de estudiantes de nivel superior* (Ruling 437/2020, SITT-UNRaf).

## References

Batthyány, K. (2020), 'The Pandemic Highlights and Reinforces the Crisis of Care, Thinking the Pandemic', Observatorio Social del Coronavirus, N° 1, CLACSO. Retrieved from: https://www.clacso.org/wp-content/uploads/2020/03/Karina-Batthyany.pdf. Accessed 5 April 2022.

Becher, P. A. (2020), 'Education in Times of Pandemic. Working Conditions and Perceptions about Virtual Teaching Work in the City of Bahía Blanca (Argentina)', *Revista Científica Educ@ção*, 4 (8): 922–45.

Castañeda Rentería, L. (2020), 'Women, Work and Pandemic. When the Atlantean Has a Woman's Body', in L. Soto, A. Daverio and N. Goren (eds), *Gender and (In)equalities. Tensions under Debate. Gender Inequalities in Times of Covid-19 in the Región no. 1*, 52–26, Buenos Aires: CLACSO.

Confederation of Education Workers of the Argentine Republic (CTERA) (2020), Annual Report. Buenos Aires.

Duhalde, L., D. Albergucci, A. Abal Medina and G. Martínez (2021), 'Situation of the Educational System and Teachers' Work in Argentina during the Pandemic', in D. Andrade Oliveira, E. Pereira Junior and A. M. Clementino (eds), *Teaching Work in Times of Pandemic: A Latin American Regional Overview*, 25–64, Brasília: IEAL/CNTE/Red Estrado, https://ei-ie-al.org/sites/default/files/docs/ebook-2-trabajo-docente-en-tiempos-de-pandemia-1.pdf.

Dussel, I. (2020), 'The Classroom in Slippers', in I. Dussel, P. Ferrante and D. Pulfer (eds), *Thinking Education in Times of Pandemic. Between Emergency, Commitment and Waiting*, 337–49, Buenos Aires: UNIPE. Editorial Universitaria.

Equipo Latinoamericano de Justicia y Género (ELA) (2022), Agenda Legislativa de Cuidado 2022, https://www.ela.org.ar/a2/objetos/adjunto.cfm?aplicacion=APP187&cnl=87&opc=53&codcontenido=4432&codcampo=20. Accessed 16 May 2022.

Faur, E. (2020), 'It Is a Myth that Men Take Care as Much as Women', *La Nación*, 11 May, https://www.lanacion.com.ar/comunidad/eleonor-faur-es-mito-varones-cuiden-tanto-nid2363981. Accessed 10 May 2022.

Gluz, N., M. D. Ochoa, V. Cáceres, V. Martínez del Sel and P. Sisti (2021), 'Pedagogical Continuity in Pandemic. A Study on the Intensification of Teaching Work in Contexts of Inequality', *Revista Iberoamericana de Educación*, 86 (1): 27–42.

Jelin, E. (2005), 'The Family in Argentina: Modernity, Economic Crisis and Political Action', in T. Valdés and X. Valdés (eds), *Family and Private Life: Transformations, Tensions, Resistances or New Meanings?*, 41–76, Santiago de Chile: FLACSO – Chile/CEDEM/UNFPA.

Jelin, E. (2021), 'The Family, a Model to Disarm', Página 12, 10 December, https://www.pagina12.com.ar/387548-la-familia-un-modelo-a-desarmar. Accessed 10 May 2022.

Morgade, G. (2020), 'The Pandemic and Women's Work in Focus: About "Care" as a Category and Axis of Policies', in I. Dussel, P. Ferrante and D. Pulfer (eds), *Thinking Education in Times of Pandemic. Between Emergency, Commitment and Waiting*, 53–62, Buenos Aires: UNIPE. Editorial Universitaria.

O'Reilly, A. (2020), 'Trying to Function in the Unfunctionable: Mothers and Covid-19', *Journal of the Motherhood Initiative*, 11 (1): 7–24.

Orsini, G. (2020), 'The Illusion of the Home Office, Riberas', 1 May, https://riberas.uner.edu.ar/la-ilusion-del-home-office/. Accessed 10 May 2022.

Passerino, L. M., and N. S. Trupa (2020), 'Experiences of Care and Work: Concerns, Discomfort and Emotions in the Context of the Covid-19 Pandemic in Argentina', *Revista Feminismos*, 8 (3): 134–48.

Pavesio, M. V. (2020), 'Teaching Work and Pandemic. A Socioanthropological Analysis of Teaching Experiences (Rosario, Argentina)', *Revista del IICE*, (48): 223–37.

Rosas, Carolina (2020), 'The (de)valorization of Paid Domestic Workers in Times of Pandemics', *Bordes, Revista de Política, Derecho y Sociedad*, 1–11.

Rosseau, S. (2020), 'Care Beyond Covid-19', in L. Soto, A. Daverio and N. Goren (eds), *Gender and (In)equalities. Tensions under Debate. Gender Inequalities in Times of Covid-19 in the Región no. 1*, 31–4, Buenos Aires: CLACSO.

Segato, R. (2020), Rita Segato analyzes the pandemic. Emerging (April 1, 2020), [Video] https://www.facebook.com/comunicacion.emergentes/videos/144417643677194/?v=144417643677194 (accessed 29 April 2022).

Tronto, J. (2009), *Moral Boundaries. A Political Argument for an Ethic of Care*, New York: Routledge.

Tuchin, F. (2021), 'The Stress, Juggling and Sacrifices of Women Raising Children alone While Working', *Redacción, Periodismo Humano*, 24 May 2021, https://www.redaccion.com.ar/familias-monoparentales-en-crisis-de-cuidados/.

Zelmanovich, P. (2020), 'Desire to Know: Zooming In on the Emergent', in I. Dussel, P. Ferrante and D. Pulfer (eds), *Thinking Education in Times of Pandemic. Between Emergency, Commitment and Waiting*, 325–36, Buenos Aires: UNIPE. Editorial Universitaria.

# 10

# 'In True Naval Fashion': Young People's Perspectives on Family Communication

Jo Bowser-Angermann, Leanne Gray, Abigail Wood,
Matt Fossey and Lauren Godier-McBard

## Introduction

In her now classic work, Segal (1986) described the military and the family as greedy institutions and therefore open to increased conflict where they intersect. It is widely accepted that military families are unique because of the exceptional demands and pressures the military places on individuals within the family unit (Burrell et al. 2006; Drummet, Coleman and Cable 2003; Segal 1986). These pressures include, but are not limited to, the risk of injury or death, geographic mobility and separation. During separation in two-parent families, the non-serving parent is thrust, in some respects, into the role of single parent. Even military families that cope well during periods of separation define it as a stressful experience that requires adjustment, not dissimilar to that experienced during grief (Segal 1986).

Families represent not only spaces within which individuals exist, but entire complex networks that affect many aspects of our lived experiences (Procentese, Gatti and Di Napoli 2019) as well as a dominant influence on the behaviours of its members (Kerr 1981). Communication, levels of openness and healthiness of interactions are usually considered as key to a satisfying family life (Procentese, Gatti and Di Napoli 2019). Mutual acceptance and open communication among family members can help them in managing stressors and negotiating adolescents' individuation, with opportunities for members to share daily concerns and issues, and to feel supported (Procentese, Gatti and DiNapoli

2019). This chapter explores the relevant literature and presents empirical data of two young people to explore their experiences of communicating with a serving military parent.

Children and young people (CYP)'s experiences of society's complex systems are discussed within the conceptual framework of Bronfenbrenner's (1979, 1994) ecological theory, which states that a child's experiences are influenced by a system of environments that are interdependent on each other. CYP's immediate environment, their microsystem, has the greatest impact on their development. This microsystem includes family, school and peers, within 'face-to-face settings' (Bronfenbrenner et al. 1996). However, this microsystem was defined prior to the development of online communication, with many interactions now taking place online and not within the young person's 'face-to-face' microsystem. It has been argued that technology should now be considered a fundamental part of the microsystem (McHale, Dotterer and Kim 2009). Some researchers go further, with Johnson and Puplampu (2008) proposing an 'ecological techno-subsystem' which sits between the child and the microsystem and includes the child's interactions with all forms of internet-based technology. More recently, Navarro and Tudge (2022) argued that, because virtual interactions are not taking place within the microsystem, modifications are required to Bronfenbrenner's microsystem. They propose three modifications to the microsystem, one of which being that individuals can exist in more than one microsystem at a time. This revised model argues that people can participate in their physical microsystem, such as home or school, whilst also participating in a virtual microsystem, such as playing an online game, using social media or sharing photos online. This proposal is particularly relevant to children within military families, who, whilst communicating with their serving parent, in a virtual microsystem, are at the same time in a physical microsystem, such as their home. It is important to explore and develop an understanding of the constant interplay of the physical and virtual environment. Within this chapter we consider how communication during military deployment can minimize both the short-term and long-term impact of separation on military families.

This chapter begins by considering how social media and internet-based communication (SM/IBC) has transformed communication over recent years, before supporting CYP in maintaining communication with their serving Naval parent.

## Transformation of the digital landscape and the role of social media

Transformation of the digital landscape, made possible by ease of access to the internet and the pervasive influence of social media, is changing the way CYP socialize (Pescott 2020). Indeed, CYP are using social media at an increasing rate. The most recent Ofcom analysis of the media habits of young people in UK aged between three and seventeen found that in 2021 nearly all children aged five to fifteen went online and 64 per cent of eight-to-eleven-year-olds used social media sites or apps, with the number rising to 91 per cent of twelve-to-fifteen-year-olds (Ofcom 2022). Sixty per cent of eight-to-eleven-year-olds said they had a social media profile, despite being under the minimum age requirement (thirteen for most social media sites). Children used a wide range of sites and apps for their social activities: WhatsApp was the most popular, used by 53 per cent of children, followed by TikTok (50 per cent), Snapchat (42 per cent), Instagram (41 per cent) and Facebook (40 per cent) (Ofcom 2022).

Leppänen and colleagues (2015) stress that each social media platform has a particular set of rules, dynamics and etiquette that users need to adhere to when posting. This makes for a complicated journey through interpretive conventions for the participants' social activity. Ultimately, digital technologies and social media add new dimensions that children have to navigate, and social media has irrevocably altered the notions of community, space, identity and the relationship between them (Pescott 2020; Thomson, Berriman and Bragg 2018).

In this chapter we view SM/IBC as an 'accommodative tool' (Vaterlaus, Beckert and Schmitt-Wilson 2019: 2182) which supports the interaction of our participants, within the virtual microsystem, with their serving parent.

## Communication and emotional arousal

An individual's experience of communication is based on the interrelationships and elicited emotional reactions leading up to, during and after the communication itself. Understanding and defining the complex relationship between communication and emotional arousal has a long sociological tradition. Debate exists around the impact of overt expressions of arousal during communication (i.e. gesturing, body language, vocal tone and cadence) and the more subtle neurological dynamics which play a significant role in how we interact (Turner 1999). A key component of emotional arousal in communication is the congruity or incongruity of what is 'expected' and then subsequently 'experienced' by individuals within an interaction, and this process is encapsulated within expectation-states theory (EST) (Berger, Cohen and Zelditch 1972; Wagner and Berger 1993; Wagner and Turner 1998). Where high levels of incongruity are experienced, there is more emotional arousal, and this, in turn, is influenced by a whole array of preconceptions between and about the actors in the communication encounter. These include, but are not restricted to, structural forces, such as the hierarchical relationship between the actors (in our case parent/child); cultural forces, that is, how to behave in certain scenarios (such as when communicating to a parent who is on board a ship) or transactional forces, whereby there is an expectation of some degree of exchange, physical or emotional, within the context of that communication. When a serving parent is on deployment, communication with a child back home increases emotional arousal for both the child and parent due to the nature of the family separation. This can result in positive communication that can strengthen the relationship. However due to the difficulty and uncertainty in the interaction taking place this heightened emotional arousal can damage the communication encounter for both parent and child.

When Berger, Cohen and Zelditch (1972) first proposed EST, communication occurred across a range of electronic platforms, for instance cinema or television as a unidirectional communication channel and the use of radio and telephony as bidirectional communication media. However, the internet and other, now widely available, forms of digital communication were not in use at the time. The relatively recent high usage of SM/IBC poses several questions about how emotions are relayed and the impact of the congruency/incongruency dyad on emotional arousal when using SM/IBC. Whilst emotional communication offline and online have been shown to be similar (Derks, Fischer and Bos 2008), there is a growing literature considering face-to-face communication over the internet and its impact on emotions (Kappas and Krämer 2011; Prikhodko et al. 2020; Serrano-Puche 2020). However, there appears to be no research that has considered SM/IBC and the bidirectional emotional arousal between serving military personnel and their children.

## Military families' experience of using social media and internet-based communication

The authors published an international scoping review of English language research, considering how military families use SM/IBC communication during periods of separation and the impact of this on their experiences (Wood et al. 2022). The review highlighted the potential for SM/IBC to both benefit military families and exacerbate challenges associated with traditional forms of communication.

Like civilians, military families appear to make considerable use of SM/IBC, including video calls, Facebook and instant messaging (Atwood 2014; Children's Commissioner 2018; Durham 2015; Goodney 2014; Gribble and Fear 2019; Konowitz 2013; Louie and Cromer 2014; Schachman 2010; Seidel et al. 2014). The literature highlights several benefits for military families in using SM/IBC to communicate during separation. SM/IBC and proliferation of personal communication devices (e.g. laptops, smart phones) can provide increased opportunities for communication for military families, and consistent access to SM/IBC aides the separated parent to better accommodate their families' schedules (Atwood 2014). SM/IBC has also expanded the number of synchronous communication options (i.e. communication that takes place in real time) available to families. This can help military parents remain involved in the daily lives of their children (Goodney 2014).

An important subsect of sychronous SM/IBC are platforms that facilitate face-to-face communication (e.g. Skype, Whatsapp, Facebook, Facetime, etc.). Several studies highlight how video communication was associated with feelings of connectedness, as well as the benefit of being able to see that the separated parent is safe (Goodney 2014; Konowitz 2013). Moreover, video-based communication was reported to help children engage better with their separated parent in some studies (Goodney 2014). However, other studies suggest that face-to-face communication is not always a better experience (Atwood 2014; Konowitz 2013), for example in instances in which CYP experienced poor connectivity and felt self-conscious about their appearance (Konowitz 2013).

Despite the potential benefits, SM/IBC also has the potential to exacerbate general communication challenges that military families experience. Military families face the challenge of balancing the increased opportunity to communicate that SM/IBC affords with the quality of that communication. Indeed, Konowitz (2013) reported that a high level of communication can simultaneously be experienced as low quality, with 90 per cent of participants reporting their communications as 'mediocre, tense, [or] limited'. Furthermore, Atwood (2014) reports that frequent communication was associated with running out of topics, arguing and a reduction in the serving parent's focus on their role in some cases. Importantly, Atwood (2014) highlights that the 'right' level of communication is subjective and based on the individual family (i.e. what is considered too much communication or damaging intimacy for some families, can be considered adequate for other families).

Several practical barriers to a military family's use of SM/IBC are discussed in the literature. Families' access to and quality of communication range from no access, inconsistent access, through to good access to SM/IBC infrastructure, and vary by location and campaign length (Atwood 2014; Children's Commissioner 2018; Durham 2015). Where infrastructure exists to support communication, inconsistent connectivity can still present a significant barrier to communication (Atwood 2014; Children's Commissioner 2018; Gribble and Fear 2019; Schachman 2010), with some families choosing not to make use of SM/IBC routes due to these difficulties. Additionally, military families may experience periods where all communication avenues are barred which can prompt anxiety as families wait for communication to be restored and for confirmation of their loved one's safety (Durham 2015).

Some limitations to our current understanding of service child–parent communication via SM/IBC exist. Firstly, most literature is US focused, therefore due to difference in communication infrastructures, deployment lengths and locations, support available to families, healthcare systems and social and military cultures, findings may not reflect the experiences of UK Royal Navy families. Additionally, the theories discuss the role of cultural forces on congruity/incongruity, and in turn CYP's emotional experiences of interactions, therefore highlighting the importance of considering the cultural differences between countries and military contexts (Berger, Cohen and Zelditch 1972; Wagner and Berger 1993; Wagner and Turner 1998). The scoping review (Wood et al. 2022 forthcoming) returned no papers published after 2019 so more recent developments in SM/IBC may not be reflected in the available research. Most of the literature discussed family communication under the assumption that communication is a desired goal, and that family relationships prior to separation are positive. In reality, not all family relationships can be characterized as safe and supportive. Indeed, research documents domestic abuse amongst military families, with ongoing debate as to whether levels are comparable to or worse than those seen in civilian families (Godier-McBard, Wood and Fossey 2021). In previous work undertaken by the authors, a subject-matter expert suggested that separation can help temporarily limit domestic abuse within family units. A participant in an earlier study stated that 'domestic abuse and so on, require a presence of some description. And even if it's a controlling relationship. And that's, again, it's very limited because of the contacts and communication controls when you're on deployment' (Godier-McBard, Wood and Fossey

2021: 89). However, this preliminary finding requires further exploration. Thus, the increased availability of communication via SM/IBC may facilitate the continuation of abusive behaviour. Further to this, most of the literature focused on experiences of heterosexual nuclear families (where specified), therefore further research is needed to reflect the diversity of family structures.

Finally, much of the literature on serving parent–child or service family communication uses parental report to explore children's experience. Therefore, current understanding of service children's communication experiences may vary from those provided by their parent's reported experience and perception. This is particularly important considering theories of emotional arousal, which highlights the role of congruity with expectations of an interaction on the quality and impact of communication. As the factors that may influence congruity can be highly personal, it is therefore crucial to engage directly with CYP to explore communication from their perspective. Due to this dearth of research, we explored the experiences of CYP with a parent serving in the Royal Navy, focusing on their communication with their serving parent during periods of separation.

## The young people's stories

To provide further insight this chapter explores the narratives of two of our participants, Arya and Bethany (pseudonyms) (Denzin 1989). As part of a larger study involving CYP aged between thirteen and twenty-one with a parent currently serving in the Royal Navy, deeper analysis of the virtual semi-structured interviews of two participants was conducted. In narrative research, the inquirer often only focuses on a small number of individuals. Narrative inquiry embodies the interest into the lived experience of individuals and the narration of those who live those experiences (Chase 2011). Arya was aged twenty-one at the time of the interview, with a father serving as an officer and Bethany was aged fifteen at the time of the interview, with a father serving as a chief petty officer in the surface fleet. Arya and Bethany were both selected because they were reflective of their personal experiences of communicating with a serving parent which allowed for a richer story.

To help facilitate deeper discussion about the experiences of communication during parent–child separation, vignettes were used during the semi-structured interviews with Arya and Bethany. These vignettes were created by the research team to present a first-person account based on (1) a young person's experience of being separated from their serving parent and (2) the experiences of a serving

174    *Reinventing the Family in Uncertain Times*

parent separated from their children, designed to encourage our participants to reflect on their own family situation and experiences. During the interviews we focused on the experiences of family communication during periods of parent–child separation, the benefits and challenges and the impact SM/IBC has on Naval CYP and their relationship with their serving parent. This is in line with Dewey, who argued that individual experience is continuous and central to understanding a person (Clandinin and Connolly 2000).

The semi-structured interviews were transcribed verbatim and then re-transcribed through the process of restorying. Clandinin and Connolly (2000) proposed the use of a three-dimensional space or narrative structure which allows for the creation of a 'metaphorical' space that encompasses and defines that narrative study. The three-dimensional structure requires the researcher to include information about the interaction (personal interaction based on an individual's feelings), the continuity (past, present and future) and the situation (contextual information). This approach was utilized to present both Arya and Bethany's restories to give a broader view of their experiences. Each restory was checked by the participants to ensure that the 'restorying' was authentic and captured their voice. As with all qualitative research, themes can be identified and separated into themes. Through re-reading each of our participants' restories, key themes were identified that encapsulate what Arya and Bethany were saying. In line with narrative researchers the themes are presented after their restories, adding depth and insight into our participants' experiences.

Both Arya and Bethany identify as white British, heterosexual girls. They are both in nuclear heterosexual families with a sibling brother. Due to their similar family contexts, this allowed us to make comparisons across how the family communicated with a serving parent.

Arya and Bethany's restories are presented here.

## Arya's restory:

It's interesting how much things have advanced since my dad was first deployed. Wi-Fi connections are better now, we only really had Skype to connect when I was younger. I was only 2 months old when he first went away on his first deployment and back then my mum would say she could only talk to him over the phone and write and receive letters … so I suppose in that respect being able to use the internet as I got older as a form of communication was a big change.

We Skyped when we got the chance to, but it wasn't often, maybe every 3 weeks. But that was how we spoke. Phone calls were clearer, but I am not sure the minutes were limited. I think the priority was to mum in terms of time to talk to my dad. My brother and I always got a couple of minutes to just chat and say hello, but it wasn't for long periods of time. I was able to have more conversation with him through Skype than anything else. We would just talk. He would ask me how school was going, how my friends are … so it was basically me talking about myself to be honest, because I didn't understand his work, and I would just say to him … . come home! And he would say, I can't! [laugh]

A memory of mine was on my 12th birthday and my dad was away, but I got to Skype him on my birthday. I remember being really sad [crying noise] I was crying because I wished he was with me. But it was ok, it passed. It was just something you got used to and in true 'naval' fashion, you just got over it because there was no point getting upset about something that was beyond your control. My mum, my brother and I normally got to Skype on birthdays though. But his internet was never good. His picture was always grainy, and you knew it would cut out. I remember it used to upset me because I couldn't speak to him properly. If he was at a port, he would have a more stable connection but when he was out at sea it was really hard. I remember there were times we would go 3 or 4 weeks without hearing from him because they couldn't connect for whatever reason. Although challenging I preferred having a Skype conversation with my dad than a telephone call because it felt more like I was having a face-to-face conversation. It was personal, he could show us things, I could show him things and I could physically look at him.

It didn't worry me when he cut out or there were times we couldn't talk, but I do remember there was a news story about a service personnel who committed suicide while they were on a deployed vessel. I remember it sparking a conversation … if you are not enjoying yourself, being on deployment must be a really isolating experience. Dad said it was really bad. There was a lapse in care or judgement. In my mind I just hoped my dad never felt like that when he was away. Maybe the person who committed suicide didn't have as much contact with their family?

Blueys were always a regular thing in our house, and it was nice when we got things back sometimes. But it took ages to get things delivered and I do also remember writing letters to Dad. I used to write them with my friend, we both had our dads away serving in common, and it was really nice to have someone to help me who understood how I was feeling. But it was all a bit bittersweet. I remember my mum saying to my brother and I, that we are going to see a school counsellor … and we were like why? She just said because you know your dad is away and it's hard for you and you're old now. And I had this session with the counsellor, she was trying her best, but she didn't understand … it would have been better if it was with someone who really understood what it was like and how I was feeling at a greater level. She just used to ask me 'how do you feel?' and I would say 'How do you think I feel? … I am not great, but [laugh] there is nothing I can do.' It wasn't for me, I had support from family and friends.

My mum used to send emails to my dad that me and brother could contribute to. I think that was a more stable communication and easier to just do and organise. Whereas when we tried to Skype, we had to make sure everyone was free at a specific time and because of time differences it would sometimes be late, and I would be in bed. My dad isn't a big social media user even now. He did have WhatsApp and we did use that to text. I can't really think of anything that would have made it any better to be honest. It's one of those things isn't it … that's just the way it is. Maybe we rely on technology too much now and it would be better to use older methods of having a phone call and writing letters?

I always say to my dad that you weren't around a lot during my childhood because you were away so much. I never held a grudge over it, but I never really felt like I had a relationship with my dad until I was 13 or 14 years old, that's when we started having more conversations and became friends. I remember sitting and watching Top Gear with my dad even though I hated it, because I wanted to spend time with him. I have this really vivid memory when I was 14, my first boyfriend broke my heart! I was so sad … I just cried and cried, and my dad was the only person home. I remember crying on his lap. He didn't ask me any questions, he didn't ask what was wrong, he just let me cry and gave me a hug. It was a strange moment for me because he would always leave and then I'd do all my crying afterwards. But also, it would have been normal at the same time, because why wouldn't your dad be somebody who could comfort you? But I am not used to seeing him cry. It would be strange when he was home, he would still be in his 'navy' head space being used to telling people what to do and my mum was like 'no, no, no, you can't do that here. We are all a team!' It must be strange being away for 9 months and then re-join society with only mundane tasks to do?

We are a lot closer now, we are friends and I like spending time with him. I would say with a full heart that our relationship was impacted by the fact he just wasn't around when I was younger. It had a huge impact on our relationship. I would never follow in his footsteps because I have been on the receiving end of what it is like … and it has impacted how I view the navy and how I view the armed forces in general. There needs to be updates, I don't want to say its toxic, but it is negative. I think it has a toxic culture if you just have to 'man up and get on'. Toxic masculinity where men are bred to not show any emotion and not be upset. It needs to be discussed that it is ok to be upset and to cry because you miss your family. It used to really upset me, I remember being on Skype calls with my dada and I could see he was trying not to cry because obviously he missed us … he could see he was missing out on things me, and my brother were doing. I think emotional development is overlooked in that line of work. My mum used to sell me a dream of one day you will meet a sailor and fall in love, and I used to think I would marry a sailor but now I am like 'F*ck no! because if I marry you, I want to you be here, I don't want you to leave for months.' It has definitely impacted my relationships with men. I feel like there is something wrong if I bottle things up and I don't like this idea of submissive women. I discovered feminism at 16 and want to be independent and career driven.

## Bethany's restory:

Adam's situation [vignette used in semi-structured interview] is 100% relatable to my own experience when my dad went away on deployment. He used to go away a lot when me and my brother were a lot younger, when he was deployed on the ship. That meant there was less communication, and it was a while ago, so I think the technology wasn't great. So, my mum was alone a lot of the time with two very young children. But me and my brother were lucky when he went away last year because we have got phones, tablets, Wi-Fi so it is a lot easier to stay in contact with him – plus he wasn't deployed to a ship. It's a lot harder when he is on a ship. I feel so bad for children who have a parent on submarines because there is no contact at all because they have to keep everything quiet and secret.

When he was away, I couldn't send him a normal text message or try and call him because it would cost a lot, so we would use WhatsApp. When he was in the Falklands, he had a landline, and we would call that. I know my mum and dad would send emails to each other if it was important, but I would email my dad. Being able to Facetime brings a sense of happiness straightaway and stops you from feeling alone all the time. I would Facetime my dad on my own once a week and then we would have a whole family conversation, with my younger brother and my mum, every two weeks. But we always had the option of Facetiming him by ourselves.

But sometimes you get black outs, or there is a glitch and then you wouldn't be able to talk for a couple of days because there was something wrong with the connection. This was really tricky, especially with the time difference as well; my dad would message to say do you want to Facetime? And we wouldn't see the message until two hours later so it would have been too late or too early call him which was horrible. The time difference was massive. For example, he would finish work at 4 o'clock and it would be 9 o'clock at night my time.

When he is away, we talk about our day and if we went out and there's like a nice sunset, I would send him a picture. One time we watched a programme and we told him to watch it so we could talk about it. My dad is really good at maths, so when I was stuck on my maths homework, I would message my dad and ask him how to do it and he would just say 'yeah of course! I will Facetime you' [laugh] and it was like a little catch up with dad to do maths! [laugh]. But if I had been arguing with mum I wouldn't tell my dad, or if something had happened at school and I was upset or if I had bad news, I wouldn't tell him at the time. I wouldn't share everything.

But me and my dad have a close relationship. When he is home, I would come home from school, and we would have a cup of tea and talk about our days. But when I used to come home, and you know he isn't there … you have to try and push past that. When he has been away for a long time you do start to worry will he recognise me? We grow up fast, I feel like I changed a lot when he left from October to May… You start to forget what his voice sounds like. When he goes on deployment it is a big event. Last year, the whole family went out for a nice meal and said goodbye to my dad, and we drove him to the airport. But the worst thing was, his plane broke, and he had to fly back home. He was only gone a day and it was like the worst thing ever, I was so sad, and I was just trying to deal with the fact my parent had gone and then he was back … and you realise that you have to go through all that sadness all over again. We have countdowns to when he returns.

I feel communication now is probably the best it could be for parents in the navy and children at home. You can't have constant communication with them when they are deployed but it would be nice to have more of it. I think it would be nice, if your parents are away, if they could put in place sports activities or days out to join in together, with others who understand. They try to do that at school but it's not the same. It needs to be something special for the 'navy kids'!

## Discussion

Arya's and Bethany's lived experiences, narrated in their restories, offer an insight into communication within the military family. By reading Arya's and Bethany's original transcriptions and restories the following four key themes were identified: distress; jealousy; relationships and toxic masculinity. These themes pull together the data from both restories allowing for comparisons between Arya's and Bethany's experiences within similar family constructions.

### (1) Distress

Despite opportunities to communicate with video and non-video-based communication during the periods of separation, both Arya and Bethany experienced emotional distress around their inability and difficulties to communicate with their fathers whilst they were on deployment. Key to this is the emotional arousal of what was 'expected' in the communication exchange and what was 'experienced' (Berger, Cohen and Zelditch 1972; Wagner and Berger 1993; Wagner and Turner 1998). Bethany considers herself and her brother 'lucky' because their father was deployed on a ship, and she feels 'so bad for children who have a parent on a submarine because there is no contact'. Even though Bethany had what she considers to be better technology such as 'phones, tablets, wi-fi … plus he was deployed on a ship', she still experienced 'blackouts … glitches' and problems with the connection. These communication issues, combined with the time difference on certain deployments, meant communicating was tricky and delayed which was 'horrible'. This caused high levels of incongruity and therefore high levels of emotional arousal which impacted the communication exchange itself and after the exchange. For military families this could mean that things are left unsaid or unclarified for days, weeks or months depending on the deployment, causing distress for the CYP and the serving parent. Arya experienced similar challenges when communicating with her father, but also admitted that during their video-based communication, via Skype, she would use it as an opportunity to ask him to 'come home!' to which he would say 'I can't'. Although the connection would drop out and there were times she could not talk to her father, which did upset her, it did not cause her worry. However, she did admit that she used to worry about her father feeling isolated. She recalls hearing of a service personnel committing suicide while on deployment and she 'hoped that he [her dad] never felt like that when he was away'. This led Arya to speculate that 'maybe the person who committed suicide

## (2) Jealousy

Throughout Arya's story there is a sense of jealousy of the relationship her father has with the Navy above their father–daughter relationship. She recalls memories of her dad not being around and her 'crying because I wish he was with me'. There is evidence that this emotion is still very raw as her restory brought her to tears. This raw emotion was juxtaposed with phrases such as, 'it was ok' and 'it was something you got used to', as it was beyond her control. Despite Arya arguing that video-based communication was like having a face-to-face conversation, being physically separated from her father was distressing and very upsetting for her. However, this separation, because of her father's career, was her and her father's reality and the only way to cope with this reality was to adopt the 'true "Naval" fashion' which was, to just get on with it. Although on a surface level this is something she accepts and confirms is 'ok', her story suggests she is envious of her father's commitment to the navy, the time he has spent in the navy and not being around when she was young, as it has negatively impacted her childhood. This is in line with Segal (1986) who argues that the demands of the military on the family are unique and that separation, particularly for naval personnel, is often longer than of that of their army and air force personnel counterparts, which causes more stress and the chance of psychological issues in children. The lack of communication and associated emotional arousal around the communication interaction with her father exacerbates this stress. In contrast Bethany's story does not express feelings of jealousy, despite being alone with her mother 'a lot of the time' and describes a positive communication at home and while her father is on deployment.

## (3) Relationships

Bethany describes her relationship with her father as 'close' and there is evidence that she has a good relationship with her father when he is away on deployment and when he is at home. She recalls happy conversations: 'we talk about our day … I would send him a picture'. In stark contrast Arya does not describe a positive relationship between her and her father when he is at home or when he is on deployment. In her case, this is suggestive that the family relationship and communication established at home reflects the family relationship online and vice versa (Procentese, Gatti and DiNapoli 2019).

Arya confesses that she openly reminds her dad that he 'wasn't around a lot during my childhood' because he was away so often. Although she states that she does not 'hold a grudge', she does not feel as though she had a relationship with her dad until she was around thirteen or fourteen years old. Burrell and colleagues (2006) found that the perception of the impact of periodic separation between a serving parent and their family negatively affected the experience of separation. Arya recalls her father missing important birthdays which has added to her negative perception of her separation from her father (Burrell et al. 2006). When she turned thirteen or fourteen years old Arya started to have 'more conversations and became friends' with her father. She remembers watching *Top Gear* with him despite hating it to try to build bonds with him. She remembers how 'strange' it felt to have her dad comfort her when she was crying even though she assumes that having a father comfort a daughter could be perfectly 'normal'. Although Arya and her father are closer now, she states, 'with a full heart that our relationship was impacted by the fact he just wasn't around when I was younger' and that 'it had a huge impact on our relationship'.

As noted earlier in the chapter Arya is a heterosexual girl and the separation between Arya and her father during her childhood has also had a lasting impact on her 'relationships with men'. Her mother used to 'sell' her the 'dream' that 'one day you will meet a sailor and fall in love' but negatively impacted by her experiences of being separated from her father as a child she wants her husband to 'be here, I don't want you to leave for months', which is again suggestive of her feelings of jealousy. She decides to end her story with her discovery of 'feminism' and an image of not being a 'submissive' woman but one who is 'independent and career driven'. Arya's aspirations to become independent so she does not ever feel left alone again can be interpreted as a means to overcome the challenges of the father–daughter separation.

## (4) Toxic masculinity

Arya's feelings of distress, jealousy and resentment have impacted on her relationship with her father during her childhood. Conversely, her experience of the separation from her father has impacted her negative perception of the navy itself and what Arya refers to as its 'toxic masculinity'. Segal (1986) argued that there are increased conflicts between the military and their families due to the intersectionality between these two greedy institutions. Arya explains in her story that the 'Naval fashion' was to just get over whatever was upsetting you and this view is strengthened when she explains that it has a 'toxic culture of you just have to "man up and get on"'. Arya witnessed this first-hand, when she saw her father was away on deployment and he would intentionally not show his emotion over Skype by 'trying not to cry' when it was clear that he was missing his family. This added to her fear of her father feeling isolated and bottling up his emotions, which she feels is encouraged by the navy. Due to hearing of another member of the navy committing suicide she sees that there was a 'lapse in care of judgement' from the navy in its personnel and their family and that 'emotional development is overlooked'. In contrast, due to Bethany's positive communication with her father at home and on deployment resulting in a close relationship, Bethany did not express the same views on the navy or toxic masculinity. She simply calls for positive events to be held to help support military families: 'it needs to be something special for the "Navy kids!"'.

# Conclusion

There is a growing body of literature exploring the impact of face-to-face communications over the internet and on emotions (Kappas and Krämer 2011; Prikhodko et al. 2020; Serrano-Puche 2020). However, because of the heightened emotions and environment military families find themselves in, this does not consider SM/IBC and the bidirectional emotional arousal between serving military personnel and their children. As highlighted by Navarro and Tudge (2022), when considering modifications to Bronfenbrenner's ecosystems, the CYP in this research were existing in both their home, a physical microsystem, whilst also communicating with their serving parent using SM/IBC, a virtual microsystem. This virtual microsystem makes it possible for the CYP to communicate with the serving parent, with no geographical limits on interactions in a virtual microsystem (Johnson and Puplampu 2008).

Families are complex networks where communication is key to promote positive family relationships (Procentese, Gatti and Di Napoli 2019). Military families have an added layer of complexity that impacts family communication due to the nature of deployment and the demands placed on them (Segal 1986). Our research suggests that although the military is a greedy institution, if positive communication is maintained within the family at home and the family can be allowed to maintain this positive communication whilst on deployment, the family can still have a positive feeling of connectedness.

However, there is evidence that the closeness of the family at home mirrors that of the family when they are apart (Goodney 2014; Procentese, Gatti and Di Napoli 2019). Bethany talked fondly of how the communication was open at home when her dad is not on deployment, sharing a 'cup of tea' when she returned from school and spending time to 'talk about our days'. This open and positive communication was mirrored when her dad was away, with the sharing of pictures over WhatsApp, individual and family Facetime opportunities and still helping her with homework. There was a strong sense of how he was there when she needed him with the help of SM/IBC. However, Arya recalls how it was 'strange' when her dad was home and describes a lack of communication where she did not feel as though she had a relationship with her dad until she was thirteen or fourteen years old. Although Arya recalls a memory of her dad giving her a hug when she was upset, no words were spoken. This closed and distant communication was mirrored when her dad was on deployment when she felt the 'priority was to mum in terms of time to talk to my dad' and that the lack of communication 'is just one of those things'.

There appears to be an association between positive communication between families at home and positive communication between families online. Both Arya and Bethany felt video-based communication made a huge difference to them by increasing their feelings of connectedness. Despite the network issues and accessibility, it was still their preferred form of communication, which contrasts with other studies where poor connectivity was a factor (Konowitz 2013). Arya explained it 'felt more like having a face-to-face conversation … personal'. Although the rise of IBC/SM has supported family communication, there are still parents who have a negative perception or refusal to engage with it. Arya hints that although she may have liked to use IBC/SM as a way of communicating with her father, he 'isn't a big social media user even now'. Our research shows that although having more SM/IBC can heighten emotional arousal in military families, it can also have a positive impact on family relationships.

# References

Atwood, K. (2014), 'Maintaining "the Family" during Deployment: Presence Work by Military Families', Doctoral Thesis, University of Calgary, Calgary.

Bronfenbrenner, U. (1979), *The Ecology of Human Development*, Cambridge, MA: Harvard University Press.

Bronfenbrenner, U. (1994), 'Ecological Models of Human Development', in Husen, T. and Postlethwaite (eds), *International Encyclopedia of Education*, Vol. 3, 2nd edn, Oxford: Elsevier, 1643–1647.

Bronfenbrenner, U., P. McClelland, E. Wethington, P. Moen and S. J. Ceci (1996), *The State of Americans: This Generation and the Next*, New York: Free Press.

Berger, J., B. P. Cohen and M. Zelditch, Jr. (1972), 'Status Characteristics and Social Interaction', *American Sociological Review*, 37 (3): 241–55.

Burrell, L. M., G. A. Adams, D. B. Durand and C. A. Castro (2006), 'The Impact of Military Lifestyle Demands on Well-Being, Army, and Family Outcomes', *Armed Forces and Society*, 33 (43): 43–58.

Chase, S. E. (2011), 'Narrative Inquiry: Still a Field in the Making', in N. K. Denzin and Y. S. Lincoln (eds), *The SAGE Handbook of Qualitative Research*, 4th edn, Chapter 17, 421–34, Thousand Oaks, CA: Sage.

Children's Commissioner (2018), *Vulnerability Report 2018*, London: Children's Commissioner for England.

Clandinin, D. J., and F. M. Connolly (2000), *Narrative Inquiry: Experience and Story in Qualitative Research*, San Francisco: Jossey-Bass.

Denzin, N. (1989), *Interpretative Biography*, Newbury Park, CA: Sage.

Derks, D., A. H. Fischer and A. E. Bos (2008), 'The Role of Emotion in Computer-Mediated Communication: A Review', *Computers in Human Behavior*, 24 (3): 766–85.

Drummet, A. R., M. Coleman and S. Cable (2003). 'Military Families under Stress: Implications for Family Life Education', *Family Relations*, 52 (3): 279–87.

Durham, S. W. (2015), 'Service Members' Experiences in Staying Connected with Family while Deployed', *Advances in Nursing Science*, 38 (4): 279–97.

Godier-McBard, L., A. Wood and M. Fossey (2021), 'The Impact of Service Life on the Military Child: The Overlooked Casualties of Conflict–Update and Review Report'. Cambridge: Veteran and Families Institute for Military Social Research.

Goodney, R. (2014), 'A Mixed Methods Study of Technological Influences on Communication and Media Exposure in Military Children Experiencing Parental Deployment', PhD thesis, University of Kentucky, Kentucky.

Gribble, R., and N. Fear (2019), *The Effect of Non-operational Family Separations on Family Functioning and Well-Being among Royal Navy/Royal Marines Families*, Hampshire, UK: Naval Families Federation.

Johnson, G. M., and K. P. Puplampu (2008), 'Internet Use during Childhood and the Ecological Techno-Subsystem', *Canadian Journal of Learning and Technology*, 34 (1), https://cjlt.ca/index.php/cjlt/article/view/26428/19610. Accessed 1 March 2023.

Kappas, A., and N. C. Krämer (2011), *Face-to-Face Communication over the Internet: Emotions in a Web of Culture, Language, and Technology*, Cambridge: Cambridge University Press.

Kerr, M. E. (1981), 'Family Systems Theory and Therapy', in A. Gurman and D. P. Kniskem (eds), *Handbook of Family Therapy*, 226–65, New York: Brunner/Mazel.

Konowitz, S. (2013), 'Understanding How Army National Guard Families with Children Cope with Deployments', EdD thesis, Wilmington University, Delaware.

Leppänen, S., J. Spindler Møller, T. Rørbeck Nørreby, A. Stæhr and S. Kytölä (2015), 'Authenticity, Normativity and Social Media', *Discourse, Context and Media*, 8: 1–5.

Louie, A. D., and L. D. Cromer (2014), 'Parent–Child Attachment during the Deployment Cycle: Impact on Reintegration Parenting Stress', *Professional Psychology: Research and Practice*, 45 (6): 496–503.

McHale, S. M., A. Dotterer and J. Y. Kim (2009), 'An Ecological Perspective on the Media and Youth Development', *American Behavioual Scientist*, 52 (8): 1186–203.

Navarro, J. L., and J. R. H. Tudge (2022), 'Technologizing Bronfenbrenner: Neoecological Theory', *Current Psychology*, 41 (1): 1–17.

Ofcom (2022), *Children and Parents: Media Use and Attitudes Report*, London: Ofcom.

Pescott, C. K. (2020), '"I Wish I Was Wearing a Filter Right Now": An Exploration of Identity Formation and Subjectivity of 10-and 11-Year Olds' Social Media Use', *Social Media + Society*, 6 (4): 1–10.

Prikhodko, O. V., E. I. Cherdymova, E. V. Lopanova, N. A. Galchenko, A. I. Ikonnikov, O. A. Mechkovskaya and O. V. Karamova (2020), 'Ways of Expressing Emotions in Social Networks: Essential Features, Problems and Features of Manifestation in Internet Communication', *Online Journal of Communication and Media Technologies*, 10 (2): https://www.ojcmt.net/download/ways-of-expressing-emotions-in-soc ial-networks-essential-features-problems-and-features-of-7931.pdf. Accessed 1 March 2023.

Procentese, F., F. Gatti and I. Di Napoli (2019), 'Families and Social Media Use: The Role of Parents' Perceptions about Social Media Impact on Family Systems in the Relationship between Family Collective Efficacy and Open Communication', *International Journal of Environmental Research and Public Health*, 16 (24): doi:10.3390/ijerph16245006. Accessed 1 March 2023.

Schachman, K. A. (2010), 'Online Fathering: The Experience of First-Time Fatherhood in Combat-Deployed Troops', *Nursing Research*, 59 (1): 11–17.

Segal, M. (1986), 'The Military and the Family as Greedy Institutions', *Armed Forces and Society*, 13 (1): 9–38.

Seidel, A. J., M. M. Franks, G. F. Murphy and S. M. Wadsworth (2014), 'Bridging the Distance: Illustrations of Real-Time Communication of Support between Partners and Deployed Members of the National Guard', in S. M. Wadsworth and D. S. Riggs (eds), *Military Deployment and Its Consequences for Families*, 21–35, New York: Springer.

Serrano-Puche, J. (2020), 'Affect and the Expression of Emotions on the Internet: An Overview of Current Research', in J. Hunsinger, L. Klastrup and M. M. Allen (eds), *Second International Handbook of Internet Research*, 529–47, The Netherlands: Springer Nature B.V.

Thomson, R., L. Berriman and S. Bragg (2018), *Researching Everyday Childhoods in a Digital Age*, London: Bloomsbury.

Turner, J. H. (1999), 'Toward a General Sociological Theory of Emotions', *Journal for the Theory of Social Behaviour*, 29 (2): 133–61.

Vaterlaus, J. M., T. E. Beckert and S. Schmitt-Wilson (2019), 'Parent–Child Time Together: The Role of Interactive Technology with Adolescent and Young Adult Children', *Journal of Family Issues*, 40 (15): 2179–202.

Wagner, D. G., and J. Berger (1993), 'Status Characteristics Theory: The Growth of a Program', in J. Berger and M. Zelditch, Jr. (eds), *Theoretical Research Programs: Studies in the Growth of Theory*, 23–63, Stanford, CA: Stanford University Press.

Wagner, D. G., and J. Turner (1998), 'The Continuing Tradition: Expectation States Theory', in J. Turner (ed.), *The Structure of Sociological Theory*, 6th edn, Belmont, CA: Wadsworth.

Wood, A., L. Gray, J. Bowser-Angermann, P. Gibson, M. Fossey and L. Godier-McBard (2022), 'Social Media and Internet-based Communication in Military Families during Separation: An International Scoping Review', *New Media & Society*, https://doi.org/10.1177/14614448221117767.

## 11

# From Active to Activist Parenting: Educational Struggle and the Injuries of Institutionalized Misrecognition

### Nathan Fretwell and John Barker

## Introduction

> We don't want to be waging this war; we do it because it's the right thing, we have no choice morally. I can't sleep at night because it makes me feel sick. I said, 'I can either be Adrian Mole[1] or you can be Erin Brockovich.'[2] You can either sit there and cry about it and write in your diary and have a breakdown over how terrible the world and the situation and the reality … and just let that swarm you, or you can actually go: 'No. I am going to question this; I am going to get answers; and I want to make this right.' (Molly, Crowley Parents Campaign)[3]

We open this chapter with Molly's account of her determination to resist the forced academization of her children's school, as it exemplifies the resolve demonstrated by parents across our study when faced with the uncertainty and anxiety arising from policy developments affecting their families and communities. As with the majority of participating parents, Molly had no prior history of activism; instead, doubts over changes to her children's education, changes over which she had little say and no control, compelled her to act. This chapter is about parents, like Molly, who respond to uncertainty by challenging rather than acquiescing to the demands of authority. Counter to discourses of families as consumers, this chapter focuses on 'active' parents reinventing themselves as parent-activists and the adversity they encountered in struggling to defend their interests.

Since the 1980s, education policy in England has promoted a culture of parenting oriented towards personal responsibility, individualism and the pursuit of family advantage (Olmedo and Wilkins 2017). Key to this has been the construction of a normative ideal of active and involved parenting that enjoins parents to become responsible consumers of educational services (Ball, Bowe and Gewirtz 1996); to provide ancillary educational support through the 'professional labour' of parental involvement (Crozier 2005) and to promote 'school readiness' by cultivating effective home learning environments (Allen 2011; HM Government 2019). Norms of active parenting tend, however, to privilege the individual family unit and scarcely extend to consider parents' collective interests. Nor are all forms of active involvement equally welcome. In practice, acceptable involvement often simply equates to 'passive acceptance of the status quo' (Crozier 2005: 43). We argue for an alternative understanding: one that recognizes parental activism as a legitimate and powerful form of collective parental involvement in education.

The chapter reports on a small-scale qualitative study of three high-profile parent-led campaign groups: Crowley Parents Campaign (CPC), Eastborough Anti-Academisation Coalition (EAC), and Protect Children's Education (PCE). Of these campaigns the latter targeted national funding cuts to education, whilst the first two sought to challenge academization within their respective locales. Academy schools were first introduced in England in 2000 and have been significantly expanded since, with the latest figures reporting that 44 per cent of mainstream schools are currently academies, alongside 41 per cent of alternative provision and special schools that serve children with special educational needs or those who are otherwise unable to attend mainstream schools due, for instance, to exclusion or illness (HM Government 2022). Academies are administratively independent from local education authorities and operate as not-for-profit companies often under sponsorship of other organizations (e.g. faith groups or businesses) and as Multi-Academy Trusts (MATs).[4] Academies have greater discretion over the governance and day-to-day operation of schools, including teachers' pay and conditions, curricula, school hours and term dates. Currently, there are two routes through which academization is pursued. In the case of voluntary conversion, school governing bodies can apply for academy status, in which case they are encouraged to join or form a MAT. Under the Academies Act (2010), however, schools can also be forced to convert and join a MAT if they are deemed liable to intervention. Of the two anti-academization campaigns considered in this chapter – CPC and EAC – the first concerns a case of forced conversion and the latter voluntary conversion.

Our specific focus in this chapter is: firstly, to detail how parental activism disrupts dominant norms of parental involvement and subverts the individualism and self-interest woven into the ideal of the active parent and, secondly, to explore parents' experiences of engaging with authorities, with particular emphasis on the conflicts and uncertainties reported by anti-academization campaigners. In explicating the latter issue, we centre on the emotions of activism (Jasper 2018) and develop our account of parents' struggles through Honneth's (1995) theory of recognition in order to foreground the powerful feelings conflict generates and the injustice of marginalizing parents' interests.

The chapter begins by outlining the normative ideal of active and involved parenting, the research on which the study is based and the motivations and goals of the campaign groups. It then proceeds to examine the emotional fallout of parents' struggles and calls for us to rethink the normative parameters of parental involvement. We argue not only that educational activism should be acknowledged as parental involvement, but that in the interests of social justice, more must be done to recognize parents' collective right to meaningfully contribute to decision-making within education.

## Normative discourses of active and involved parenting

Neoliberalism has redefined relationships among citizens, public institutions and the state. We see this in Britain and elsewhere, for instance, in the coupling of public sector marketization and welfare-reduction strategies with programmes of active citizenship geared towards broadening citizens' responsibilities (Newman and Tonkens 2011). Discourses of active parenting are fundamental to this model of citizenship, representing a key avenue through which citizens are pressed to fulfil their obligations in post-welfare contexts. In education and family policy this is reflected in the flawed conviction that parents are the ultimate determinants of children's future outcomes and a corresponding fixation on *what parents do* rather than the structural conditions shaping family life (Jensen 2018). Indeed, the refrain that 'it is what parents do that matters, not who they are' has echoed across political administrations (Allen 2011; DfES 2006; DfE 2018). According to this rhetoric, parents must respond to an increasingly uncertain educational landscape by striving to provide optimal developmental environments so that even the most unfortunate family circumstances can be overcome. In other terms, as former UK prime minister David Cameron articulated: 'what matters most to a child's life chances is not the wealth of their upbringing but the warmth of their parenting' (Cameron [2010], cited in Jensen 2010: 2).

Active parenting is primarily constructed in educational contexts through policy and practice around parental involvement.[5] Although concern in the UK regarding parents' role vis-à-vis education dates back to the Plowden Report (1967), parents have come under increasing pressure over recent decades to 'inhabit and perform certain responsibilities and obligations in order that they might become more "active" and "effective" as parents' (Olmedo and Wilkins 2017: 577). One effect of expanding parental responsibilities has been to blur boundaries between home and school, with parents expected to adopt the role of surrogate educators (Crozier 2019). From the purview of neoliberal economic rationalities, this transforms parenting into an instrumental, goal-oriented activity in which it becomes reconceived as a matter of human capital development centred on making good choices and investments in children's development to maximize later dividends (Rosen 2018). Hence parents are increasingly encouraged to strategically nurture their children's talents through the provision of extra-curricular activities (Vincent and Maxwell 2016) or turn even the most mundane aspects of everyday life, such as riding the bus or grocery shopping, into educationally enriching experiences (HM Government 2019).

Education policy contrives to sanction an ideal of active and involved parenting. The active parent, on this account, exercises choice in the educational marketplace, supports schools and undertakes pedagogical work at home and maximizes their child's potential by carefully crafting their repertoire of talents and abilities. The obvious flipside to this logic, however, is the spectre of the inactive and irresponsible parent. Crozier (2019) argues that whereas white middle-class parents are routinely perceived as active regardless of their actual involvement, the engagement of parents from working-class and minoritized backgrounds is often misrecognized or misrepresented. This suggests that normative constructions of active parenting cohere around white middle-class forms of participation that can result in greater institutional scrutiny of non-dominant parents, thereby further entrenching their marginal status.

Alongside these problematic exclusions, active parenting also privileges the individual family unit. Like active citizenship discourse more generally, which de-collectivizes citizenship and valourizes individual responsibility (Newman and Tonkens 2011), active parenting promotes individualism (Crozier 2019; Vincent 2000). Any sense that parents might realize collective aspirations through concerted action is occluded by the overwhelming tendency to posit parents as self-interested individuals solely concerned with securing competitive advantage for their families:

The injunction to choose is translated into an injunction on behaviour – the need to be calculating, moralizing (acting in the best interests of the child), self-regarding and committed to pursuing competitive familial advantage above consideration for any notion [of] public interest, public orientation, public ethos, fairness or equity. (Olmedo and Wilkins 2017: 579)

Our data reveal a different story. This is a story about parents collectively defending their common interests and pursuing a vision of educational justice that disrupts the imperatives of neoliberal individualism. These are active parents, parents deeply invested in their children's education and the well-being of their communities, who channel incredible energy into fighting for what they believe is right. Yet the authorities' hostile reaction to parents engaged in anti-academization struggles suggests that active parenting ideals do not extend to genuine opportunities to influence policy or shape institutional practice. There appears to be something paradoxical then about active parenting discourse: parents are to be active, just not too active. Focusing primarily on the experiences of anti-academization activists, the analysis that follows traces their struggle to be heard and the resistance they encountered.

## The study

This chapter reports on qualitative data collected between 2018 and 2020 from a sample of three parent-led campaign groups:

### Protect Children's Education (PCE)

PCE was formed in 2017 to oppose national funding cuts to education. The campaign is notable for combining innovative online activism with more traditional methods and for having spawned a network of regional groups all operating under PCE 'branding'. Our focus, however, is on the original, founding group based in a large city in the south of England. Despite the campaign having waned somewhat in the face of the Covid-19 pandemic and other pressures, PCE remains active and continues to maintain a social media presence.

### Eastborough Anti-Academisation Coalition (EAC)

EAC was established in late 2017 to consolidate opposition to academization in a large outer-London borough. The group primarily comprised parent and teaching union activists from three primary schools facing imminent threat of conversion: Old Leaf, Grovelands and Fenside. Key participants from EAC were interviewed after the school campaigns had concluded, but whilst the coalition itself was still active to a degree. By 2020, EAC ceased to exist although many members had moved on to further advocacy work in the community.

### Crowley Parents Campaign (CPC)

CPC was formed by parents seeking to prevent the conversion of Stonefield Primary School in Crowley, a town bordering London. Between 2017 and 2019 they rana rancorous campaign that attracted significant media attention and resulted in one of the most protracted academy conversions on record. Interviews were conducted with the two parents driving the campaign, both during the conversion process and after the school formally converted to academy status.

Data used in this chapter were collected through semi-structured interviews, focus groups and observations. In total, sixteen parents participated in the study: seven each from PCE and EAC, and the two parents driving CPC. A further interview was conducted with a figure from EAC who helped coordinate the campaign. In most cases, those interviewed self-identified as core members with lead roles in the respective campaigns. The sample was a purposive one – we decided to focus on the three parent-led campaigns listed earlier as each had a distinct focus, methods of campaigning and levels of publicity. For each, we initially approached key informants, and through them, recruited parents to the study. The majority of our interviewees were female, and participants from EAC and PCE indicated this was true for membership of the campaigns more broadly. The predominance of mothers in the campaign groups is perhaps indicative of the persistence of gendered divisions of labour around schooling (see Reay 2006), although this is not a line of questioning that we pursue here. The socio-economic backgrounds of parents were complex and varied across the campaigns. The EAC campaign brought together parents from a range of ethnically diverse, often working-class backgrounds. PCE's membership consisted mostly of white, middle-class parents with professional employment histories, whilst the two parents interviewed from CPC had varying social and ethnic backgrounds. Data were also collected from three 'campaign advocates' (individuals involved in promoting and advising educational campaigns). Of these, one had coordinated a parent-led campaign, one was a campaign manager for a prominent teaching union and the other volunteered for a nationwide network coordinating opposition to academization. However, it is the data collected from parent activists that we predominantly draw upon here. Ethical approval was secured in advance and standard ethical procedures were followed throughout. All relevant proper names have been assigned pseudonyms to protect the identities of participants, including the names of the campaign groups themselves.

The study was centrally concerned with the experiences, motivations and meaning-making activities of families engaged in educational activism. We sought to investigate the goals and organizational structures of the campaigns, the emotions, values and motivations driving parents' activism, and the affinities and dynamics among parents, children and other key actors. However, it is important to note that our account is partial and one-sided. We report here solely on parents' experiences of fighting their campaigns. We have no independent means of verifying the events reported and offer no account of the perspectives of other protagonists. What is certain, however, is that this is how parents *felt* about events and it is precisely the affective dimension of parents' activism that the study sought to explore in large part. Our aim is to do justice to parents' experiences, to their feelings of disenfranchisement and their anger at being silenced and ignored. It is in this spirit that we trace their struggle for recognition.

## Activist parenting

Activism, as we understand it, is the practice of engaging in concerted action aimed at securing social and political change. It can involve protest, direct action and organized campaigning, but may also adopt more implicit, less confrontational forms (Horton and Kraftl 2009). Our specific concern here is with educational activism – activism that is explicitly centred on educational policies, practices or institutions and, in our case, led by parents.

Although parental activism in education has attracted substantial scholarly interest in other national contexts, particularly the United States (e.g. Cortez 2013; Fennimore 2017; Jasis 2013; Stitzlein 2015; Warren and Mapp 2011), it represents an under-researched field in Britain. Despite some notable recent work (Sibley-White 2019; Stevenson 2016), the most extensive treatment of the topic remains Carol Vincent's (2000) study of parent-centred organizations. In this work, Vincent observed that parental activism appeared to be a relatively uncommon phenomenon, but much has changed in the intervening years, and parent-led campaigns have become a more visible feature of the educational landscape. This is attributable in part to the growth of social media as an organizing tool (Heron-Hruby and Landon-Hays 2014), but it is also a likely consequence of the sweeping reforms imposed on the sector over this period.

The relentless pursuit of marketization through the expansion of the academies and free school programmes, greater emphasis on high-stakes testing and an attendant narrowing of school curricula, policies and practices surrounding Special Educational Needs (SEND) provision, and significant cuts to educational spending have all contributed to producing uncertainty and anxiety in the sector and provoked considerable opposition from parents.

We argue that it is through engaging in collective action to defend common interests that parent-activists disrupt dominant norms of active and involved parenting and the individualism around which they cohere. As we explore shortly, our data reveal a closer binding between universal and particular concerns than was evident in Vincent's (2000) study, where parents' action tended to centre on securing improvements for individual children and families. It also presents a more radical challenge to neoliberal orthodoxy than is suggested by Sibley-White's (2019) conclusion that *Let Our Kids Be Kids*, a campaign opposing high-stakes testing in primary schools, which ultimately remained complicit with the underlying logic of the regime being contested.

Of all the campaign groups comprising our study, PCE was perhaps the most straightforwardly altruistic in outlook. Whilst members acknowledged that funding cuts would inevitably impinge upon their children's education and that repealing them was therefore to their own benefit, it was the desire to protect education provision for all that really galvanized the campaign:

> The desire to make a change, the desire to make a difference, the desire to do something not for my children because they're always going to be okay, even if I end up having to home school, they'll be fine. I earn enough money to send them off to dance classes and study textiles and drama. It costs probably £200 to £300 a term extra for me to do that; I can afford the £1,000 plus per school year, but most families can't and so, this is for a campaign that is saying, 'Every child matters and we're doing this for the community, not for ourselves' and it's that passion, that drive to change something. (Lynn, PCE)

Universal and particular concerns also coincided within the anti-academization campaigns. Parents were clearly anxious about the implications of academization for their own children's education, but this was often framed as a collective issue affecting all families as well as the wider community. For EAC campaigners these anxieties translated into general opposition to the very principle of academization and a demand for greater community participation in education:

*From Active to Activist Parenting*          195

I think that for us it's about inclusion, it's about democracy, it's about listening to parents, it's about being together and work together as a community to improve anything that affected us, rather than just getting a few people who don't know us to make those decisions. It's about democracy. It's about true democracy in the way our educational system is run. So, I think, yeah, that's what we're fighting for, that's the key. (Floyd, EAC)

The CPC campaign, on the other hand, mainly concentrated on the decision to pursue conversion at Stonefield primary and the suitability of the academy trust awarded the school. The lead campaigners, Molly and Mina, were adamant they were not opposing academization per se, they simply wanted parents (and staff) to be afforded a genuine say in the future direction of the school. As Mina explained, 'We want the right education and the right trust for our school because we understand the bigger picture and we feel Amphora Academy Trust are not right for us.' Even here, though, parents' efforts were often couched in a demand for greater parental voice in education more generally and clearly sought to improve circumstances for the whole school community.

It would be a mistake, then, to view the campaigns as motivated primarily by self-interest. Of course, individual families had something to gain from the campaigns – should they prove successful at least – but collective aspirations and wider educational goals equally played a part. Moreover, once the pressures of campaigning are considered – the demands on time and energy, the strain on family life and the danger of becoming alienated from powerful institutional figures responsible for your children's education – we see that actively opposing policy might actually work *against* families' immediate interests. It would undoubtedly have been easier, less risky and less stressful for parents to simply acquiesce, but, as Molly indicated in the quote with which we opened the chapter, parents felt morally compelled to act.

## Struggling for recognition

In this section, we explore how parent-activists in our study were involved in a struggle for recognition. Each campaign engendered different relationships with those in positions of power, which resulted in different levels and types of conflict. The extent of conflict in each case was largely determined by the degree of alignment between parents' interests and those of the authorities, with conflict figuring much more prominently in the reports of anti-academization activists

(EAC and CPC) than in the school funding campaign (PCE). Indeed, working collaboratively with schools was a key aspect of PCE strategy, and consideration was given throughout to avoid alienating headteachers: 'I think we've always been if the heads don't like it, if the heads aren't on side with this, then we're not going to do it' (Yara). The overriding image presented was one of working in concert *with* school leadership.

Anti-academization activists, in contrast, were often pitted against an array of forces with vested interests in pursuing conversion, from school leadership and governing bodies, through to local authorities and the Department for Education itself. The urgency of the threat posed by academization and its proximity to families' everyday lives further exacerbated tensions and uncertainties. As David, one of the 'campaign advocates' we interviewed, noted:

> Fighting against academisation is extremely difficult … Fights against academisation are on a school-by-school basis and what you have to have and what you have to do, and it isn't easy, you literally have to confront the governors and the head of the school to which your children go to and that's difficult.

It is this combination of diametrically opposed interests and the proximity and urgency of the issue that helps explain the prevalence of conflict within the anti-academization campaigns. Whilst prejudice may also have been a factor, insofar as some EAC campaigners suggested the authorities held patronizing views of parents and the local area, it is unlikely they would have encountered such opposition had their campaigns been less antithetical to the interests of the authorities.

Parents across the campaigns, particularly those engaged in anti-academization struggles, were fighting to be heard and fighting for the right to meaningfully contribute to key decisions affecting their children's futures. In *The Struggle for Recognition* (1995), Honneth argues that it is precisely the denial of recognition which motivates social struggle and propels social change. 'Motives for social resistance and rebellion', he writes, 'are formed in the context of moral experiences stemming from the violation of deeply rooted expectations regarding recognition' (Honneth 1995: 163). Honneth's starting point is that individual self-realization and identity-formation are crucially dependent upon intersubjective regard: it is only through the process of being recognized by others that we recognize ourselves and can develop the practical relation to self, which secures our sense of ourselves as fully individuated beings. Mutual recognition thus constitutes the normative core of social interaction, and it is the experience of misrecognition (*Mißachtung*), the experience of having recognition denied or withheld, Honneth suggests, that drives social conflict and, with it, social change.

Honneth's contention that struggles for recognition drive progressive societal change has been much debated (see Fraser and Honneth 2003). However, it is not our intention to enter into this debate here. Instead, we draw on Honneth's ideas about recognition as a tool for illuminating and deepening our understanding of parent-activists' accounts, focusing in particular on the profoundly affective nature of experiences of misrecognition. Honneth writes, for instance, that 'all social integration depends on reliable forms of mutual recognition, whose insufficiencies and deficits are always tied to *feelings of misrecognition*', and that 'the experience of disrespect is always accompanied by *affective sensations* that are, in principle, capable of revealing to individuals the fact that certain forms of recognition are being withheld from them' (Honneth 2003b: 245; Honneth 1995: 136; emphasis added).

That misrecognition felt, not simply cognized, is central to our analysis. It is now firmly acknowledged that emotions play a fundamental role in social movements and protest activity (Goodwin, Jasper and Polletta 2001; Jasper 2018). Emotions spur us to action and sustain our involvement, they nurture solidarities and shape our aims and goals. Not only were our data replete with emotion talk, interviews themselves were often punctuated with affect as parents relived key events. This was particularly acute in connection with anti-academization activists' contemptuous treatment by the authorities. Parents were angry, upset, outraged and aggrieved. They felt ignored and excluded; disregarded and belittled. Such feelings are symptomatic of the injuries of misrecognition. They also served, however, as motivation for parents to continue their fight.

The EAC and CPC campaigns originated with inquisitive parents seeking information about why academization was being pursued and what it would entail. In each case, however, their efforts were frustrated. Consultation processes were invariably represented as bogus, designed to legitimate preordained decisions without any genuine intention of hearing parents' views. There were even suspicions that they were intentionally rigged to prevent participation:

What happened is, consultations – which are meant to be *meaningful*, right? – were pretty much done as a paper exercise and the schools were essentially just trying to get through the consultation process without having to actually consult anyone. So, meetings were held that were sort of at strange times, they weren't well communicated, and so you had really poor turnouts. (Mark, Old Leaf Primary, EAC)

Such experiences are not unique. Martinez-Cosio (2010) and Stevenson (2016) also highlight how ostensibly participatory processes can be used to contain and control parents. Parents' experiences at Grovelands Primary School (EAC) were particularly telling in this regard. Despite the school serving a multi-ethnic population from a wide variety of linguistic backgrounds, consultation took place entirely in English, and although interpreters were supplied, albeit at the behest of parents, it was generally felt they were utilized in ways that stifled discussion:

> They were very patronising in that we had parents there who had language issues, the interpreters wouldn't sit with the parents, they were standing on the side, and it was just … the whole thing was just … it was just mismanaged, it was just poor. It was a poor excuse for a consultation exercise. (Isra, Grovelands Primary, EAC)

Forestalling debate and the disregard this displays for parents' interests, constitutes, for Honneth, a form of misrecognition he captures in terms of the denial of rights. On this account, denying parents the right to speak or air dissenting views deprives them of the status of equal partners to interaction with equally valid rights claims, thereby violating 'the intersubjective expectation to be recognized as a subject capable of forming moral judgements' (Honneth 1995: 133–4).

Another form of misrecognition concerns the negation of individual self-worth and value. Often manifested through insult and belittlement, this involves 'evaluative forms of disrespect' that 'downgrade individual forms of life and manners of belief as inferior or deficient, [robbing] the subjects in question of every opportunity to attribute social value to their own abilities' (Honneth 1995: 134). Many parents reported feeling undermined by the authorities in an effort to discredit their campaigns and comments like the following were not uncommon:

> But I think, you know, at every opportunity, they tried to make us inferior by the wording they used on their reports, on their letters; you know, 'Some parents …', 'A few …', 'A small number of parents'. No, we're not small actually, but you know, I felt like that was a sort of manipulative and quite bullying tactic that they were using within their sort of letters to make us seem insignificant. And they did – they used the word 'insignificant' (Aalia, Grovelands Primary, EAC)

Such condescending treatment, moreover, was a source of considerable frustration for parents:

That's the thing, who did they think we are that we don't have a clue about how things work. That's the other thing. I think they were so hellbent on their own ideas and initiatives, that they just forgot that we are also professionals, that we have an understanding of how things work. (Isra, Grovelands Primary, EAC)

Contempt and condescension function as mechanisms for withholding recognition. To show contempt for someone or to view them condescendingly is to assert one's superiority over the presumed inferiority of the other. But it can also carry a darker inflection, morphing in some cases into outright intimidation:

Because they've done, bullied me, in governors where they all ganged up on me [and] it was really hard. Seven governors against you. Everybody shouting at you, not allowing you to speak. Not trying to get your points across. You emailing them, they're not listening to you. It's, it's really hard as a person to go through that, you know. I've fled from a bloody dictatorship, you get me. I thought we had democracy in this country and I'm seeing that as really unfair to what, the way they were treating me. (Floyd, Fenside Primary, EAC)

For Floyd, as for other parents, feeling disrespected elicited intense and sometimes painful emotions. Indeed, this was one of several instances in Floyd's interview where he became visibly angry and upset – the gravity of his feelings accentuated here through comparison with the experience of fleeing political violence. This reminds us that the research interview is an affective practice in its own right (Wetherell 2012). In recounting their emotions participants were often also reliving them. In cases like this, where there is a doubling of emotion, as recounted and relived, we see just how deep injuries of misrecognition can cut.

Similar experiences were reported by CPC campaigners. Molly and Mina's forensic investigation of the academization process surrounding Stonefield primary brought them into direct conflict with the local authority, the incoming academy trust, the Regional Schools Commissioner, and the Department for Education. Although the pair relished their notoriety to a degree, it also came at a cost:

This is where the DfE … and I know why they hate me so much, yeah, and it is a personal thing, because I've seen emails about myself, yeah. Like, 'Shut this woman up', and all that, yeah? What did she [senior figure in the local authority] call me? 'That fucking FOI[6] woman', yeah? You know, like, that's horrible. If I was actually a bit more of a, like, all airy fairy, I'd find that really offensive, that could be a bit damaging to someone's character really, you know like if someone was saying that about you. (Molly, CPC)

Again, we get a sense here for the wounds that misrecognition can inflict, the damage it can cause to an individual's integrity and self-worth. Even Molly's apparent stoicism was belied, for instance, by acute doubts, fears and insecurities: 'I think they're listening to my calls and that ... and they're looking at me emails.'

However, one of the most pronounced examples of contempt concerned parents' vilification as 'troublemakers' and 'bullies':

> [Senior leadership at the school] were actually trying to portray us as troublemakers and, do you know, as bullies. We were called bullies. We were called all sorts. (Aalia, Grovelands primary, EAC)

> And I can tell you now: when they ... when we found out we were classed as anti-academy boisterous parents I was quite taken aback by that. I was like, 'No, I'm not that; I just don't think Amphora Academy Trust is right for my school.' (Mina, CPC)

Conferring pathologized identities onto parents is an act of 'affective-discursive positioning' (Wetherell 2012) that delegitimizes parents' feelings and discredits their struggle whilst simultaneously working to secure a hegemonic affective order in which parents are expected to display compliant attitudes. Parents' feelings thus constitute 'outlaw emotions' incompatible with the dominant order (Jaggar 1989). Yet, parents resisted this positioning. Some, like Mina, sought to reclaim value by appealing to the justice of their actions: 'We're two mums who just wanted some unjust done right. We've annoyed so many people just because they've always got away with it, could think they could keep getting away with it.' Others harnessed their anger as fuel to further propel their campaigns, thereby demonstrating how counterproductive contempt can be. As Aalia commented, 'it just became this thing of feeling so downtrodden that nobody's listening and then you think, "Right, I'm going to shout louder now. I'm going to scream even more if you're gonna do that." And that's what we did and that kept us going.'

Wider research on parental activism indicates that the experiences documented here are by no means uncommon, which confirms the sense that active parenting appears desirable only insofar as it aligns with dominant interests (Cortez 2013; Fennimore 2017; Mediratta and Karp 2003; Pazey 2020; Stevenson 2016). McKay and Garrat (2013: 743) suggest, for instance, that 'the degree to which the voice of the parent is fully incorporated into decision-making is largely contingent upon the extent to which what is being said actually conforms to the received discourse and the normalising gaze of prevailing authorities and professionals'. When parents challenge the dominant narrative, on the other hand, when they transition from being active parents to parent-activists, they are instead pathologized as confrontational troublemakers (Stevenson 2016). Our argument is that we need to rethink the narrow and loaded construction of active and involved parenting in ways that can recognize and appreciate the power of collective parental involvement and through doing so secure genuine spaces for parental participation in decision-making structures within education.

## Rethinking parental involvement

In the context of uncertain education policy landscapes, parental involvement is framed in terms of a relatively narrow range of pedagogical behaviours, for example supporting learning; relationships with schools and the quality of the home learning environment. To fully appreciate its potential, however, it needs extending to encompass parents' collective efforts to influence education policy and provision. Parental activism, in other words, *is* a form of parental involvement, albeit one that disrupts traditional models (Fennimore 2017). It might even be considered parental involvement par excellence. These are parents deeply invested in their children's education, who devote considerable time and energy to fighting for what they believe is right, often at significant cost to themselves. Moreover, as many parents conveyed, their actions are themselves educational, teaching children about democratic processes and the value of civic engagement, amongst other things. In many respects it thus represents the very epitome of active and involved parenting.

A broadened conception of parental involvement would recognize parents' right to collectively contribute to decision-making processes within education and legitimate action undertaken to secure that right, at least insofar as the goals in question prove morally defensible.[7] This requires thinking beyond the individualism and instrumentalism enshrined within current languages of parenting to evoke instead an alternative ethico-political horizon of childrearing, one shaped by and through parents' conception of the kind of people they themselves want to be and the moral example they wish to set for their children (Ramaekers and Suissa 2011). The present study affords a glimpse of such an alternative, with parent-activists demonstrating the power of parenting for the common good rather than mere self-interest.

Rethinking parental involvement also requires challenging ingrained perspectives on the role of parents vis-à-vis education. Despite expanded opportunities for exercising 'choice' and the rhetoric around increasing parents' power and 'voice' (DfE 2016), we remain in a situation where parents have limited scope for genuinely influencing education policy and practice, as the recent dilution of school governing bodies' accountability to parents exemplifies (Belger 2021). Following Wright (2012), we might argue, then, that active parenting is built on a 'fantasy of empowerment'. Its promise is a chimera, a simulacrum of empowerment that masks proliferating responsibilities without any corresponding expansion of rights. Moreover, the construction of active parenting around the model of the individual family unit inevitably excludes consideration of parents' collective interests. Little has changed in this regard from Vincent and Martin's (2000: 474) observation that 'parents are located within a discourse that defines them as passive where collective issues are concerned, and active only in terms of fulfilling their individual responsibilities around their own children'. To the extent that policy does address parents collectively this is often limited to forms of parent blame, where social and educational problems come to be located in the perceived inadequacies of certain family structures and cultures – as we find in the explanation offered for racial inequalities in contemporary Britain by the Sewell Report (Commission on Race and Ethnic Disparities 2021). A different narrative is needed, one that affirms parents' collective rights not merely their individual responsibilities. Moving in this direction means opening up deliberative fora that are genuinely participatory and imbued with an 'emotional morality' underscored by 'recognition and respect for the emotional content of experiences and values and the authentic expression of these as a necessary part of dialogue on issues that are directly relevant to such experiences and values' (Barnes 2008: 473). It is precisely this element that was missing in anti-academization campaigners' dealings with the authorities. A necessary step towards genuinely empowering parents both individually and collectively is therefore to establish deliberative structures that recognize not only parents' right to speak and contribute, but their right to feel, so that fears, concerns and anxieties, for example, might be disclosed without recrimination.

Parent Carer Forums (PCFs) offer an instructive example of both the potential and limitations of formally recognized participatory structures. Originally established by parents of disabled children in the mid-2000s to provide mutual support and lobby for greater voice in SEND policies and procedures, PCFs subsequently acquired official recognition and funding from central government. Whilst the formalization of PCFs has created expanded opportunities for parents to contribute to SEND policy, such as 2015 Code of

Practice, it also binds groups to legal requirements that may ultimately work against parents' interests by restricting campaigning activity and the pursuit of wider social justice agendas (Runswick-Cole and Ryan 2019; Smith 2019). Given the risk that formalization may serve to nullify more progressive and far-reaching demands, the challenge, then, is to devise participatory structures that are flexible enough to accommodate both voice *and* action. There must be spaces, in other words, for parents to meaningfully contribute to policy without thereby relinquishing advocacy and activism.

There is also a pragmatic point to be raised here. If increasing parental involvement is a strategic educational goal, then the intransigence and hostility encountered by anti-academization campaigners strikes a cautionary note. In some cases, like CPC, academization destroyed previously strong relationships between the parent body and the school. In other cases, it had the effect of alienating individual parents. This was represented most acutely in Floyd's account of feeling victimized by the leadership at Fenside (EAC): 'I can't go near the school, I feel traumatised, you know. It's like a war-zone for me.' The fact that campaigning served to create a stronger, more unified and more coordinated parent body at each of the schools suggests there is much to be gained from working constructively with parents, but it also indicates the potential that can be lost through opposition:

> Surely you would want parents that are actually caring, passionate, and proactive? All this fucking energy we're putting into this position we could've raised thousands for that school. All the extra things; we could've had, I could have had bake sales, we could have had a new library, we could've had all sorts of stuff; but no, we're trying to fight the government. (Molly, CPC)

Jasis (2013) maintains that parental activism can create new avenues for collaboration, but for this to happen, he argues, it is important that 'concerned parents not be seen as threats to established school norms or to the perceived power status of teachers and administrators'; instead, schools must recognize 'the value of welcoming parents at the education table as indispensable, knowledgeable, and contributing partners in the schooling of their children' (128). Although the bitter experiences of anti-academization campaigners indicates we may be some distance from realizing this goal, loosening the hold of individualism by recognizing parents' collective rights constitutes a step in the right direction through which we might begin to release the transformative democratic potential of parental involvement (Crozier 2019).

## Conclusion

Educational activism has come under increased critical scrutiny of late (Spielman 2021). Yet, as our data indicate, it can be a legitimate response to the uncertainty and insecurity generated by policy developments affecting children's education, particularly when parents are confronted with obstacles that frustrate meaningful discussion. That parents' efforts were not recognized as a token of their involvement, that they and their claims were disregarded, is indicative of the narrowness of dominant models of active parenting, which paradoxically delegitimize action challenging the status quo even where that action arises from and is evidence of parents' investment in their children's education. Policy primes parents to pursue self-interest and familial advantage through instrumental engagement with the education system whilst simultaneously discouraging collective solutions to the challenges they encounter. The campaigns featured here, however, reveal the promise of collective parental involvement. Parent-activists' resoluteness in the face of institutionalized misrecognition demonstrates the progressive potential of a cohesive and coordinated parent body actively invested in shaping education policy, with strong parental networks acting as a buffer against uncertainty and strengthening the school community. To harness this potential, though, we need to rethink the normative parameters of parental involvement. We need a model that recognizes parents' collective rights and values their contribution. We need a system that secures deliberative spaces for parents to genuinely contribute to decision-making processes and we need authorities receptive to and respectful of parents' feelings.

We close this chapter on a celebratory note. Despite their challenges, the families involved in each campaign secured some notable successes, suggesting that parental activism can lead to system-level change, not merely benefits for individual campaigners (Vincent 2000). The data have also shown how families are able to subvert and challenge dominant discourses of individualism and self-interest by working together for the collective good. The pressure exerted by PCE activists, for example, helped establish school funding as a key election issue and arguably influenced the decision to inject additional funding into schools following the 2017 general election. EAC, for its part, had a considerable impact on the local educational landscape, thwarting two planned conversions and securing a commitment from the local authority to desist from pursuing further academization within the borough. Even though CPC failed in its immediate goal of blocking conversion, it nevertheless had an impact in terms of developing a methodology for combatting academization that campaign groups

_From Active to Activist Parenting_ 205

around the country have emulated as well as purportedly influencing the DfE's own guidance and practices around academization. These successes speak to the power of parental activism and the value of working with rather than against parents and families.

## Acknowledgements

We would like to express our gratitude to all the participants in the study for generously giving their time and for sharing their experiences with us.

## Notes

1  An introspective, intellectual character appearing in a series of novels written by Sue Townsend.
2  An American environmental activist renowned for successfully campaigning against several large-scale corporations.
3  Throughout the chapter, pseudonyms have been allocated to all research participants, schools and parental campaigns.
4  The recent schools White Paper – 'Opportunity for All: Strong Schools with Great Teachers for Your Child' (HM Government, 2022) – has renewed the drive to turn all English schools into academies by enabling local authorities to establish their own MATs.
5  Parental involvement refers here to both involvement with schools and parents' engagement in supporting children's learning.
6  This is a reference to the statutory right of access to public information that is enshrined in the Freedom of Public Information Act 2000; something that Molly and Mina were particularly adept at using throughout the campaign in order to stall the conversion process.
7  As Honneth observes, not every demand for recognition can be considered morally legitimate: 'we generally only judge the objectives of such struggles positively when they point in the direction of social development that we can understand as approximating our ideas of a good or just society' (Honneth 2003a: 171–2).

## References

Allen, G. (2011), _Early Intervention: The Next Steps. An Independent Report to Her Majesty's Government_, London: Crown Copyright.

206     *Reinventing the Family in Uncertain Times*

Ball, S. J., R. Bowe and S. Gewirtz (1996), 'School Choice, Social Class and Distinction: The Realization of Social Advantage in England', *Journal of Education Policy*, 11 (1): 89–112.

Barnes, M. (2008), 'Passionate Participation: Emotional Experiences and Expressions in Deliberative Forums', *Critical Social Policy*, 28 (4), 461–81.

Belger, T. (2021), 'RSC's Push to Get Communities On Board Not Matched by Academy Guidance', *Schools Week*, Saturday 19 June, https://schoolsweek.co.uk/rscs-push-to-get-communities-on-board-not-matched-by-academyguidance/?f&fbclid=IwAR123VCEw1Uv9VW_F2gBFhRhrBodbchoy8BAeL6tmF7FWG-hdxIBOjPCojw. Accessed 1 July 2022.

Commission on Race and Ethnic Disparities (2021), *Commission on Race and Ethnic Disparities: The Report*, London: The Stationery Office.

Cortez, G. A. (2013), 'Occupy Public Education: A Community's Struggle for Educational Resources in the Era of Privatization', *Equity & Excellence in Education*, 46 (1): 7–19.

Crozier, G. (2005), 'Beyond the Call of Duty: The Impact of Racism on Black Parents' Involvement in Their Children's Education', in G. Crozier and D. Reay (eds), *Activating Participation: Parents and Teachers Working towards Partnership*, 39–55, Stoke-on-Trent: Trentham Books.

Crozier, G. (2019), 'Interrogating Parent–School Practices in a Market-Based System. The Professionalization of Parenting and Intensification of Parental Involvement: Is This What Schools Want?', in S. B. Sheldon and T. A. Turner-Vorbeck (eds), *The Wiley Handbook of Family, School and Community Relationships in Education*, 315–31, Hoboken, NJ: John Wiley.

Department for Education (DfE) (2016), *Educational Excellence Everywhere*, London: Crown Copyright.

Department for Education (DfE) (2018), *Improving the Home Learning Environment: A Behaviour Change Approach*, London: Crown Copyright.

Department for Education and Skills (DfES) (2006), *Parenting Support: Guidance for Local Authorities in England*, London: Crown Copyright.

Fennimore, B. S. (2017), 'Permission Not Required: The Power of Parents to Disrupt Educational Hypocrisy', *Review of Research in Education*, 41: 159–81.

Fraser, N. and A. Honneth (2003), *Redistribution or Recognition? A Political-Philosophical Exchange*, London: Verso.

Goodwin, J., J. M. Jasper and F. Polletta (2001), *Passionate Politics: Emotions and Social Movements*, Chicago: University of Chicago Press.

Heron-Hruby, A., and M. Landon-Hays (eds) (2014), *Digital Networking for School Reform: The Online Grassroots Efforts of Parent and Teacher Activists*, New York: Palgrave Macmillan.

HM Government (2019), *Hungry Little Minds: Campaign Toolkit*, https://assets.publishing.service.gov.uk/government/uploads/system/uploads/attachment_data/file/919947/Hungry_Little_Minds_Campaign_Toolkit_Web_Final.pdf. Accessed 22 August 2021.

HM Government (2022), *Opportunity for All: Strong Schools with Great Teachers for Your Child*, London: Crown Copyright.

Honneth, A. (1995), *The Struggle for Recognition: The Moral Grammar of Social Conflicts*, Cambridge: Polity Press.

Honneth, A. (2003a), 'Redistribution as Recognition: A Response to Nancy Fraser', in N. Fraser and A. Honneth (eds), *Redistribution or Recognition? A Political-Philosophhonnethical Exchange*, 110–97, London: Verso.

Honneth, A. (2003b), 'The Point of Recognition: A Rejoinder to the Rejoinder', in N. Fraser and A. Honneth (eds), *Redistribution or Recognition? A Political-Philosophical Exchange*, 237–67, London: Verso.

Horton, J., and P. Kraftl (2009), 'Small Acts, Kind Words and "Not Too Much Fuss": Implicit Activisms', *Emotion, Space and Society*, 2 (1): 14–23.

Jaggar, A. M. (1989), 'Love and Knowledge: Emotion in Feminist Epistemology', *Inquiry*, 32 (2): 151–76.

Jasis, P. (2013), 'Latino Families Challenging Exclusion in a Middle School: A Story from the Trenches', *School Community Journal*, 23 (1): 111–30.

Jasper, J. M. (2018), *The Emotions of Protest*, Chicago: University of Chicago Press.

Jensen, T. (2010), 'Warmth and Wealth: Re-imagining Social Class in Taxonomies of Good Parenting', *Studies in the Maternal*, 2 (1): 1–13.

Jensen, T. (2018), *Parenting the Crisis: The Cultural Politics of Parent-Blame*, Bristol: Policy Press.

Martinez-Cosio, M. (2010), 'Parent's Role in Mediating and Buffering the Implementation of an Urban School Reform', *Education and Urban Society*, 42 (3): 283–306.

McKay, J., and D. Garratt (2013), 'Participation as Governmentality? The Effect of Disciplinary Technologies at the Interface of Service Users and Providers, Families and the State', *Journal of Education Policy*, 28 (6): 733–49.

Mediratta, K., and J. Karp (2003), *Parent Power and Urban School Reform: The Story of Mothers on the Move*, New York: The Institute for Education and Social Policy.

Newman, J., and E. Tonkens (eds) (2011), *Participation, Responsibility and Choice: Summoning the Active Citizen in Western European Welfare States*, Amsterdam: Amsterdam University Press.

Olmedo, A., and A. Wilkins (2017), 'Governing through Parents: A Genealogical Enquiry of Education Policy and the Construction of Neoliberal Subjectivities in England', *Discourse: Studies in the Cultural Politics of Education*, 38 (4): 573–89.

Pazey, B. (2020), 'Ya Basta! Countering the Effects of Neoliberal Reform on an Urban Turnaround High School', *American Educational Research Journal*, 57 (4): 1868–906.

Ramaekers, S., and J. Suissa (2011), 'Parents as "Educators": Languages of Education, Pedagogy and Parenting', *Ethics and Education*, 6 (2): 197–212.

Reay, D. (2006), 'Compounding Inequalities of Gender and Class', in B. Francis, C. Skelton and L. Smulyan (eds), *Handbook on Gender and Education*, 339–49, London: Sage.

Rosen, R. (2018), 'Poverty and Family Troubles: Mothers, Children, and Neoliberal "Antipoverty" Initiatives', *Journal of Family Issues*, 40 (16): 1–24.

Runswick-Cole, K., and S. Ryan (2019), 'Liminal Still? Unmothering Disabled Children', *Disability and Society*, 34 (7–8): 1125–39.

Sibley-White, A. (2019), 'A Critical Discourse Analysis of the Let Our Kids Be Kids Protest', *Power and Education*, 11 (3): 327–45.

Smith, S. L. (2019), 'The Construction of the "Effective" Parent in the Special Educational Needs and Disability (SEND) Code of Practice (2015)' MA Diss., Institute of Education, University College London.

Spielman, A. (2021), Amanda Spielman's speech at the Festival of Education, 23 June, https://www.gov.uk/government/speeches/amanda-spielmans-speech-at-the-festival-of-education. Accessed 22 August 2021.

Stevenson, H. (2016), 'Challenging School Reform from Below: Is Leadership the Missing Link in Mobilization Theory?', *Leadership and Policy in Schools*, 15 (1): 67–90.

Stitzlein, S. M. (2015), 'Improving Public Schools through the Dissent of Parents: Opting Out of Tests, Demanding Alternative Curricula, Invoking Parent Trigger Laws, and Withdrawing Entirely', *Educational Studies*, 51 (1): 57–71.

Vincent, C. (2000), *Including Parents? Education, Citizenship and Parental Agency*, Buckingham: Open University Press.

Vincent, C., and J. Martin (2000), 'School-Based Parents' Groups – a Politics of Voice and Representation?', *Journal of Education Policy*, 15 (5): 459–80.

Vincent, C., and C. Maxwell (2016), 'Parenting Priorities and Pressures: Furthering Understanding of "Concerted Cultivation"', *Discourse: Cultural Politics in Education*, 37 (2): 269–81.

Warren, M. R., and K. L. Mapp (2011), *A Match on Dry Grass: Community Organizing as a Catalyst for School Reform*, Oxford: Oxford University Press.

Wetherell, M. (2012), *Affect and Emotion: A New Social Science Understanding*, London: Sage.

Wright, A. (2012), 'Fantasies of Empowerment: Mapping Neoliberal Discourse in the Coalition Government's Schools Policy', *Journal of Education Policy*, 27 (3): 279–94.

# 12

# Conclusion

Cynthia Okpokiri, Marie-Pierre Moreau and Catherine Lee

*Reinventing the family in uncertain times: Education, policy and social justice* brings together multiple perspectives and framings of families. This volume is fundamentally underpinned by social justice paradigm, as we have sought to privilege notions of family that reside at the periphery of traditional Western family discourses and practices. Key themes drawn from the various works in the volume include sociological interpretations, education and social care practice-informed evidence, narratives and the influences of language on family life, family practices of people of various marginal identities and finally, activism and manoeuvrings within family relations. In other words, but in no particular order, the volume has interrogated transformational ideas vis-à-vis power, discourse, forms, systems and practices in contemporary domestic spaces.

In respect to the book's main ethos to engage marginalized perspectives of the family as a phenomenon, attempts to disrupt entrenched classifications of intimate relationships can take several avenues; some theorists argue that significant social change can only be achieved through radical means, a total upheaval of the systems that created and sustained the status quo (see Kaufman 2016). Some chapters in this book including those by Carmichael-Murphy, Fretwell and Barker, and English, subscribe to this notion of radical change regarding how family is understood and enacted. They make no apologies for not only resisting existing structures of family relations and their conceptualizations, but also supporting the forging of completely new systems. Other chapters follow more subtle processes of change by seeking more incremental ways to circumvent the stifling prescriptions for what should be framed as acceptable norms of domestic relationships. Like Morgan (1996) in his influential work on family practices, the authors did not seek to recommend a particular type of discursive disruption, but have strived to create spaces for inclusion of other voices; being and doing family should not have a prescribed nomenclature, where other potentially nonconformist possibilities are excluded.

It is impossible to explore developments in family relationships without analysing the role of gender. The continued subjugation of women in domestic and professional settings are mirrored in the experiences of LGBTQ+ people who identify as sexual minorities (see Moreau 2022). Conversely, some of the hard-won legal and moral rights of these groups are being rolled back in present times by increasingly right-wing and autocratic governments around the world. The reversal of the landmark *Roe versus Wade* 'settled law' on abortion in the United States by their Supreme Court in June 2022 has opened the way to murmurings across the world, *re-questioning* women's bodily autonomy and the rights of sexual minorities, in particular, the existence of transgender people. In July 2022, UK government removed references to sexual and reproductive rights and bodily autonomy of women in the updated International Agreement on the Freedom of Religion or Belief (see Davies 2022). Tinkering with the rights and well-being of women is certainly going to impact significantly on family realities, not the least in the number of children a woman (or girl) would have, and the resulting extensive implications. Several chapters in the book including those by Passerino and Zenklusen, Lee and Carmichael-Murphy speak to women's clamour for increased self-determination, as women around the world continue to seek more equal rights. The three editors of this volume are women, and vigorously resist the prospect of going back to blatantly gender-oppressive conditions of decades past.

In presenting the family as a verbed concept, Carvalho and Casimiro drew on well-established literature to emphasize that family is not a situated entity but a web of actions and interactions. The authors credit LGBTQ communities in the United States with the evolution of *families of choice* when people felt it essential to draw on friends to enact family relationships. An important missing element of this notion of *family of choice* is that long before the advent of autonomous LGBTQ communities in the United States, African families either in diaspora or in urban cities in African countries had perfected families of choice through *families of necessity*. Many African persons were willing to raise other people's children as their own, and parents and carers asked friends and sometimes acquaintances to do so for various reasons, including financial, access to opportunities and convenience (see Colder and Maclean 1982). This phenomenon was easily understood in African circles but poorly conceptualized in Western discourses until the advent of congregating LGBTQ people. The general perspective in London in 1965 was that African 'mothers who relied on [private] fostering inevitably demonstrated a "curious lack of concern for their children"' (Bailkin 2009: 107). The increase in Black African children in private foster care arrangement in UK and the United States in the 1960s up to the 1990s can be explained through the concept of *families of necessity*. In fact, the notorious case of a child named Victoria Climbié in UK, who died in 2000 following months of abuse by her great-aunt, who was only a family member through necessity, is often reported as failure of private fostering. Many analysts saw such cases as good examples of why non-consanguine family relations are problematic, calling for the prohibition of the practice based on a few similar cases, and failing to appreciate the potential strengths of the practice (see Bailkin 2009).

White children growing up in UK do not also wholly subscribe to adults' limiting understandings of *who* constitutes a family member. Kinship care in Western contexts is underpinned by utilitarian calculations of state actors including social workers and social care policymakers, but Shuttleworth's chapter presents children's considerations quite differently, in ways that mirror the developments of *families of choice* and *necessity*. Again, this reflects the chapters by Lee and English. The frequent use of the singular *we* by the young participants in Shuttleworth's work in describing their experiences negates the individualism inherent in Western ideals of private life (see Fevre, Guimarães and Zhao 2020). These ideas compel us to reframe not just how we *see* and *do* family, but invites us to let children and young people cross the restrictive familial boundaries set by adults in their lives.

This book does well to amplify children's voices. Children and young people in the twenty-first century largely find ways to connect, and manage some of their needs and fears, through social media. In the case of children of military parents in the chapter by Bowser-Angermann, Gray, Wood, Fossey and Godier-McBard, such communication is made more complex when a parent is away on military deployment. The Covid-19 pandemic also highlights the increased use of social media as a major means of communication among family members, especially those who live apart (Drouin et al. 2020). Telecommunications provide opportunities for power to shift between family members; an individual can, for instance, decide not to respond to a telecommunication message, or do so when they choose. There are of course widely recognized oppressive uses of such media; partners and parents have been known to use them as monitoring tools, sometimes with sinister motives of control (Leitão 2021). The objective here though is to acknowledge the shift in agency within the family that social media institutes and to explore how online connections can produce new positive permutations of family membership.

Anti-racist thinking, as centred in Carmichael-Murphy's chapter, guides us to contemplate how non-Western, particularly Black, knowledges and practices are accorded little respect in Western spheres, while any negative implications from those perspectives are accentuated (Okpokiri 2021). Colonial legacies evident in the continued disruption of Black ways of being suggest it is not outrageous to imagine that atomizing close relationships in ex-colonies and among previously colonized peoples is a neo-colonialist aim. Adzahlie-Mensah's chapter speaks to language as a bearer of culture, and the colonizers historically sought to change the *natives'* culture (see Malinowski 1936). This book joins the calls for resistance to the continued colonialism of thought, culture and relationships of persons and groups from former colonies.

Resistance to forces of oppression is a thread that runs through this book. Fretwell and Barker's discussion of activist parents indicates that collective citizenships are essential to overcome dominant seats of power. We are convinced that reinvigorated ancient policies that lock girls out of schools in Afghanistan or ensure that American girls as young as ten years bear the children of their rapists can be overturned through multi-pronged concerted acts of solidarity. In their chapter, Gusmeroli and Trappolin bristle against outdated laws and social processes that ultimately work to undermine the parenting aspirations of lesbian and gay adults in Italy. We are not unaware that in too many countries LGBTQ people are not able to live their authentic lives openly, let alone be allowed, like other heterosexual adults, to have and care for their own children while in same-sex relationships. Nevertheless, we actively argue that the joys and pains of parenting should be extended to every responsible adult who would choose to be a parent, not only in Italy but across the world.

In concluding this important body of work, it is useful to evaluate what is included in the volume and what is missing, the types or ways of being family that are outstanding and where the opportunities are for future evolutions of conceptualizations of family. Countries covered in the book are drawn from northern and southern hemisphere, allowing for North American postmodernist arguments to be juxtaposed with African emancipatory ones. Contemporary Asian debates on constructions of family are not overtly visible in this volume. Core themes of the book do nonetheless represent current points of inquiry in academic and public discourses and practices in the region, particularly southern and eastern Asia, covering China and India who together comprise more than a third of the world's population (see Evans 2021; Kowalski 2021; Zuo 2013). The chapters by Shuttleworth, Gusmeroli and Trappolin, and Adzahlie-Mensah all resonate with struggles for a reconfiguring of family forms, hierarchies and responsibilities, recognition and respect for other ways of being, and genuine post-colonial liberations similarly sought by Asian entities on the margins. The

*Conclusion* 213

concept of ageing and who cares for ageing family members is as old as the gendering of caring as a female preserve, across peoples and of all nations of the globe; Lee and English engaged with sentiments and practicalities around ageing through queer lenses with multifaceted trajectories. They both however write from separate but similar Western contexts, and it would be useful to see how persons from the Global Majority grapple with the issues both authors discuss. Future academic endeavours in the subject area should thus consider non-Western debates and experiences.

Poverty and class struggles remain exigent within and across families, epitomizing society. Interestingly, three pivotal contested arenas such as childhood education, caring and class are scrutinized in the chapter by Passerino and Zenklusen. Just like the care for ageing family members, education of children, especially younger age groups, is heavily gender-skewed towards women (Moreau 2022). While Passerino and Zenklusen touched on how middle-class teachers navigate caring and work, an equally robust working-class reimagining of family would have enriched this volume even more. Likewise, the voices and changes impelled by other social experiences including religion and dis/ability, among others, require interrogation in future volumes of similar interests.

# References

Bailkin, J. (2009), 'The Postcolonial Family? West African Children, Private Fostering, and the British State', *The Journal of Modern History*, 81 (1): 87–121.

Colder, S., and J. Maclean (1982), 'Private Fostering in Lambeth', *Adoption & Fostering*, 6 (2): 16–37.

Davies, L. (2022), 'UK under International Pressure over Deletion of Abortion Commitments', *theguardian.com*, https://www.theguardian.com/global-developm ent/2022/jul/22/european-countries-pressurise-uk-over-removal-of-abortion-comm itments-liz-truss. Accessed 9 August 2022.

Drouin, M., B. T. McDaniel, J. Pater and T. Toscos (2020), 'How Parents and Their Children Used Social Media and Technology at the Beginning of the COVID-19 Pandemic and Associations with Anxiety', *Cyberpsychology, Behavior, and Social Networking*, 23 (11): 727–36.

Evans, H. (2021), '"Patchy Patriarchy" and the Shifting Fortunes of the CCP's Promise of Gender Equality since 1921', *China Quarterly*, 248 (S1): 95–115.

Fevre, R., I. Guimarães and W. Zhao (2020), 'Parents, Individualism and Education: Three Paradigms and Four Countries', *Review of Education*, 8 (3): 693–726.

Kaufman, C. (2016), *Ideas for Action: Relevant Theory for Radical Change*, Oakland: PM Press.

Kowalski, J. (2021), 'Between Gender and Kinship: Mediating Rights and Relations in North Indian NGOs', *American Anthropologist*, 123 (2): 330–42.

Leitão, R. (2021), 'Technology-Facilitated Intimate Partner Abuse: A Qualitative Analysis of Data from Online Domestic Abuse Forums', *Human–Computer Interaction*, 36 (3): 203–42.

Malinowski, B. (1936), 'Native Education and Culture Contact', *International Review of Missions*, 25 (3): 480–515.

Moreau, M. P. (2022), 'Performing the "Feminine" Subject of Education: Lessons from Matilda', in S. Kerger L. and Brasseur (eds), *Gender and Education in Luxembourg and beyond: Local Challenges and New Perspectives*, 158–70, Luxemburg: Mélusine Press.

Morgan, D. (1996), *Family Connections*, Cambridge: Polity Press.

Okpokiri, C. (2021), 'Parenting in Fear: Child Welfare Micro Strategies of Nigerian Parents in Britain', *British Journal of Social Work*, 51 (2): 427–44.

Zuo, J. (2013), 'Women's Liberation and Gender Obligation Equality in Urban China: Work/Family Experiences of Married Individuals in the 1950s', *Science & Society*, 77 (1): 98–125.

# Index

absentee father 6, 56
Academies Act (2010) 188
active and involved parenting
  discourses 189–91
  individualism 190
  norms of 188
activist parenting 193–5, 212
additive and cumulative hypothesis of
  family disruptions 50
adoption 1, 3, 6, 21, 29–31, 69, 109–10,
  117, 130
Advocacy and Services for LGBTQ+
  Elders (SAGE) 125, 135
Adzahlie-Mensah, V. 6, 212
affective discursive positioning
  200
affective sensations 197
affiliation 42
affinity 42
African-American communities
  15
African family
  conceptualizing 49–50
  economic production unit 49
  English as language of instruction in
    Ghana 54–60
  extended family 49–50
  family disruptions 50–1
  kinship relationship 49
  language of instruction and family
    disruptions 51–4
  psycho-biological unit 49
  social unit 49
African Union Plan of Action on the
  Family 49–50
ageing 213
  healthy 125
  transgender 134–5
Ageing Without Children 125, 135
Aletta, E. G. 127
allostatic load 137–8
ambivalence relationships 34–6

anti-academization 202–3
  activists 191, 195–7
  campaigns 188–9, 196
anti-immigration Leave campaign 67
Argentina
  education workforce in 7
  family, care relations and professional
    practices 154–7
  female education workers 157–62
  gender inequalities 108, 153, 157, 162–3
ART, *see* assisted reproductive technology
assisted reproductive technology (ART)
  107, 109, 117
Atkin, K. 16
Atwood, K. 171
Australia
  cultural and linguistic sensitivity 13
  family arrangements 13

Bandura, A. 123, 132
Barker, J. 7, 209, 212
Beck-Gernsheim, E. 12
Behavioral Risk Factor Surveillance
  System survey 135
Berger, J. 170
Berghs, M. 16
Bernini, S. 109
Bertone, C. 105, 118
betweenness 113, 117
Bhaskar, R. 42
Bhat, M. A. 51–2
Bian, Y. 18
Biden, J. 126
biological/legal parent 111
birth rates 13
bisexual women 84; *see also* lesbians, elder
Black African 70
Black British families 65–7
  Blackness in British education 70–2
  Britain, Brexit and 'Britishness' 67–8
  British values 69–70
  discrimination 65

exclusion of 67
liminality and the liabilities of
language 73–4
marginalization 74
meritocracy 72–3
misrecognition 74–6
politicization of 76
racial disparities 66
single-issue policy 73
social inequalities 65
Black Caribbean 70
Black identities 70
Black Lives Matter 1
Black mothering 67
blended families 2, 115
Blume, L. B. 5
blurring, domestic space and
workspace 158–60
Bourdieu, P. 86
Bowen, M. 133
Bower, K. L. 88
Bowser-Angermann, J. 7, 211
Boza, C. 124, 132
Braukmann, S. 87
breakdown thesis 11
Breen, R. L. 90
Brexit 67–8
British education 68
British morality 66
Britishness 69
Bronfenbrenner, U. 130, 168, 182
Bronfenbrenner's ecological theory 168
Brown, C. 131
Brown, R. 19
Brynin, M. 19
Budgeon, S. 1
Burgess, M. 134
Burrell, L. M. 181
Butler, J. 105
Butler's theory of gender performativity 5

Cameron, D. 189
care functions 19
Carlile, A. 136
Carmichael-Murphy, P. 6, 209–10
Carmona, M. S. 128
Carvalho, J. P. M. 5, 210
Casimiro, C. 5, 210
centrality of personal communities 17

chain migration 28
child adoption by same-sex couples 1
child-centred narratives 114, 116
childhood sentimentality 13
childlessness 87–8
child protection practitioners 42
children and young people (CYP) 168
restories 174–8
semi-structured interviews 173–4
and social media 169, 211
Civil Partnership Act (2005) 84
civil unions 107–9
Clandinin, D. J. 174
Clarke, V. 85, 87
Climbié, V. 211
Clinton, H. 28
close family 32
Coard, B. 70
cohabiting couples 68, 112, 116
non-married 109
same-sex 108
Cohen, B. P. 170
Cohen, O. 127
Cohen, P. N. 12
coming out 113
and parenting 115–16
timing of 114
community activism 67
Confederation of Education Workers of
the Argentine Republic (CTERA) 150
'conjugalisation' of family life 21
Connolly, F. M. 174
continuity thesis 12
contraceptive technologies 14
couples 'living apart together' 13
Covid-19 pandemic 4, 7, 17–18, 27, 31,
88–9, 108, 142
blurring, domestic space and
workspace 158–60
education sector 150
emergency services 149
family, care relations and professional
practices 154–7
female education workers 157–62
gender inequality 157
lockdown period 150
social media 211
teleworking 152
Cox, N. 85

CPC, *see* Crowley Parents Campaign
Cronin, A. 16–17
Crowley Parents Campaign (CPC) 188, 192, 197
Crozier, G. 190
CTERA, *see* Confederation of Education Workers of the Argentine Republic
cut-rate education 52
CYP, *see* children and young people

Dawson, M. 12
DeCrescenzo, T. 141
defacto criminalization of trans people under laws 126
deinstitutionalization of marriage 13
De Jong, G. 17
democratization thesis 11–12
Department for Children, Schools and Families (DCSF) 69–70
Department for Education (DfE) 69
detraditionalization 108
Dewaele, A. 85, 87, 93
displaying family 16
distress 179–80
divorce–marriage ratio 20, 28
doing family 5, 8, 14–15, 22
domestic violence 51
Donovan, C. 87, 105
Durkheim, E. 12
Dussel, I. 160
Dyson, S. 16

EAC, *see* Eastborough Anti-Academisation Coalition
Eastborough Anti-Academisation Coalition (EAC) 188, 191–2, 197
ecological techno-subsystem 168
Educationally Subnormal Schools (ESN) 70
education of children 49
education policy
 parental involvement 201–3
 parenting 187–8, 190
 racial inequity 72
Edwards, R. 19
Eldén, S. 18
emotional arousal 169–70
emotional reflexivity of women 19
English, S. J. 7, 209, 211, 213

English language in Ghana 54
 family disorganization 60
 institutionalization of 58
 of instruction and family disruption 54–9
 as medium of instruction 57, 59
 speaking 56
 value of 55–6
Epstein, D. 85
equalitarian gender-role dynamics 21
Equality, Diversity and Inclusion (EDI) 73
Equality Act (2010) 84
Equal Marriage Act (2015) 84–5
Ermish, J. 19
EST, *see* expectation-states theory
ethnicity 2–3, 71–2
European Union Agency for Fundamental Rights 108
expectation-states theory (EST) 170
extended families 2, 32, 49–50, 60, 108, 113, 118

*Famiglie Arcobaleno* (Rainbow Families) 106–7
families 123, 126; *see also* kinship care
 of choice 83
 definitions 2, 5, 12–13, 127–8
 dismantlement 18
 disruption 50
 diversity 2, 4
 doing family 5, 8, 14–15
 dysfunctional 129
 estrangement 128–30
 extra-blended 115
 formation 2, 32
 forms 2
 of friends 2, 6, 97–8, 101
 FST 133
 functioning 129
 health and wellness 124
 idea of 1–2
 intersectionality 4
 make-up 31–3
 norms 2–3
 performative act of 5
 pets 32–3
 Portuguese context 20–1
 relational frame of dynamics 14–15
 set of daily practices 14

social support 124
sociological interest 12–14
sociological overview 15–20
solidarity 108
trends and social implications 20–1
families networks 112–13, 115
families norms 1–4, 28, 30, 113, 117
family-building policies 20
family communication
  child–parent 172
  digital landscape, transformation of 169
  distress 179–80
  and emotional arousal 169–70
  jealousy 180
  military families, SM/IBC
    communication 170–3
  relationships 180–1
  toxic masculinity 181–2
  young people's stories 173–8
family of chance 7, 128, 130–3, 138, 140
family of choice 7, 128, 210–11
family of necessity 210–11
family practices and strategies, female
  education workers
  blurring, domestic space and
    workspace 158–60
  transformations, teaching organization
    and conditions 160–2
Family Systems Theory (FST) 133
family time 37
Fannin, A. 88
Fante 59
fatherhood
  IBC/SM 183
  Navy kids 174–8
female education workers
  family practices and strategies 157–62
  kindergartens 154
  middle-class teachers, Argentina 154–7
  Santa Fe 151–2
  unpaid care work 157
feminization of care work 19
Fenge, L. A. 88
fictive kin 130–1
2008 financial crash 31
Finch, J. 14, 18, 40
Findlay, L. 13
Fioravanti, G. 110
Five X 67

Fleishman, J. 125
foreign language 54
Fossey, M. 7, 211
fractured relationships 129
fragmented relationships 128–9
frail relationships 124, 128
Franchi, M. 110
free time 37
Fretwell, N. 7, 209, 212
Freud, A. 30
friendly groups of divorced parents 107
friendship ties 14–17
FST, see Family Systems Theory
fuzzy generalisations 90

Gal, S. 52
Gavriel-Fried, B. 127
gay fathers 106, 108, 115
gender
  identity 124, 127
  inequalities 108, 153, 157, 162–3
  minorities 125, 136–7, 141–2
  roles 20
George, C. 133
Giammattei, S. V. 5
Gillespie, R. 88
Gillie, V. 19
Giunti, D. 110
Godier-McBard, L. 7, 211
Goldstein, J. 30
Gonzales, G. 124
Gray, L. 7, 211
Guasp 88
Gusmano, B. 110
Gusmeroli, P. 6, 212

Halberstam, J. 4
Hamilton, C. E. 133
Hao, M. 18
Heaphy, B. 87, 105
Hertrich, V. 49
heteronormativity 30
heterosexuality
  families 5–7
  kinship 110–13
  marriage 85, 93–4, 97, 101, 106, 108,
    114, 116
heterosexual peers 97
HIV/AIDS 51

Holmes, M. 19
home language 51
homophobia 97, 106
homosexuality 84
Honneth, A. 189, 196–8
Hook, G. 4
*How the West Indian Child Is Made Educationally Subnormal in the British School System* (Coard) 70
Hudak, J. 5
Hull, K. 15

ILGA, *see* International Lesbian, Gay, Bisexual, Trans and Intersex Association
ILGPs, *see* intentional lesbian and gay parents
Immigration and Asylum Act 1999 68
INDEC, *see* National Institute of Statistics and Census of Argentina
Indigenous languages 55, 60
individualization 13
inequalities, social class and gender 3
information and communication technology (ICT) 17
intentional lesbian and gay parents (ILGPs) 106, 118
  in familialist Italy 108–10
  heterosexual kinship 110–13
intergenerational solidarity 109, 113
International Agreement on the Freedom of Religion or Belief 210
International Lesbian, Gay, Bisexual, Trans and Intersex Association (ILGA) 135
interracial marriages 3
intersectionality 3–4, 182
*Intersectionality and Difference in Childhood and Youth* (von Benzon and Wilkinson) 4
Irvine, J. T. 52
Italian familism 6
  *Famiglie Arcobaleno* 106
  heterosexual kinship 110–13
  ILGPs 108–13
  lesbian and gay parents 106–7
  PHLGPs 108–10, 113–17
Italian National Statistical Institute 108
*Italian Rainbow Families' Census* 108
Italy

heterosexual kinship 110–13
ILGPs 108–13
lesbian and gay parents 106–7
PHLGPs 108–10, 113–17

Jamieson, L. 19
Jasis, P. 203
jealousy 179–81
Jelin, E. 155
Johnson, F. L. 53
Johnson, G. M. 168
Johnson, R. 85
Juster, R. P. 137

Katz-Wise, S. L. 129
kin 130
  family of chance 130
  fictive 130–1
King, A. 93
kinship care 2, 5, 27–8
  absence/presence 33–4
  ambivalence relationships 34–6
  arrangements 32
  children's views of family life 31–43
  cost-effective placements 29–31
  family make-up 31–3
  grandparents 28
  heterosexual 110–13, 116
  historical-socio-political understandings 28–9
  intergenerational cycles of abuse 29
  permanence 40–1
  permanence discourses 29–31
  recognition of family 39–40
  shared narratives 39
  sharing narratives 42–3
  sharing of time, place and space 42
  sharing space 37–9
  sharing time 36–7
  siblings and birth parents 34–6
  social work 29–31
  working with ambivalence and change 41–2
kinship system, LGBTQ people 105
kithship
  allostatic load 137–8
  discrimination, old age 135–6
  family 123–4, 126–8
  family estrangement 128–30

kin 130–1
legal considerations 126–7
persona 123
protective aspect 131
social exchange 133–4
social theory of promise 139–41
support and 131–2
transgender community 134–5
youth and emerging adults 136–7
Kitzinger, C. 90
Kohen, D. 13
Konowitz, S. 171

language as symbol of identity 51
Lee, C. 6, 210–11, 213
Lee, Catherine 6
Leppänen, S. 169
lesbian and gay parents 106–8
lesbianism 84
lesbian mothers 3–4, 106, 108
lesbians, elder 6, 83–4; *see also* same-sex
    care requirements 89
    childlessness 87–8
    children 96–7
    families of choice 87
    forming groups 91–4
    later life, planning for 99–101
    lesbian visibility 97–8
    literature review 84–6
    marginalization and disempowerment
        85
    methodology 90–1
    norms of reciprocity and trust 83
    pandemic, connecting in 88–9
    pandemic, coping in 89–99
    relationships with families of
        origin 94–6
    social network 83
    theoretical framework 89–90
*Let Our Kids Be Kids* 194
LGBT lobbying group 87
LGBTQ+ families 2, 4, 15–16, 85, 94, 125,
    135, 137, 141
LGBTQ+ identities 85
LGBTQ+ persons
    family support, sexual identity 124
    non-kin relationships 136
    ostracism 125
Li, Y. 18

linguistic imperialism 52
Lister, S. 135
living apart together 14
long-distance relationships 17
Lottman, R. 93

Malinowski, B. 53
Mallon, G. P. 141
Marchetti-Mercer, M. 13
Marks, S. R. 5
marriage to divorce ratios 13
Martell, M. E. 86
Martinez-Cosio, M. 198
maternal mortality 67
MATs, *see* Multi-Academy Trusts
May, V. 12, 15
McEwen, B. S. 137
#metoo 1
Meyer, I. H. 136
middle-class teachers, Argentina
    family, care relations and professional
        practices 154–7
    kindergartens 154
    pandemic education 155
military family 7
minority stress 136–7
Mock, S. E. 88
Morgade, G. 154
Morgan, D. 5, 14, 16, 40, 209
Morphy, F. 13
motherhood 96, 110–11
Motterle, T. 110
Multi-Academy Trusts (MATs) 188
mush time 37

Natalier, K. 19
National Association of Social Workers
    127
National Center for Transgender Equality
    135
National Health Service (NHS) 68
National Institute of Statistics and Census
    of Argentina (INDEC) 157
Nationality and Borders Act 2022 68
National Survey 'Health and Teacher's
    Working Conditions 150
Navarro, J. L. 168, 182
Nedelcu, M. 17
neoliberalism 68, 76, 189

Nicholson Perry, K. 124, 132
non-consanguine family relations 211
normative family 4
Norqvist, P. 15
nuclear family 15, 66
  norms 30

Obama, B. 126
older transgender persons
  discrimination 135–6
  isolation, feeling of 136
  kithship 7, 123–42
  negative experiences and mindsets 138
  social support 137
  vulnerabilities 125
oocyte donors 112
Ortyl, T. 15
ostracism 125, 140
Oswald, R. M. 5
'outsiderness,' 117

Painter, D. W. 52
Pallotta-Chiarolli, M. 105, 118
pandemics 51
parental activism 188, 193, 200–1, 203–5
parental life disruptions 50
Parent Carer Forums (PCFs) 202
parenthood
  biological/legal parent 111, 115
  same-sex couples 110–11
  social 111
parenting 212
  active 189–91
  activist 193–5
  discourses 189–91
  parental involvement 201–3
  parent-led campaign groups 191–3
  struggle for recognition 195–201
parent-led campaign groups
  CPC 188, 192, 197
  EAC 188, 191–2, 197
  PCE 188, 191, 196
Passerino, L. M. 7
Passerino, L. M. 7, 210, 213
Paton-Imani, S. 3–4
PCE, see Protect Children's Education
PCFs, see Parent Carer Forums
pedagogical continuity 154–5
Perlman, H. H. 123

permanence 29–34, 40–1
persona 123
pets 43
PHLGPs, see post-heterosexual lesbian
    and gay parents
Plowden Report (1967) 190
PORDATA 20
Portugal
  divorce to marriage ratio 20
  family trends and social
      implications 20–1
  social changes 21
postcolonial psychology 52
post-heterosexual lesbian and gay parents
    (PHLGPs) 106–7, 118
  in familialist Italy 108–10
  transition to same-sex
      intimacies 113–17
post-separation parenting 115
Potvin, L. 136
Power, J. 124
power relationships 2
preservation of family 30
privatization of schooling 72
proper family 32
Protect Children's Education (PCE) 188,
    191, 196
psychological parenting 30
Puplampu, K. P. 168

queering familialism
  heterosexual kinship 110–13
  ILGPs 108–13
  Italian lesbian and gay parents 106–7
  PHLGPs 108–10, 113–17
*Queering Family Trees: Race, Reproductive
    Justice, and Lesbian Motherhood*
    (Paton-Imani) 3
queer Latino 15

racialization 70
racial neoliberalism 68
Ragan, C. 136
Reay, D. 3
relationships
  and communication 180–1
  familial 124, 126, 128–9, 131
  fractured 126, 129, 131
  fragmented 126, 128–9, 131

frail 124, 128
  kin 130–1, 136
  negative familial 129
  non-kin 136
  social exchange 133–4
  social support 123–4
relatives 32
*Rete Genitori Rainbow* 107
Reynolds, T. 66–7
Riggs, D. W. 124
right to abortion 1
*Roe vs. Wade* 1, 210
Root, E. 136
Rosario, M. 129
Roseneil, S. 1
Russel, S. 19

SAGE, *see* Advocacy and Services for
  LGBTQ+ Elders
same-sex; *see also* lesbians, elder
  couples 86, 88
  marriages 1, 4, 6, 14, 21, 135
  parents 28, 112
  parents having children 28
  partner 85, 105, 107, 109
Samuel, O. 49
Saraceno, C. 109
Schmauch, U. 87
schooling norms 3
Schout, G. 17
screen time 37
SEF, *see* Social Exchange Framework
Segal, M. 7, 167, 180–1
Segato, R. 163
Selmi, G. 110
SEND, *see* Special Educational Needs
sense of belonging 42
Sewell Report 202
sexual abuse 51
sexual identity 95, 112, 114, 124, 126
sexual relationships 14
Sharma, R. 127
Shilo, G. 127
Shuttleworth, P. 5, 211–12
Sibley-White, A. 194
siblings 43
  and birth parents 34–6
  relationships 35
Silva, E. 20

Simmel, G. 12
single-parent families 2, 4, 21, 156, 160
Smart, C. 12, 20
SM/IBC, *see* social media and internet-
  based communication
social bi-directionality 132
social capital theory 6, 83–4, 89–90
social classes 3, 12
social exchange 133–4
Social Exchange Framework (SEF) 133
social hostility 106
social inequalities 18, 65
socialization 35, 49
social justice 8, 117, 142, 189, 203,
  209
social legitimacy 5
social media and internet-based
  communication (SM/IBC) 168
  and CYP 169, 177–8
  emotional arousal 170
  military families 170–3
social mobility 3, 108
social movements 1
social ostracism 125, 140
social parenthood 111–12, 116
social support 124
  non-familial 131
  relationships 123–4
  transgender 131–2, 138–9
Social Theory of Promise 134, 139–41
social work policy 38
social work theory 29–30
socio-cultural diversity 2
sociological interest in family 12–14
sociology 12–20
sole parents 4
Solnit, A. J. 30
Southall Black Sisters 67
space sharing by children 38–9
Special Educational Needs (SEND) 194
sperm/egg donors 106, 111
Spirzzirri, G. 135
Stellar, E. 137
stepchildren 110
Stevenson, H. 198
Stonewall 87
street children and beggars 51
*Struggle for Recognition, The* (Honneth)
  196

# Index

surrogacy 107, 109, 112
surrogate mothers 106, 112
'Survey on Unpaid Work and Use of Time,'
    157

Tam, B. 13
telecommunications 211
Thomas, S. J. 50
Törnqvist, M. 17
toxic masculinity 181–2
traditional kinship 110, 117
Traies, J. 85–6, 89, 98
transgender; *see also* LGBTQ+ families
  ageing 134–5
  description 124–5
  kithship 134–5
  as protected class 126–7
  protective factors, kithship 138
  rights 126
  social support 138–9
  social theory of promise 140
transnational families 2, 14
Trans PULSE Canada 132
Trappolin, L. 6, 212
Tronto, J. 156
Trujillo, M. A. 131
Trump, D. 126
Tsappis, M. 129
Tudge, J. R. H. 168, 182

universalism 65

Van den Berghe, W. 85
Vincent, C. 193–4
virtual communication 17
von Benzon, N. 4
von Doussa, H. 124

Wallace, B. 85
Waters, E. 133
Weeks, J. 87, 105
Weinfield, N. S. 133
West, M. 133
Weston, K. 105
Westwood, S. 88, 98
White, R. G. 136
Wilkinson, C. 4
Wood, A. 7, 211
work–life balance 20
Wright, A. 202
Wyss, M. 17

YouGov 87
youth and emerging adults 136–7, 141

Zelditch, M. 170
Zelmanovich, P. 155, 159
Zenklusen, D. 7, 210, 213

Printed in the USA
CPSIA information can be obtained
at www.ICGtesting.com
LVHW011617260424
778545LV00003B/271